Silence
Is the Answer

To All the Noise of Doubt

By Robert E. Draper

For Kathy

You have navigated with raging soul
far from the paternal home;
passing beyond the sea's double rocks,
you now inhabit a foreign land.[1]

—Medea

Contents

It has been said that man is a rational animal.
All my life I have been searching for evidence
which could support this.

— Bertrand Russell[2]

Preface

THIS WORLD IS SUCH A DUPLICITOUS PLACE. For example, we pass by a car, and the bumper sticker proclaims, "Life Is Good!" No, it's not! At least not for the countless millions for whom life is either a physical, psychological, or material challenge, or simply a disappointing prelude to death. Not that it seems so for those viewing it through the mist of present satisfaction, serene in their cocoons of relative safety because, at the moment, things are going their way. Yet what happens to these people when the underpinnings of their contentment are swept away, when they unexpectedly lose their job, a loved one, their home, their wealth, or their health? Is life still good then? Or has it, in an instant, turned into a distressing and vulgar affair? And if it has turned into something painful and tawdry for them, are we then to believe that the ensuing despair they feel is any more tangible and real than the fleeting self-satisfaction they had experienced before? Or is their despair merely more mental machination, another insubstantial and impermanent state of mind that will disappear the instant another form of stimulation comes along?

A good question for all who, like us, are at times caught up in such nightmares of vacillating emotions is simply, "Do we have to put up with it?" In other words, do we have to remain the prisoners of our own minds, experiencing external events as the cause of our emotions, both good and bad, or is there a way out of this pitiless and pitiful entrapment? Yes, it is true that the world we live in is a mess: our bodies are both vulnerable and slowly disappearing, a number of people we encounter are far from friendly, we often don't get what we want, and our minds are frequently filled with worrisome noise. And, yes, it is true that most of our teachers and religious leaders have taught us from childhood that the answer to our questions about this precarious state is to accept it as a mystery, stuff the questions out of sight, and then just live and hope for the best.

Yet, what if this is not just the way things are? What if these ubiquitous purveyors of tales of weakness are mainly ill-instructed, accordingly misinformed, and, therefore, wrong? What if we—who seem to be subject to the whims of the many and of fate alike, and who are told to obey the rules of a decaying society and, above all, not to disturb the status quo—decide instead to revolt and say to this untidy package of propaganda, "Says who?" Not to say, "Says who?" and then disobey the rules. That's too childish. Rather, to say, "I will no longer live under the influence of my simple-minded acceptance of my past learning," and then, in an almost Cartesian way, begin again with a completely open mind. With this as our personal declaration of independence from reliance on the old, we could begin to reassess the evidence put forth by the many merchants of meaninglessness we've met, being unconvinced, unconvicted, and in search of wiser teachers; willing to learn how little we may know, and glad to be freed to learn anew.

How Little I Knew

The eldest son of a school custodian, I grew up in a tough, tenement-filled section of the Bronx. I was bright in school but found no satisfaction there. As time went on, I grew fiercely resistant to what I felt to be the dogma and the domination of an unreasoning and unreasonable authority, both at home and in my parochial school education. By high school, this eventually led to my becoming a master truant and frequent runaway, making it to Virginia at fourteen, Daytona Beach at barely fifteen, and again later Palm Beach while still fifteen, remaining at a beach hotel for the winter as a page boy.

At sixteen, I returned home and, not long after, joined the army. Upon discharge, now a little more mature, I decided to get an education, working and going to college at night on the G.I. Bill, while spending much of my free time in the dark world of the bars of the Bronx. It wasn't long before I got married, more to get out of my parents' apartment than anything, and just because that is what people where I lived did. Then I had children, also because that's what people where I lived did. Finally, due to my continuing dissatisfaction with life, I concluded that success in business and the money it brought would be the answer to the unrest I was experiencing within.

And so, with a background in accounting and a penchant for sales, I worked at building a career with great determination, rapidly moving forward in positions of increasing responsibility: first in sales, and then in sales management, branch management, division management, and finally corporate management. By thirty-five, I was the president and CEO of a successful and growing nationwide company, a position I remained in for over twenty years. Yet under the cover of my achievement, I was still restless. I had all the trappings of my position: plenty of money; a seaside home in La Jolla, California; membership in two exclusive country clubs; trips to here, there, and everywhere in first class, on the Concorde, or on private jets; reservations at the finest restaurants; name recognition at the Carlyle and like places; and, last but not least, the hard-to-swallow realization that, as far as I was concerned, this "success" wasn't adding up to much at all.

As I was doing my best to wrap my mind around this uncomfortable discovery, as well as my failing marriage, my children began to develop problems that sincerity and determination on my part could do very little to resolve. At sixteen, my oldest daughter became ill with leukemia, a disease she eventually overcame through aggressive treatment, though not without side effects that continue to haunt her terribly today. My oldest son got lost in drugs and alcohol, which eventually destroyed him. And while my two daughters went through graduate school and onto successful careers in academia, my two surviving sons made the painful choice to follow their older brother into the world of displaced values and general displeasure. To say that all of this left me—a man who'd had early hopes of a Norman Rockwell-type family life—beside myself is to put it mildly.

As a result of these unexpected developments and my distress over them, even while continuing to experience great success in my career, I began to think more deeply about my general disappointment, not just with my family life as it was turning out, but with everything. Eventually, I came to what was, for me, the surprising conclusion that what I was seeking was not greater achievement, but a deeper understanding of what I was experiencing. This, in turn, led me to embark upon a period of serious introspection, along with a careful examination of what a number of the wiser people in the world have had to say about life's sundry surprises and seeming embitterments. From them, I learned something else that surprised me: that disappointment is not the enemy it appears to be, but is rather, when seen properly, a friend pointing all determined to go beyond the tyranny of emotions in the direction of a better way. Concomitant with the acceptance of this idea—an idea that was, for me, revolutionary—came the increasing desire to learn more; and, strangely enough, in my new dedication to do so, I settled down and began to feel comforted. There, in the realm of study, contemplation, and the daily practice of what such learning teaches, I have spent the last thirty years gaining greater insight into both myself and what Camus once termed, "this absurd world."[3]

As I became more and more convinced that learning was the answer to what I was beginning to see as a meaningless life, I also began to understand that being bright enough didn't mean that I was wise. In fact, I started to appreciate how little I knew about what was really important, and how necessary it would be to become more open-minded if I was to make any progress at all. As Tolstoy once said,

> The most difficult subjects can be explained to the most slow-witted man if he has not formed any idea of them already; but the simplest thing cannot be made clear to the most intelligent man if he is firmly persuaded that he already knows....[4]

Being successful, egotistical, and, in my own mind, somewhat "already knowing," reaching toward open-mindedness was often not easy. Like many other more-successful-than-average people, I was, if anything, immodest, and being a quick study, at least when it came to business problems, I was also, in a number of ways, arrogant. Yet, thanks to my disappointment and general unhappiness, I had growing suspicions about what I really knew and, thankfully, access to the writings of people far wiser than seemingly "bright enough" and successful I.

A good example of what helped me become more modest about my "understanding" can be found in Plato's account of Socrates's final acceptance of his own greater wisdom. It seems that the Oracle at Delphi had responded "yes" when asked if Socrates was the wisest man in the land. Being puzzled by such a proclamation, Socrates then set upon a careful examination of men of renown in every field. This research led to the realization that what made him wiser than others, with a reputation for being wise as well, was that he understood how little he knew, while those "with the greatest reputations were almost entirely deficient" because they believed that since they knew a little about something, it meant they knew a lot about everything.[5]

For most of us, then, an admitted ignorance would be the beginning of wisdom, with a professed wisdom being a sign of ignorance. Earlier than Tolstoy, the German philosopher Arthur Schopenhauer, also writing about how difficult it can be to learn anew when one has set beliefs, said,

A "dictate of reason" is the name we give to certain propositions which we hold [to be] true without investigation, and of which we think ourselves so firmly convinced we [cannot even] call them provisionally in doubt. We credit these propositions so completely because when we first began to speak and think we continually had them recited to us and they were thus implanted in us; so that the habit of thinking them is as old as the habit of thinking as such and we can no longer separate the two.[6]

This is important, even vital, information for us. That is, unless we come to the place of understanding how much of our certainty is merely the result of early indoctrination and habits of thought based on secondhand knowledge, we'll unlikely be open to the "unlearning" that is the prerequisite for gaining real knowledge.

Accepting the idea of how little I actually knew about what was important and what was not helped me enormously in better understanding my frustration with not understanding. Prizing wealth and what it could bring and then discovering that it did nothing to relieve my mind's discontent was a difficult but necessary step out of my personal fog of war; learning that worldly learning was equally inadequate was another step. Steps leading me toward what? The recognition that I needed to master something that I was sometimes good at and at other times woefully dismissive of: the simple idea that in every situation into which I entered, *kindness trumped all.*

Introduction

I N RESPONSE TO THE TITLE *Silence Is the Answer: To All the Noise of Doubt*, you may wonder, "What does silence do?" Absolutely nothing, which, once you learn that the problem is but a phantasm of the mind, you begin to see is the entire point. The "noise of doubt" refers to all of the anxieties and questions and restlessness that come and go in the uncertain mind, especially the fitful raging against others and against the uncooperative fate that leads us finally to death. Dylan Thomas, speaking about death, famously said,

> Do not go gentle into the good night,
> Old age should burn and rave at close of day;
> Rage, rage against the dying of the light.

Dylan Thomas was wrong! As are we when we rave and rage about not getting what we want and are so sure we should have.

It should be clear to anyone who is honest that there are many times when we are not the "rational animal" Bertrand Russell was searching for. And while a preliminary solution to that problem may be to discipline ourselves to behave better, it does nothing to solve the mental state that generates the uncertainty and fear, which ultimately causes us to struggle in life.

I once had a dream in which I was in a cave with a number of others near the sea, taking shelter from a storm. As the storm grew in intensity, I held my arms out and pushed my wife Kathy and a friend of ours back, saying, "Stay here, and I'll go and quell the waves." Like Dylan Thomas, I was wrong, because I was trying to solve an unsolvable dilemma. Using the storm in the dream as a symbol of the mind's fitful state, "silence is the answer" really means that watching the mind's storms without interfering in their passing *is* the answer to their fitful uprisings—not struggling against them in some heroic notion of being the one who can "quell the waves." People who are adamant that their efforts to learn a better way to live must result in a peaceful mind before the noise in it subsides miss the happy step into this mental state—that state of simply and peacefully watching the mind's unrest each time it rises until it disappears. And as a result, they either go back to their private wars, or they distract themselves with rituals, such as concentrated meditation, chants, or prayers, and never really progress. Said another way, because they insist that peace of mind come to them where they are, instead of meeting the "observational conditions" that will lead them within, where it quietly awaits, they never experience peace at all.

In light of the idea that each of us should take steps toward reaching this inner silence, in order to attempt to achieve peace as a society, this book has three primary objectives. The first is to examine a wide variety of written accounts spanning two millennia to help us take off our rose-colored glasses and look at the world for what it really is. As Charles Dickens said, and I concur, "It's a mad world. Mad as Bedlam!"[7] The second objective is to learn that it is our minds, and not others or the world around us, that are the determiners of our experiences here. As Shakespeare said, and, here again, I agree, "There is nothing either good or bad but thinking makes it so."[8] The third goal is to help us slow down enough to take a thoughtful look at what a number of wise and not-so-wise people have had to say about this experience we seem to be passing through, which we call life, that we may expand our horizons, shed some light on our self-imposed limitations, and increase our capacity for discernment and independent thought.

I should also make the point here that this book is *replete* with excerpts from numerous sources, not because I consider myself incapable of expressing the ideas here fully, but because the same ideas seen at different times and in various forms and places can serve nicely to remind us of what we all already innately know.

Finally, be aware that although this book is philosophical in nature, it is not meant to be an academic textbook so much as an inquiry into the nature of the human mind, a venture into what each of us might do to improve our thinking and become more peaceful citizens in this conflicted and mad world. In that light, as you delve into what may sometimes be foreign ideas, bear in mind the following: in order to grow and expand our minds, we all must learn to consider and reconsider concepts, accept and reject what we will, and then decide for ourselves what we believe. The alternative is to think like the religious-minded politician who recently said, "I never read anything that might conflict with my beliefs." The refusal to question and doubt leaves us as fountains spouting forth information supplied to us by others, making us pretenders to the throne of wisdom in what would otherwise be our own very capable minds. To accept the ideas of others without examination is to disrespect our power of discernment and dismiss as unworthy whatever feels right for us, which, after serious evaluation, is what we should honor above all else.

An Instinct for Self-Destruction

One major thread that runs through this book is what some might consider "stating the obvious"—that the world is firmly in the grip of a gathering storm and that, as such, things in general are getting worse, not better. Many writers, often eloquently, make similar statements, so to add to that concern wouldn't seem much of a contribution. My stating this obvious fact, however, is to stress the less evident: that things have been so bad for so long that we have become accustomed to them being that way and, in the mental shrugging of our shoulders, are robbing ourselves of the ability to recognize *our own* roles in disturbing our peace and contributing to the general mess. My hope is that this book's exposition of the central problem, in some of its grimmer forms, will evoke a reaction and uproot our complacency about what we've settled for and should no longer continue to accept. As Sigmund Freud said, "The fateful question for the human species seems to me to be whether and to what extent [it] … will succeed in mastering … the human instinct of aggression and self-destruction."[9]

Or, perhaps you think Freud and those like him overstate the problem. Perhaps you feel that it is *not* obvious that the world is pretty bad off and only getting worse. Maybe you believe that, given time, we will work things out, and that humankind is gradually evolving to a more civilized state. If this is your belief, I respectfully beg to differ. At present, no matter how obscuring the patina with which we seek to disguise our state, we remain warlike and selfish. Yes, many of us give generously of our money, our goods, or our time to aid the less fortunate, while still others enter religious orders, join the Peace Corps, or volunteer at hospices or Habitat for Humanity. Then there are those who dedicate themselves to pursuits such as teaching, keeping the order, fighting fires, healing the sick, giving encouraging lectures, or writing informative books. Noble pursuits all. Yet, few approach, much less address, the possibility that we ourselves are the problem we have been so futilely attempting to solve.

Under the superficial covers of its acquired manners and developed culture, the world is a grossly unfair place for many. Not so much because it has to be this way, but because we, who too often honor cleverness over common decency, have made it so. And in our rush to get ahead, or, alternatively, to think ourselves superior to those who are striving to do so, we have either accepted the system as it is, and used it to our supposed advantage, or chosen to be in opposition to others within it—two approaches that have proven dangerously ineffective in bringing any semblance of contentment to our restless minds. The reality of finding harmony in relationships is that, unless we begin to set aside our drives to be the stars of the show or the critics of the same, we are certain to remain fearful in our isolation, angry in our outlook, and incapable of perceiving those who are essentially the same as us as anything but different.

Perception and Reality

If you are, at present, a satisfied character in the grand play, this book is probably not for you. If, however, you are concerned about the chaos that surrounds you and, more importantly, your own inner turmoil over it, the ideas here should interest you. To look at what we've done and failed to do, and to disallow rationalization to continue to deceive us, is to become aware that we have devolved into a state of interpersonal anarchy that is utterly senseless. This makes rationalization the problem that hides the problem and, therefore, the first problem to be addressed and undone. How is this accomplished? By letting honesty disclose to us how often our wishes influence our perceptions and leave us in the unfortunate condition of perceiving things as we want them to be and not as they are. This solution will be examined more thoroughly later in the book. For now, drawing on a few different sources, I will use a situation related to the Iraq War to demonstrate what I mean by the dangers of rationalization found in common and significant disconnects between perception and reality.

> **Perception:** In *The War Within,* author Bob Woodward recounts the following conversation between General David Petraeus's mentor, General Jack Keane, and President George W. Bush, after one of Keane's many trips to Iraq. Keane speaks first.

"At the risk of sermonizing … I have to say to you, this military that we have in Iraq may be the most idealistic force we've put on the battlefield since the Revolutionary War."

"Maybe includes the Civil War," the president said.

"That's possible," Keane said. "But the American people have soured on this effort and are no longer supporting the war.… But nonetheless every single day [our troops] go out there and are willing to risk everything that they care about in life!"[10]

Reality #1: Sergeant John Crawford's version of such "idealism" from his book, *The Last True Story I'll Ever Tell*:

Two years ago … the world seemed uncomplicated. Now all I can say for sure is that … my quiet optimism has been replaced by something darker, a kind of hatred—of what I cannot even grasp.…

[This is] what war is really like. When Third ID [Infantry Division] arrived, they told us … we were part of them now.…

We were put on a water and food ration. No supplies came our way.… Our retooled Vietnam-era rifles began to show their age, falling apart with the slightest usage. We became shadows of the shock-and-awe troops that Americans saw on television. My uniforms were torn beyond repair and my boots had no soles on them. Still we walked on, day and night, sloshing through the sewage-filled streets.…"[11]

Later, in his description of watching a wounded enemy die, Crawford tells us more about war as it really is:

He was looking at us, both eyes perfectly focused despite the fact that half his brain was all over the car.…

His breath was coming in wheezing gasps, and the hole in his head glistened in the streetlight like fairy dust....

When he fell over onto the seat of the car, the rest of his brain became dislodged and slid onto the floor of the car.... the whole squad was standing there, unable to speak.

After his discharge, Crawford continued to reminisce, saying,

The smell [everywhere] is what I remember most. Burned human flesh.... Sometimes you ... feel like someone is just in your head screaming at the top of his lungs so that you can't think....

It certainly could have been worse. One of my buddies got locked up in an institution by the police for being a danger to himself. Another woke up in the hospital ... not for being a danger to himself, but to everyone else. One guy got a brain infection and wakes up every morning expecting to be in Iraq. Two more are in Afghanistan, having re-upped rather than deal with being home....

This is a true story.

Reality #2: More on what was experienced by the "idealistic force" from *House to House* by David Bellavia:

I decide I need to move. I get to my feet and zig down the alley-way, then turn a corner. I stop short. I've come up behind a man smoking a cigarette. His golden armband denoting membership in the Mahdi militia has fallen around his wrist....

At first I think I'm hallucinating....

My weapon comes up automatically.... In the second it takes to set the rifle on burst-fire, my surprise gives way to cold fury. The muzzle makes contact with the back of his head....

My finger twitches twice. Six rounds tear through his skull. His knees collapse as if I'd just broken both his legs.... I lower my weapon ... and trigger another three-round burst into his chest just to be sure. He flops to the ground with a meaty slap....

I convince myself that this is the man who shot [my buddy] Fitts, and I am aroused to a full fury. His face looks like a bloody Halloween mask and I stomp it ... until he finally dies.... My entire boot is bathed in ... gore....

We ... don't mind doing the nation's dirty work....

We're the infantry.

War's a bitch; wear a helmet.[12]

Toward the end of the book, Bellavia confesses to the attraction of the excitement he experienced while at war and to calling the recruiting station when his wife was not around, hoping to be called back. He says,

My thought process is that I would be wrong to volunteer, but if Uncle Sam called me back, that is okay. At one point I was on a list to go back. I feigned like it was the worst news in the world. But inside I thought I would pass out from excitement.... I want back in the game. I can't help it. It is who I am, who I always wanted to be.

Adrenaline is better than any painkiller.[13]

Reality #3: From an October 2008 article in *Vanity Fair* about a group of soldiers in Afghanistan:

Patriotism on its own couldn't take a hilltop from a troop of Boy Scouts, but … rage will win battles, change wars….

"The high point of our day is killing someone else," [Sergeant Brendan] O'Byrne told me one night…. "I mean, what's that say about us? What's it going to be like when we go home?"

… Combat is a rush, and once it has blown out your levels, it's hard to appreciate the more mundane pleasures of life….

"I like firefights," he admitted, scratching a design in the dirt with his boot heel….

"I know," he said with a shake of the head, "the saddest thing in the world."[14]

Reality #4: From *American Sniper*, the autobiography of Chris Kyle, who, by official count, killed a hundred and sixty enemy combatants:

I loved what I did. I still do. If circumstances were different—if my family didn't need me—I'd be back in a heartbeat. I'm not lying or exaggerating to say it was fun. I had the time of my life being a Seal.[15]

To summarize, the perception, from the perspective of what some with perhaps unrecognized hidden agendas want us and themselves to believe is true, is that our troops are idealistic warriors for freedom. The reality, however, is that, for many young men who put themselves in harm's way in order to participate in what is, for some, a highly addictive "game," such a designation is a misnomer of the first order.

How many other differences exist between perception and reality, not just among our leaders, but among the rest of us as well? How many rationalizations have we embraced that cover secret wishes waiting to be discovered? And, most of all, how does one embark on a real journey of escape from the dark forest of ignorance and confusion in which most of us are scurrying around aimlessly?

Certainly the wise have some possible answers. They tell us that the first step out of our sleepiness—our often unseen dishonesty about our motives—is to look without condemnation at what we are up to. What they would ask of us is to shake off our sleepiness and look closely at accounts of war, such as those above, as well as the following, from the highly decorated Vietnam veteran, Rhodes Scholar, and prize-winning author Karl Malantes:

> When I was fighting … either I felt nothing at all or I felt exhilaration akin to scoring the winning touch-down.…
>
> In combat you are already over some edge. You are in a fierce state where there is primitive and savage joy in doing in your enemy.… There is a very primal side to me. I suspect we all have this, but are so afraid of it that we prefer to deny its existence. This denial is more dangerous than acceptance.… It's why a good Baptist can get caught up in a lynching.…
>
> The least acknowledged aspect of war, today, is how exhilarating it is. This aspect makes people uncomfortable.…
>
> Combat is the crack cocaine of all excitement highs—with crack cocaine costs.[16]

Looking at all this, perhaps the real bell that "tolls for thee" is simply the alarm clock, saying it's time to wake up.

CHAPTER 1

Separate Interests

O N AN OVERCAST SATURDAY MORNING, as I began writing this chapter, my attention wavered between what I intended to write and a call I was expecting from my youngest son. He had been released from prison in Alaska the Tuesday before, after serving a year for writing bad checks to feed his addiction to alcohol and drugs. He was in his late thirties at the time and, with the exception of one relatively short period of sobriety, had been in almost constant trouble of one sort or another since he was sixteen. Over those years, I had tried to help him in various ways, taking him on trips, talking to him, paying for counseling, and placing him in numerous recovery programs, the latest being the Betty Ford Center in Palm Springs, where he left a ninety-day program after thirty days, proclaiming himself cured.

After that, as had happened before, he did seem to be "cured" for a while. He returned to his home in Anchorage, went back to work with enthusiasm, almost doubled the size of his wife's eyewear business in a matter of months, and, along with her, started making lots of money. One day soon after, he called and said, "I'd like to know what you think about this," and proceeded to inform me that he and his wife had just bought a house costing three times as much as the condo they'd been living in, along with a couple of new Lexus automobiles for the commute, since the house was farther away.

This kind of after-the-fact question was typical of him. Not wanting advice contrary to what he had already decided, he rarely asked my opinion beforehand, and, instead, sought my approval after the deed was done. This time, being an old hand at the game by then, instead of offering criticism for what was obviously a rash decision for a newly recovering addict, I focused on encouraging him to continue working hard while directing every extra dollar the business earned toward paying off their new mortgage.

Within months, he was back into abusing alcohol and drugs, and, soon after, wrote the bad checks on the business that led to prison. There, because it seemed a safer and easier way to do time, he talked his way into a special nine-month drug rehabilitation program, where, following a familiar pattern, he was thrown out after four months for lack of cooperation. He served the balance of his sentence in a maximum-security prison, where I assume they put him to teach him a lesson. When we talked on the phone during that time, I kept suggesting that he look around with open eyes at what could easily become his future home if he didn't make the decision to stop abusing drugs.

Today, the reason I somewhat uneasily anticipated the phone ringing was that I suspected he might be in trouble again. Not knowing what else to do to help him—he couldn't return to his old life, because his wife, fed up with his behavior, was now his ex-wife and had a restraining order on him—I had agreed to relocate him to Honolulu and provide him with a fresh start.

With full awareness of his potential for failure, yet with hopes for possible success, I arranged for his nonrefundable airline ticket to Honolulu, sent him a cashier's check for two thousand dollars to get started, told him I would pay three months' rent on whatever studio apartment he found, and offered to help him further if he stayed sober. After that conversation, the last time I heard from him, he had just been released. After going to the DMV to get a new copy of his driver's license and to the bank to get traveler's checks, he told me that he was looking forward to going to his favorite taco shop to order what *he* wanted to eat for the first time in a very long time. He was excited about leaving the cold and darkness of the Alaskan winter for the sunshine of Hawaii, a place he had visited more than once and liked very much.

While I reasoned it was possible that I had not heard from him because he was still searching for a place to live and waiting until he found one before phoning me, I also knew this might not be so. Despite his recent release from prison and a year of sobriety, it was not impossible that he had taken the money I sent him and gone right back into the drug world. Yet, while I had serious doubts that, after years of slipping and falling, he was all at once going to be straight forever, in no way did I believe he would revert to his old habits without at least giving Hawaii a chance. On the other hand, being aware that he was a troubled person, I wasn't going to be shocked if that also turned out not to be the case.

Regardless of what happened, I knew I would not buy into his behavior as some failed expectation. After years of experience with my children's travails, I had come to realize that things are simply what they are; therefore, I was willing to deal with this as it was, with kindness toward my son—which doesn't mean stupidity. Acting kindly was something more important to me than any form of resentment.

The telephone finally rang. He was calling from Honolulu: high, paranoid, almost broke, and half-babbling, as he described his sad but deliberate journey into that condition. His first step, he said, had been a conscious decision he'd made at the bank in Anchorage to get cash instead of traveler's checks as we had agreed, this being the initial expression of his unconscious desire to hurt himself again. Then he passed on the taco shop, went to the drug dealer instead, and, for a day and a half, had a huge party, spending three-quarters of his fresh-start money in the process.

On the third day, still high, he convinced a pastor he met to take him to the airport and, with the clergyman's help, managed to use the previous day's ticket to get on a flight to Hawaii. According to his version of reality, when he arrived in Honolulu that evening, he went downtown in search of a cheap hotel in order to conserve his remaining money, but since "drugs were everywhere," he got "waylaid" again, spending most of his remaining cash on another party over the following two days. Now he was in a strange city, with little money and no sensible connections, in search of a solution he had used many times before: to find a way into a "lockdown facility" in a hospital, where he could get tranquilizers to help him come slowly off of his high.

In one sense, even in his senselessness and distress, he was still being quite clever. He didn't want to go to a detox center, where they would just lock him in for a while and then let him go. He wanted a hospital with a psychiatric unit attached, where he could find drugs that would calm his comedown. Still, this was yet another version of his long-time modus operandi—binge, go to rehab or something similar, come down, get straight, and soon after do it all over again. It was repetition compulsion writ large and in stark form: attraction to a painful pleasure that always costs far more than it is worth, the participant refusing to see the obvious cause-and-effect relationship between the pleasure and the resulting pain.

As I listened to him talk for a while about how he was going to accomplish his plan, I didn't really doubt him. He was, sometimes unfortunately, a great salesman, and I believed he would probably pull it off. My son, at this time, was a good example of someone with a deeply divided mind: one part of him gifted, charming, and as reasonable as can be; the other part devious, careless, and self-indulgent beyond measure. As I wished him luck and told him that, as far as I could see, there was nothing more I could do for him at the moment, I thought, *Only time will tell when he will listen to reason and what his next step will be.* And while I had no plan to write about him at all—his entry into the book being coincidental to the day I began writing this chapter—since he has now become part of the narrative, I will continue writing about him, as his ongoing struggles with life parallel the challenges we all face, both as individuals and as a society.

Behind the Façade

In this frequently challenging world, there is great difficulty in learning to live in peace, with reason as our only guide. While it does appear that a fortunate few live somewhat untroubled lives, there is no question that many struggle—for example, my other children. My oldest son was a nice-looking young man with a good sense of humor, who, for some unknown reason, lay down on the doorway of life and refused to enter. He was a good athlete who spurned group sports, a bright-enough child who wouldn't complete his homework, and a person so unwilling to cooperate with the norm that he preferred living on the beach to participating in society, dying at the age of twenty-eight after never having worked a day in his adult life.

My second son's difficulties also started in his teens, though he finished high school and went on to college. We sent him there with high hopes, a decent used car, an allowance, and the single require-ment that he take no fewer than twelve credits and maintain passing grades. After three driving incidents involving alcohol, we took the car back. After he flunked out in the first semester, we gave him a second chance. After he flunked out on his second try, we gave him a reason-able financial start and told him that it was time for him to stand on his own. For the following twenty years, to him—another decent guy with a good heart—that meant little more than partying for a while and then getting into trouble, getting straight and then getting bored, and finally, returning to the party life only to get back into trouble. He repeated this pattern time and again. Then, for some inexplicable rea-son, he made the decision to get sober. He settled down, married a nice woman, and now works hard, goes to church, and lives a responsible and sedate life. Go figure.

My middle child, a daughter, went off to college after her junior year in high school to help take care of her ailing sister, whom she roomed with. She sailed through undergraduate and then graduate school, her only voiced complaint being about the one *B* she got in graduate school on her otherwise straight-*A* record. She has a beer or two now and again, but doesn't really drink and doesn't do drugs, and while she did get divorced, she's been happily remarried for quite a while. She's truly a nice person, a schoolteacher living the quiet and respectable life we would wish for all our children.

Her older sister has had nowhere near the same good fortune. This child, as I mentioned earlier, became ill with leukemia at sixteen. She went for weekly chemotherapy treatments for a very long time and was hospitalized more than once. After four years or so, she fell out of remission, and, while being given little hope of survival, was heavily dosed with full-brain radiation. To everyone's surprise, she survived, but the extreme doses of radiation "overcooked" the fluid around her brain, leaving one arm and one leg partially paralyzed, and making it a struggle for her to get around without the aid of first a cane and then a walker. After a while, she became a professor at a local community college, but her situation later deteriorated again, due to a medically unexpected reflux from the over-radiation. She eventually became unable to perform her duties at work and is now in a wheelchair in a nursing home, reasonably content most days, but suffering from slowly increasing paralysis and growing dementia for which there is no cure.

Now, while these problems are relatively severe and somewhat unusual in that they are clustered among a group of siblings, they are not that uncommon in our troubled world. Look at all the maimed and troubled soldiers returning from war; the many families with autistic children; the starving, the poor, and the downtrodden in so many different places; the self-shamed religious and political leaders; the incestuous fathers; the murdered and their murderers; the homeless; the millions with AIDS and cancer and other deadly diseases; the severely depressed and the joyless; and all the fevered bigots who burn with hatred, condemning others for no better reason than these others look strange or think differently. Even when there is no particular problem in a family, at least not yet anyway, in some places in the world, the struggle just to survive is enormous.

Putting this latter struggle into perspective, author Carl Hoffman describes a typical day in the life of two drivers of a matatu (a kind of small bus), whom he spent time with in Nairobi, Kenya:

> Back and forth from the Town to Ngong we went all day as the traffic built; in places it took fifteen minutes to move two blocks—wall-to-wall, bumper-to-bumper matatus honking and flashing their lights and blasting music … each matatu spat a continuous, visible plume of gray exhaust, and the fumes were intense, overwhelming. Kimani kept the music at earsplitting volume…. In America people flipped out if you talked too loudly on your cell phone; in the rest of the world there was so much noise, the very idea of silence was unheard of….
>
> Kimani rarely actually stopped the bus—Phillip was like an acrobat climbing over passengers to collect fares, hanging out the doorway to spot them and hurry them on and off the vehicle, banging on the side and whistling loudly to signal Kimani.
>
> On it went, at a grueling pace … [the two working] very long hours … scratching for pennies.
>
> At noon we snapped a main front leaf spring, and Kimani sped off to the garage. But it was no garage; it was a place that boggled my mind, that stretched my imagination. It was Dickensian: block after block of mud passageways littered with garbage and upended vehicles and men sleeping on tires and the sparks of welders and the smell of smoke and oil and diesel and Bondo. It was one lane wide, with two-way traffic. It was hot and glaring, a place of burning fires and braziers and hammering and music, and the mud was so dark, so black, so viscous, it was like oil….
>
> The heat was searing. Hammers smashed and banged and generators roared and flies landed on our

arms, our faces. Children walked barefoot through the greasy mud with tubs of packages of cashews and cigarettes on their heads.... Across the mud a man welded ... against the eye-burning white light of the arc welder he held a shard of dark glass in front of his face.... Smoke filled the air from hundreds of fires. Broken, rusted, and smashed cars lay stacked on each other like books in a used book store. A pair of eight-year-olds in ragged T-shirts slowly swept by, collecting bits of wire, stray nuts and bolts, which they dropped into a plastic bag....

[F]ourteen hours after I'd met them, sixteen hours after they'd started their day, Kimani and Phillip were at the Nairobi train station for the last time—they'd end their day when they dropped the last passengers off in Ngong Town....

I was delirious with fatigue, beaten up, my neck, back, knees, and shoulders aching; hungry for solitude and quiet and cleanliness; my nerves frayed from the constant jangling noise and crowds. Kimani and Phillip had four more days to go before the weekend...."[17]

There is a story about Sigmund Freud that touches on our common plight. It seems that as he and his daughter Anna were strolling around one of the nicer sections of Vienna one day, Freud said, "You see those houses with those lovely façades! Things are not necessarily so lovely behind the façades. And so it is with human beings too."[18] In other words, even the most seemingly successful people and families often have unseen burdens, skeletons in their closets, or unresolved issues they are wrestling with in some way, and we shouldn't let supposed exceptions, or what appears to be personal good fortune, delude us into thinking it is otherwise.

As the old song lyric goes, "All God's chillun got trouble."[19] If this is so in most of our lives, and to a degree it is in mine, then it seems to me that the sensible answer is to learn to deal with it without resistance or giving into the uselessness of complaint. A different way to say this is that fretting about, moaning over, or quarreling with situations I can do little or nothing about is an exceedingly poor use of my time.

This is a lesson I learned slowly, but well, while dealing with my children in their numerous difficulties. When my oldest son, the one who died, would not engage in life as people ordinarily do, nothing I tried—and I tried just about everything—had any real influence on his thinking or behavior. When my oldest daughter became ill, all my worldly power and best efforts to ameliorate the situation were for naught. With my younger sons, it was no different. Drug programs, different forms of counseling, interminable father-son talks, sternness, cajoling, soothing, rewards, and other attempts at motivation—they made no difference whatsoever. That's not to say that I shouldn't have done what I did, or do what I do, but only to say that if I'm to find any peace of mind, I must fully erase expectation, since the failure of harbored expectations is what produces my complaining to begin with.

Protecting Self-Interests

Everywhere one looks in this world there is violence, chaos, and the stunning confusion born of differing values and their clashing interests. Yes, as a race, we have made substantial technological progress, going, for example, from covered wagons to space flight in a century. Yet along with this "progress" have come weapons of mass destruction, a growing sense of animosity among nations, further evidence of the age-old sickness of mind that breeds intolerance between religions, a widening acceptance of the immature idea that greed is good, and an increasing appetite for more of this and more of that, much of it relatively useless. And that's not to mention the not-too-subtle expansion of means and methods developed by the clever and the mighty, such as many on Wall Street, aimed directly at exploiting the weak, the uninformed, and the unwary.

Why is there such a dearth of goodwill between people in this world? Is it that most are so wrapped up in what they consider to be their own—or their family's, religion's, or nation's—best interests that they do not see beyond these borders except dimly? Does confusion reign supreme in a mind like that of my son who was imprisoned simply because he put reason in second place to his own false desires? And, even though the form it took may appear less respectable, was his difficulty with self-centeredness all that different in content from the selfishness so often expressed by all of us?

Let me give you an example of what I mean. As an inveterate channel-flipper, I was going about my routine of checking the news one morning while having breakfast, when I paused to watch three guest commentators on a Fox News financial show. They were addressing a viewer's e-mail question, which asked, "Do you believe that the current administration and the general attitude of business are contributing to the increasing disparity between the rich and the poor?" The responses of these three well-dressed and successful men were informative of their mindsets.

The first answered, "Well, the rich have worked hard for their money, and no one should have the right to take any of it and give it to those who haven't."

The second said, "The gap between the rich and the poor has been growing since the 1970s. Therefore, it can't be laid at anyone's door. It's just the way things are."

And the third replied, "I don't even want to talk about that. That's the kind of nonsense that leads to class warfare."

What was interesting about this was that not one of the three paused to consider whether the disparity itself was justified, or whether, perhaps, the whole system of reward and remuneration might be askew. Why? Because each was responding from the basis of the self-protection of his convictions, which meant that, for him, what he was saying was true.

Here is another example of self-interest and its clashes: In March 2008, the U.S. Congress held a hearing on executive compensation at companies engaged in the subprime mortgage debacle. The first person to testify was a compensation expert who called the salaries, stock sales, and severance packages of the executives who were about to testify "outrageous." Then the committee chairman, a Democrat, grilled the ex-CEOs of Merrill Lynch, Citibank, and Countrywide Mortgage on the justification for their multimillion dollar severance packages in light of their companies' shabby performances and rapidly declining stock prices. The executives rallied together to defend their incomes and were quickly supported in those efforts by the Republican members of the committee, the whole thing amounting to another tempest in a teapot, all for show and essentially a waste of everyone's time.

As we viewed it, I said to my wife, "Watch and I'll say what each person is going to say before he or she says it." And I did, which wasn't all that hard to do once I perceived them as actors in a play, spouting forth their preprogrammed and "assigned" lines. The compensation expert called by the Democrats attacked the wealthy businessmen. The committee chairman and the other Democrats, in effect, called the executives a bunch of hypocrites and crooks. The executives proclaimed themselves the innocent victims of market forces beyond their control, recipients of tens and hundreds of millions of dollars that were simply their pre-earned and just due. And the pro-business Republicans, as could be expected, stood foursquare behind them all.

Among this elite group with such opposing opinions, who was right? From their own viewpoints, all of them. Who was wrong? From another viewpoint, none of them and all of them. None of them, because people functioning from beliefs solidified into convictions are merely expressing their devotion to those convictions. All of them, because they engaged in a clamoring brawl, showing little, if any, restraint, consideration, or respect for others' rights to be heard. Were the businessmen selfish? Probably. But, in a different way, so were the Democrats who hauled them before Congress to embarrass them about something they really couldn't do anything about. As were the committee's Republicans who so vigorously defended them, probably, at least to some degree, to look good to the business community whose campaign donations would enhance their chances for re-election. As are, at times, and in different ways, the rest of us as well.

Looking objectively at the above scenarios and others like them help us also see what we do objectively. For instance, how often do we function in relationships with complete honesty; that is, without allowing our supposed needs and selfish desires to envelop and distort our perceptions? How in touch are we with the mean-mindedness behind the belief in separate interests, with mine being more important than yours? How aware are we of self-importance as the unrecognized foe of harmony, the outgrowth of our secreted wish to be different, better, and special? In his book *Form versus Content,* Dr. Kenneth Wapnick, president of the Foundation for *A Course in Miracles*—and the best and wisest man I know—uses Freud's assessment of Marxism to state the general problem of self-importance, saying, "In the 1920s, Freud insightfully wrote that Marxism would inevitably fail, not because of anything external, but because Marx and his followers did not recognize the inherent aggression and self-centeredness of homo sapiens."[20] What disguises this elemental problem and thereby protects it is everyone's first line of defense: the idea that there are substantial differences among the Democratic-Republican, Christian-Muslim, American-North Korean, Israeli-Arab definitions of self we perceive as reality in the shadowy world of your interests or mine. Our desire that it *be* so—our egos finding vim and vigor in the process—becomes the proof that it *is* so, protecting the belief that these differences are based on something inherently real, that they are far more than skin deep.

The Orwellian notion that some of us are more equal than others, which seems ingrained in our thinking, is the source of an untold host of miseries. What else but self-centeredness could produce the abject "reasoning" behind such attitudes as "My country, right or wrong," or the worldwide educational inequities that result from the attitude "My child first, no matter the cost to yours"? I mean, ask yourself, can the human family heal and cohere while thoughts like these hold sway?

What we don't seem to recognize, at least not consistently, is that to see others as equals in sentiment and theory, but not in actuality and practice, is not to see at all. As Kenneth Wapnick often reminds his students, the preamble to the charter of UNESCO states, "Since wars begin in the minds of men, it is in the minds of men that the defenses of peace must be constructed." For us as individuals, this means that if we don't realize the contribution our own retreat into a little corner of selfishness is making to the expansion of unfairness in the world, we'll be of little help to anyone, least of all ourselves.

With Malice toward None

To be truly helpful to ourselves and others requires learning new lessons, the first lesson being to face, without evasion, our participation in the incredibly disturbing act of inflating self-importance. How else but by exposing it for what it is and recognizing its general harmfulness can we come to understand that this is the basis of our motivation to dominate those whom we perceive as different? Krishnamurti, who, like Dr. Wapnick, understood where the real problem lay, cautioned us against thinking that the answer is to improve the external circumstances of the world:

> Learning has been the ancient tradition of man. Not only from books, but also about the nature and structure of the psychology of a human being. As we have neglected this [latter aspect] entirely, there is disorder in the world; terror, violence and all the cruel things that are taking place. We have put the world's affairs first and not the inner. The inner, if it is not understood, educated and transformed, will always overcome the outer, however well organized it may be politically, economically and socially. This is the truth which many seem to forget. We are trying politically, legally and socially to bring order in the outer world in which we are living, and inwardly we are confused, uncertain, anxious and in conflict. Without inward order, there will always be danger to human life.[21]

A good example of how "danger" caused by inward disorder can express itself in what is, in effect, our common state of paranoia was evident in my old crowded neighborhood in the Bronx. There, a number of the guys I grew up with would fight at the drop of a hat for the sole purpose of demonstrating that they weren't the kind of people one should mess around with. After considering the incongruous nature of that as a principle, let's examine the following from Bob Woodward's *State of Denial,* reflecting the thinking of political leaders like Dick Cheney and Henry Kissinger, and see if we find any real difference between their outlooks and those of the young men of my old neighborhood:

> Cheney [having] worked closely with Kissinger in the Ford administration ... found his hard-line advice useful after 9/11. They shared a world view that international relations were a matter of military and economic power. Diplomatic power derived from threatening to and then actually using that power. In its rawest form, using the military sent a useful message to the world: It's dangerous to be an enemy of the United States.[22]

Woodward, claiming Kissinger remained embittered about America's failure to prevail in Vietnam, said that his constant litany to both the president and vice president was that victory is the only option.[23] Whether we approve of Cheney and Kissinger or not, the foregoing should give us all pause. Does this belligerence in attitude mean, for example, that it might have been acceptable to drop an atom bomb on Hanoi, as General Curtis LeMay, the vice chief of staff of the Air Force, advocated in his day? How far does one go to have it his or her own way? And does building up arsenals actually save us or merely make everyone engaged in the process that much more frightened and paranoid?

We need to shake our heads and realize that most of us have been listening to less-than-helpful and unreasonably aggressive teachers and leaders, such as Kissinger and Cheney, and accepting their opinions at face value, when we should have been learning to think for ourselves. One of the things we seem not to have learned is that acting belligerently toward others not only alienates them, but also generates fear and guilt that cloud the aggressor's mind, hiding the understanding that real strength grows only in peace. In simple terms, war weakens, and sometimes seriously, even the conqueror. Therefore, using force against anyone, except when absolutely necessary for self-protection, is patently stupid. And as long as we as a people engage in force for little good reason, as we have in Iraq and Vietnam, we set our sights on self-defeating goals such as feeding the pride of nationalism or conquering equals. Yet, even in the midst of this almost universal penchant for viciousness toward those who appear different, such as that among the exuberantly righteous in all religions, some have refused to give in to xenophobia, allowing the light of reason to shine out from their minds onto a world darkened by fear. Two noteworthy examples follow.

After the Civil War and on the occasion of his second inaugural, President Abraham Lincoln said,

> With malice toward none; with charity for all ... let us strive ... to bind up the nation's wounds, to care for him who shall have borne the battle ... to do all which may achieve ... a lasting peace among ourselves, and with all nations.[24]

That attitude of generosity toward all was later convincingly exemplified by two Dutch women who found themselves—perhaps literally as well as figuratively—in extraordinary circumstances. In Holland, during the Second World War, two sisters, Corrie and Betsie ten Boom, were arrested for hiding Jewish people. As a consequence for their actions, the two were sent to a concentration camp. In her book *The Hiding Place,* Corrie relates an incident in which she and Betsie witnessed a camp guard whipping a feeble-minded girl. As they observed the beating, Corrie whispered to Betsie, "What can we do for these people?

Afterward, I mean. Can't we make a home for them and care for them and love them?"

Betsie responded, "Corrie, I pray every day that we will be allowed to do this! To show them love is greater."

Following this, Corrie recalled, "And it wasn't until I was gathering twigs later in the morning that I realized that I had been thinking of the feeble-minded, and Betsie of their persecutors."[25]

CHAPTER 2

Returning to the Trunk

A FEW DAYS AFTER OUR LAST conversation, my son called from the lockdown section of a psychiatric hospital, having talked his way in exactly as he said he would. Being sober, he was, as he usually is when he is sober, quite reasonable, once more promising himself and the world that he would now make something of his life that he could be proud of. No longer Pollyannaish about believing such promises, I took what he said with a large grain of salt, thinking he would likely do drugs again at the first opportunity.

As we talked, I remained encouraging, reinforcing the idea that if he really wanted to make it, he most certainly could. He said he would, and I said, "Good." What was left between us at that moment? On my part, a continued commitment to myself to look upon his behavior impersonally and to remain patient in our interactions until he turned his life around. On his part, his best efforts—and even if they sometimes seemed much less than adequate, they *were* his best efforts—toward that solely important goal.

Evil-Doers or Mistake-Makers?

My son is certainly not the only one unaware of his mind's attraction to instant gratification and self-destructive behavior, without due regard for their potential cost. A number of otherwise very bright people are right there with him. For example, in early 2008 the governor of New York, Eliot Spitzer, was forced to leave office in disgrace after being caught up in a scandal involving a young woman and a prostitution ring. When the story broke, the governor's opponents in the state legislature threatened to impeach him unless he resigned immediately. Without exception, the news shows castigated him; he publicly apologized to his wife, his family, and the voters, yet for days on end the attacks on him continued unabated. As this furor went on, how many of the newscasters, who were expressing their great sorrow for "his poor wife and family," perceived Eliot Spitzer through the eyes of a Betsie ten Boom and also said, "Wow, that poor guy"? Of the many I heard, only one, and he was a close friend of the family.

Before we go further with this, let's pause for a moment and explore a different and what might seem unusual question. Taking into consideration the ideal of the eventual improvement of the mental states of all concerned, was what happened to Mr. Spitzer and his family actually all bad? First, let's look at the situation as it relates to him, but through the eyes of a man with a far wiser-than-average perception.

In Plato's *Gorgias,* Socrates teaches that when a man "has need of it, he must suffer to be disciplined if he is to become happy," saying,

> Of those who suffer evil ... which is the most wretched, the man who [is treated] ... and gets rid of the evil, or he who is not treated but still retains it? It is a just penalty that disciplines us ... and cures us of evil.... Then the happiest of men is he who has no evil in his soul ...
>
> And the second in order is he who is delivered from it, and [this] we found [is] the man who is [discov-

ered] and rebuked.... Then [he] is most unhappy who is afflicted with evil and does not get rid of this.[26]

From Socrates's viewpoint, what happened to Eliot Spitzer was, for him, actually an improvement in a miserable situation. But was it an improvement for his wife as well? From a fully inclusive perspective, and in the longer run, it certainly could have been. Why? Because once a festering wound in any marriage has been exposed to the light of day, the sickness behind it can be understood as sickness and the foundation of the relationship possibly repaired. As for their two daughters, were they, too, given an opportunity to benefit from the situation? If so, how? By learning that the world they live in, where no one is perfect, will continue to appear painful until the day they learn that what will heal their pain is not time, but forgiving their dad for having clay feet. And since everyone can learn, hopefully the unpleasant exposure also ended up turning the young woman involved in the direction of a less self-hurtful way to live.

Who else can benefit from this scenario? All who perceive it as an opportunity to refuse safe harbor to any condemnatory thoughts that arise in their minds about Mr. Spitzer, thus arriving at a better place from which to perceive not only him, but all others who are in distress.

Along those lines, in that same *Gorgias*, Socrates tells a friend that he agrees with Homer's assertion that "The just are gentle."[27] So what about us? Are we truly just and therefore gentle? As gentle as the Amish people who went, en masse, to comfort the non-Amish family of the man who had shot and killed a number of their schoolchildren? As just as the Japanese family who, after their exchange-student daughter was killed in San Diego by another student, traveled to the States and hired an attorney to defend the life of their child's killer?

In the introduction to Plato's *Republic* it says,

> The Republic lays down a standard for human life. To order a state rightly men's [minds] must be raised to behold the universal light. There is a truth beyond this

shifting, changing world, and men can seek and find it. The just state may never come into being, but a man can always be just, and only the just can know what justice is. Of this Socrates himself was the proof....[28]

I once saw this warning on a graffiti-covered wall in a New York subway: "Give to mental health or I'll kill you." In a not-so-humorous way, not giving of our understanding to those who are presently in trouble might not kill us, but it will certainly retard the germination of compassion toward ourselves. As Shakespeare said in the *Merchant of Venice,*

The quality of mercy is not strain'd,—
It droppeth as the gentle rain from Heaven
Upon the place beneath: it is twice blessed,—
It blesseth him that gives, and him that takes;[29]

Is this the way of thinking we are meant to evolve into and then find reason to apply universally? The ten Boom sisters seemed to think so, as did Socrates, Plato, and others. Or, are these examples deviations from the norm and exceptions to the rule, with Homer mistaken, Plato impractical, and true justice the natural cohort of punishment? Are people like these the odd ducks who don't get what the world is really like? Or are they, perhaps, the swans we don't recognize for what they are, because our minds are still darkened and our perceptions limited? And while it is obvious that most of us are not as advanced in our ways as was Socrates, should we not, as Epictetus (the freed Roman slave and stoic philosopher, ca. 100 CE) suggested, "live as though we were doing our best to become like Socrates"?[30]

Are some things simply unforgivable? Or is the cruelty so often encountered in our world not only rooted in, to quote Robert Burns, "man's inhumanity to man,"[31] but equally in our own unwillingness to understand the perpetrator of the crime in his or her own misery and wretchedness? Said another way, should people be looked down upon because of their errors or recognized as mistake-makers who will one day do better?

If it is true that everyone has the same capacity for goodwill, then the logical course of action for anyone seeking to grow in this goodwill would be to disapprove of his or her every thought that speaks out against it. In simple terms, the question is, "If the just don't condemn, should we?"

Did the Apple Fall Far from the Tree?

A philosopher and early church father named Origen (ca. 250 CE) used an interesting metaphor to explain humanity's limitations in perception. A deliberately simplistic description of his idea is that, in the beginning, we were like apples on a tree. We were connected to one another through the tree's trunk and branches, at rest in the knowledge that we were one and the same. Then, something inexplicable happened, causing the apples to fall, a few close enough to the trunk and to one another that these apples could remember the unity they had descended from and yet continued to share, some farther away and somewhat stupefied, and still others so far removed that they lost all conscious memory of that original state.

It should be clear to any thoughtful person that living in a world as riddled with hatred, blame, and judgment as is ours means something has gone terribly wrong. This *cannot* be our natural state, and something like Origen's conception of "the fall" and its attendant confusion might well serve as a metaphorical premise for explaining this state of the world, which we seem unable to understand or undo. One benefit of the metaphor is that it offers a more generous basis from which to look upon the destructive and self-destructive behaviors of others. Beginning to perceive people who make mistakes as unknowing, we eventually see that they stumble and fall not because they are bad, but because they are unaware of what they are doing. This is the meaning behind Socrates's statement, "to act beneath oneself is the result of pure ignorance."[32]

Accepting Socrates's teaching and Origen's metaphor as benchmarks for our interpretations of the actions of others leads to the possibility that those we consider evil-doers may be more like bewildered fallen apples than anything else. Perhaps these ideas also explain why some come more easily to a benign perception of mistake-makers than do others; an absence of generosity toward others representing no more than the darkened outlooks of those who, like the mistake-makers they are condemning, simply fell farther from the trunk.

A different way to say this is that everyone is returning to reason and gentleness at the speed at which he or she is capable of doing so. If this is true, it means—and this is absolute or it is not true at all—that despite all appearances to the contrary, everyone is doing his or her best at any given moment. And, since the world is made up of people, this hypothesis would apply equally to nations and religions and other groups caught up in insisting that theirs is the right way and there can be no other.

It is easy to conclude that those who continue repeating the same mistakes should be doing better and leave it at that. It is not so easy to accept that, while their potential is certainly greater, their actions are an expression of where they are in their process of returning to the trunk, and therefore, at the moment, they cannot do better. What makes this latter viewpoint more difficult to accept is that such acceptance would mean the end of our fitness to judge *anyone*. And this assumed power of judgment is a critical defense of our treasured belief in our own great worth. In other words, if the only real flaw to be found in another apple were his or her unawareness, and the scales of judgment we hold so dear were thereby rendered questionable at best, would not our beloved self-importance be questionable as well?

Only the Self-Accused Condemn

I mentioned earlier that I grew up in an interesting neighborhood. Here's one lesson I learned there about my own faults and the ineffectiveness of attempting to escape from them through projection and judgment.

One Friday night, I went with a bunch of the guys to the finals of the Golden Gloves in Madison Square Garden. The main reason we went was that one of my friends was a boxer, and his younger brother was fighting for the heavyweight championship. The brother put forth a good effort and was never knocked down, but he ended up losing the fight on points. This so disturbed my friend that when we arrived back home and walked into a neighborhood bar, and a guy we all knew well said something innocuous to us, my friend yelled at him. The other guy thought he was kidding and said something flip back to him, at which point, my boxer friend, without notice, clocked him. The guy put his hand up and yelled, "Hey, what the hell!" and my friend hit him again, this time so hard that he broke a couple of the guy's front teeth.

Now, violence in that neighborhood, in those days, was far from uncommon. (Once, after I had moved away, I took a friend from New Jersey back there for a night of drinking, warning him that if a fight broke out, he was to stay out of it. We were in three bars in the first couple of hours, and in every one we saw a fight.) Even so, this situation was so unexpected and unreasonable that I started to step in to try to break it up, but as I did so, another friend grabbed me, saying, "Stay out of this, Bob." Since the guy who was doing the punching was so enraged and could also hit like a mule, fortunately for me—and for him, too, since he would have felt even worse about himself if he had also hit me—I stepped back. Instead, as soon as things settled down, I took the guy who had been punched into the bathroom. I helped him wash his bloody face and tried to comfort him as he kept repeating, "What'd I do? What'd I do?"

After that night, and for quite a while, I silently condemned my friend the boxer. I mindlessly judged him as being somewhat of a bad guy. In this unjust perception, I found in his seeming fall from grace not the expression of ignorance it was, but a convenient excuse to over-look my own similar mistakes. Only as I grew older did I realize where the lesson in this lay, not so much by coming to understand the insanity of thwarted familial pride that led to his mistake, but by recognizing that my judgment of him had its roots in a secreted condemnation of myself for doing like things. Further, had I been capable at the time of assessing the situation as a whole, I would have understood that the puncher was, albeit in a different form, in just as much trouble as the one being punched—and in just as much trouble as I was for feeding the idea that we are all seemingly separated into better and worse people by empathizing with one at the expense of the other.

Simply put, those who attack, even in the most violent outbursts of rage, are people in trouble and pain and, in some ways, may be in even greater distress than those whom they are treating so badly. Second, when we find ourselves justified in joining with one and excluding the other, *we* are the ones in need of correction.

This scenario, more or less, depicts one of our more difficult problems. In a common certitude that we understand whatever we perceive, we either identify with the victor—often out of a desire to gain his approval, because the victor seems stronger—disregarding the rights of the victim, or, instead, join with the victim in an equally careless disregard, this time for the suffering of the victor. Either way, we, who see only one side, unknowingly perpetuate the unhappy myth of real differences among apples. Secure in the unfounded notion that we know whom to join with and whom to oppose, we delude ourselves into believing we are choosing rightly or, heaven help us, "doing good."

In my case, I had lost my sense of common decency, a fatal error for anyone wishing to maintain a balanced perspective, meaning one that is inclusive, with goodwill toward all. Plato offers a little insight into taking our focus off the mistakes of others and solving our own problems first:

> A man can only attain freedom by fighting the cowardice within himself and vanquishing it. Without experience and discipline in that contest, no man will ever be half the champion he might be.[33]

34

When I finally realized that the problem I was having with my friend wasn't about him, but was a cowardly attempt on my part to shift the burden of my hidden guilt for similar actions onto him—a process called projection—it turned into a valuable lesson in personal accountability. This, in turn, brought me closer to accepting that the emotional content of my problems with others is *always* about me. *A Course in Miracles* (*ACIM*), a most profound discourse on spirituality and psychology, describes it this way:

> Only the self-accused condemn. As you prepare to make a choice that will result in different outcomes, there is first one thing that must be overlearned. It must become a habit of response so typical of everything you do that it becomes your first response to all temptation, and to every situation that occurs. Learn this, and learn it well, for it is here delay of happiness is shortened by a span you cannot realize. You never hate your brother for his sins, but only for your own.[34]

While this means that only the guilty blame, it does not mean we are to foolishly condone an aggressor's bad actions any more than we are our own. Nor does it mean that the form of the other's error is always the same as ours. What it does mean is that if we find ourselves unwilling to understand the suffering in the mind of the mistake-maker, and are condemning him right along with his error, we should question in whom our unforgiveness really lies. In his book *Parents and Children,* Kenneth Wapnick says,

> *A Course in Miracles* teaches that "projection makes perception," that the world is "the outside picture of an inward condition." Therefore, our perceptions of an external situation reveal the thoughts in our minds that we wish to deny. It goes without saying that, for example, accusing someone of being a sinner because of [a crime] does not mean that I am accusing myself of the

specific form of [that crime]. However, the *meaning* of such an aggressive act is surely in me as well—the need at times to dominate another through sheer force of will or physical strength in order to have my desires filled; not caring about the other person, but only me. Again, that tendency may not be nearly as extreme or as violent in expression as [the crime I judge], but it exists in all of us nonetheless. And it is our guilt over such a wish that finds its projected scapegoat in actual [criminals]. Their blatant "sin" nicely serves this need of finding a suitable object for projection, obscuring the fact of our common unity.[35]

Leo Tolstoy, echoing Socrates, said, "People aren't punished *for* their sins, but *by* their sins, which is the most difficult punishment."[36] This also means that while punishment for punishers and "an eye for an eye" are common themes of the world, there is no way to attempt to hurt another without suffering for it in turn. Therefore, if we are to learn to be truly charitable, we must come to see that even in the most difficult of situations, the victimizers are as deeply enmeshed in pain and sorrow as the people they attack.

Any honest examination of how badly we feel after *any* form of assault on another proves Tolstoy was right. Accordingly, if we would take the time to magnify any of our errors to the degree of some attacks made by others, and then imagine how great the suffering in those attackers' minds, we'd grieve for them right along with their victims. After that, while taking every precautionary step to restrict the really violent ones, especially the psychopaths—and clearly there *are* psychopaths—we could better ask ourselves whether we are justified in adding to their distress by trying to hurt them further.

Common sense and a reasonable modesty tell us that there is nothing meritorious or particularly admirable in gaining a perspective that is generous toward everyone engaged in the human struggle. Understood properly, a generous perspective is merely evidence of having taken a logical step in the right direction.

The Guard Within

The means by which we come to understand the dangers of fragmentation into good guys and bad are unimportant, but if we want to escape the painful consequences of our isolating self-centeredness, then understanding this danger, and understanding it well, is beyond important. One person who made this shift from separation to inclusion in a powerful way is Claude Anshin Thomas. In his book *At Hell's Gate: A Soldier's Journey from War to Peace,* he describes its beginnings in Vietnam:

> Every time it rains I walk through war. For two rainy seasons I experienced very heavy fighting ... Now when it rains, I am still walking through fields of young men screaming and dying. I can still see the tree lines disintegrating from Napalm. I still hear seventeen-year-old boys crying for their mothers.... Only after re-experiencing all of that can I come to the awareness that, right now, it's just raining.[37]

Thomas goes on to speak about his experiences on a gunship helicopter, where he logged over six hundred combat missions. He says, "The only experience I had with the Vietnamese was, they were my enemy. Every one of them: shopkeepers, farmers, women, children, babies."[38] He describes once passing three or four men dressed as Buddhist monks who, when thirty meters beyond him, turned and opened fire on his group of seven, killing three and wounding two.

He admits to eventually reaching a state of mind where "indifference and terror were completely intermingled," recounting one tragic interaction this way:

On another occasion the infantry unit that our company supported began to receive heavy automatic weapons fire from a village, so they radioed us and asked for help. We flew in with a heavy-fire team, opened fire, and without thought ... killed everything [people, children, animals] that moved. All that remained when we were finished were dead bodies, fire, and smoke.[39]

Thomas speaks of numerous atrocities on both sides, including accounts of friends picking up crying babies to comfort them and being blown up because the babies were booby-trapped. Yet, believing himself to have been on the side of truth and justice, when a beautiful girl approached him upon his arrival home at Newark Airport, with his chest full of medals, he fully expected to be greeted with a kiss. To his shock, she spit right in his face.

After a period of great confusion adjusting to society, he went to college, joined a peace movement, suffered terribly from flashbacks, and always slept with a gun under his pillow. After more years of emotional struggle, he finally recognized his need to stop avoiding his suffering and to, instead, face it, making what he called "a commitment to living in conscious awareness" and offering to others the wisdom that he had learned. Similar to what Plato once said about "fighting the cowardice within," Thomas said he learned this: "I [cannot] stop ... war ... I can only stop the war that is within me."[40]

After years of effort, he described his part in a peace pilgrimage to Auschwitz and what he had learned about himself to that point:

One of the things I understood while I was there is that even today, at any moment, the Holocaust can repeat itself; it exists now. Each of us, under certain circumstances, could act with this kind of horrendous cruelty. I know this personally to be true. [There and then] I became acutely aware not only of the suffering of the prisoners of the camps, but the suffering of all the soldiers who had been guards.… I realized that I must look at their suffering and not only at that of the prisoners. I must see the guard that is within me.[41]

He then finished his description of the trip to Auschwitz with another expression of the remarkable extent to which his compassion had grown. Speaking of the Polish people who then lived in the town just outside the walls of the camp, he said that to be "aware of what was going on inside the camp: to have breakfast every morning, go to work, come back home … it must have been terrible to live in such a state of denial and numbness."[42]

Regardless of how Claude Thomas arrived at his way of thinking, it is clear that his outlook, like that of Plato, Socrates, the ten Boom sisters, Kenneth Wapnick, and some others, is not the usual one. Yet should it be? Here's a little syllogism we might consider: war is madness; the world is constantly at war; therefore, the world must be mad. "I'm not mad!" you or I might exclaim. Yet, like so many others, we *are* at war—in our every angry thought or spiteful deed, even in our reticence over considering the suffering of the oppressor along with that of the oppressed. Therefore, to some degree, and at some times, we too must be somewhat mad.

It takes a while to realize that the only real difference between Claude Thomas's description of the village they tore asunder in Vietnam and the Holocaust is simply one of size and number, and that punching someone, slandering another, or hating an oppressor for his or her actions, are all, while different in form, in content one and the same. They *all* emanate from a sickening love of self to the detriment of others, and healing that sickness—through the removal of ignorance—is, as we'll see in future chapters, the real life's work of everyone.

CHAPTER 3

Our Shared Responsibility

I HEARD FROM MY SON AGAIN a few days later, and according to his best recollection, his latest serial misadventures went something like this: He was released from the hospital as scheduled, leaving with twenty-five Vicodin tablets someone had issued him as part of his comedown program. Being faithful to his antecedents, he immediately went to a drug dealer and traded the Vicodin for crack. He then wandered the streets in a daze for a couple of days. After he ran out of crack and started to withdraw, he went back to the same lockdown section of the hospital he had just left and rang the bell over and over until someone came out. He then talked that person into helping him get into a short-term recovery home. From that recovery home, and with their assistance, he applied for and was accepted into a ninety-day Salvation Army drug program he would be able to enter a few days later.

In our again sober, reasonable, and seemingly rational conversation, he said he felt that this was exactly what he was looking for; that ninety days sober, while out of prison, would change everything. While I'm sure he meant it, I'm sorry to say I didn't believe a word of it, thinking that once he felt better, he would revert to his pattern and find a way to drink and use drugs again.

Is my son a tragic figure? Or is he just one more of the many in the world who are still singing, "I did it my way," and refusing to listen to their own good sense? For example, as he passed on going to the taco shop in Anchorage to begin partying, had the voice of reason said something to him like, "Don't fall under the spell of false desire and do this to yourself again"? Certainly. Had he severed his connection with this voice of reason by tuning it out? Surely not. Rather, it was waiting patiently for the day when he became disgusted enough with the results of following his own bad advice to tune back in, this being a valid description of not only his state but also of one of humanity's main problems—perhaps, humanity's only main problem. In other words, *everyone* has this same reason and good sense within, but far too often, we reject its counsel in favor of the senseless dictates of what Claude Thomas referred to as "the guard within." And since the consequences of this tendency are always so dire, it seems logical that the question we all should be asking ourselves is, "If I'm not possessed, then why in heaven's name do I continue such harmful practices?"

Knowing Ourselves

Stepping back from the wrong-minded beliefs of the guard within, which tell us that the selfishness that surrounds us is just the way things are and must be, let's consider again the possibility that many of us are contributing to the worldwide phenomenon of selfishness by acting carelessly, if not badly. To aid in our investigation of what we spend very little time thinking about, let's look at the following statement from *Global Capitalism*, a book of essays by people such as Paul Volcker and George Soros, the preface of which opens

> The Third World is being environmentally despoiled by
> the First World, which uses its power to ensure that the
> international rules of the game benefit it.[43]

In support of this idea, one of the book's contributors, Dr. Vandana Shiva, begins her essay "The World on Edge" as follows:

> For the poorer two-thirds of humanity living in the South, nature's capital is their source of sustenance and livelihood. The destruction, diversion and takeover of their eco-systems in order to extract natural resources or dump wastes generates a disproportionate burden for the poor. In a world of globalized, deregulated commerce in which everything is tradable, and economic strength is the only determinant of power and control, resources move from the poor to the rich, and pollution moves from the rich to the poor.[44]

If the world is indeed this selfish, why don't we see that and take it seriously? Could it be that we don't look because we don't want to see, hiding from the recognition that if things are really this gross, then we are no less than the accomplices of those who have their hands in the pockets of the poor?

Some sincere people believe so, and more. In his *Confessions of an Economic Hit Man*, author John Perkins begins a description of his career as an international business consultant with the following:

> Economic hit men (EHMs) are highly paid professionals who cheat countries around the world out of trillions of dollars. They funnel money from the World Bank, the U.S. Agency for International Development (USAID), and other foreign "aid" organizations into the coffers of huge corporations and the pockets of a few wealthy families who control the planet's natural resources. Their tools include fraudulent financial reports, rigged elections, payoffs, extortion, sex, and murder. They play a game ... that has taken on new and terrifying dimensions during this time of globalization.
>
> I should know; I was an EHM.[45]

Perkins fills his book with various tales detailing how he and others aided corporations in getting what they wanted in many parts of the world, but an excerpt from his visit to Ecuador will suffice for all the rest:

> Quito, Ecuador's capital, stretches across a volcanic valley high in the Andes. The city of Shell ... hacked out of Ecuador's Amazon jungle to service the oil company whose name it bears, is nearly eight thousand feet lower than Quito....
>
> Much has changed in thirty-five years.... A trans-Andean pipeline built shortly after my first visit has leaked over a half million barrels of oil into the fragile rain forest.... [I]ndigenous cultures have been driven to the verge of collapse, and pristine rivers transformed into flaming cesspools....
>
> Because of my fellow EHM and me, Ecuador is in far worse shape today than she was before we introduced her to the miracles of modern economics, banking and engineering ... the official poverty level growing from 50 to 70 percent, under or unemployment increasing from 15 to 70 percent, and public debt from $240 million to $16 billion.....
>
> For every $100 in crude taken out of the Ecuadorian rain forest, the oil companies receive $75. Of the remaining $25, three-quarters must go to paying off foreign debt. Most of the remainder covers military and other government expenses—which leaves about $2.50 for health, education, and programs aimed at helping ... [those] whose lives have been so adversely impacted by the dams, the drilling, and the pipelines; and who are dying from a lack of edible food and potable water....
>
> How, I asked myself, did a nice kid from rural New Hampshire ever get into such a dirty business?[46]

What relevance do such examples of unfairness in faraway places have for us who are neither economic hit men nor heads of exploitive corporations? Not much, if these people who take without consideration are different from us, but a great deal if their actions are expressive of what can happen to anyone who listens to the self-dealing advice of his or her own selfishness.

What it comes down to is this: if those who exploit the weak and poor are actually like the rest of us, then we have much to learn from them about what we may be hiding *from* ourselves *about* ourselves. Denial helps no one. Without getting in touch with our own inclinations toward what is, to put it plainly, avarice, we will never find freedom from its influence.

Only by acknowledging our acquiescence in the ego-driven scheme of worldwide greed can we grow in awareness and learn to go beyond our wrong-minded notions of what we are and what we are meant to be to one another. As Krishnamurti puts it in his *The First and Last Freedom*:

> So long as I do not understand myself, I have no basis for thought ... for action....
>
> Without knowing yourself, without knowing your own way of thinking and why you think certain things, without knowing the background of your conditioning and why you have certain beliefs about ... your country and your neighbor and yourself, how can you think truly about anything?...
>
> The more you know yourself, the more clarity there is.... Only when the mind is tranquil—through self-knowledge and not through imposed self-discipline ... can [there] be creative action.... Without this ... experience, merely to read books, to attend talks, to do propaganda, is so infantile ... whereas if one is able to understand oneself ... then perhaps there can be

transformation in the ... relationships about us and so in the world in which we live.[47]

Can you and I learn to do this, not just for ourselves, but for everyone? Can we, for example, through a dedication to understanding ourselves better, come to a perception of the exploiters and the bullies and the users of others not as evil people, but as what they more likely are: fellow apples who have forgotten who they are, where they come from, and what their true relationship is to those whom they presently regard as less important than themselves? And, while we are at it, can we not also discover that it is possible to disapprove of their actions without condemning them, if, in actuality, they don't really understand what they are doing?

What if We've All Been Wrong?

The following from *Escape from Evil* by Pulitzer Prize-winning author Ernest Becker provides a good example of an idea that can make us want to turn away because it's so personal and uncomfortable to conceive of as true.

> Modern man lives in illusion, said Freud, because he denies or suppresses his wish for the other's death and for his own immortality; and it is precisely because of this illusion that mankind cannot get control over social evils like war. This is what makes war irrational: each person has the same hidden problem, and as antagonists obsessively work their cross purposes, the result [being] truly demonic.... Not only enemies but even friends ... are fair fuel for our own perpetuation, says Freud. In our unconscious we daily and hourly deport all who stand in our way, all who have offended or injured us. This is the price of our natural animal narcissism. Very few of us, if pressured, would be unwilling to sacrifice someone

else in our place.... Thus ... we see how right Freud was
[when he pointed out our] enslavement by our illusions
based on our repressions....[48]

If we are indeed enslaved "by our illusions based on our repressions," it would make the pertinent question not how we should solve the problems we perceive as so important "out there." Rather, we should ask, "How do we uncover and resolve the problem of our desperate craving for self-importance and self-perpetuation, which has led us so far from reconciliation and the remembrance of our unity?" When we look without blinders at what otherwise decent people are willing to stoop to in personal, international, or corporate affairs to get their own ways, or in the political process to get elected, it becomes difficult to deny that aggrandizement of the self has a terrible attraction. Be it in an argument, business, or war, the stultifying belief seems to be that winning at any cost is the only acceptable option, although it is a self-centered idea that experience proves is false.

Here is a seemingly minor example from my childhood, yet one that speaks unequivocally to what I mean. When I was about ten, I was fighting with another boy. I was winning the fight until his brother jumped in, after which I lost. I went home in a tearful rage over the unfairness of it all and asked my mother if I should go back out and beat the boy up, which by then I knew I could do. My mother, being wiser than my rage, said I shouldn't, and I didn't. Since knowing in advance that I would have won the fight and going through with it anyway would have been unfair, as is any form of taking advantage, not doing so turned out to be a significant victory over my wounded pride, and the other boy later became one of my closest friends.

Knowing when it is appropriate to defend oneself and when it will end up unhelpful is a complicated subject. Are there times when one is stuck with the need to put a limit on another's activities? Yes. Are there also ways to step aside from much of the neediness and hostility that we, as individuals, corporations, and nations, engage in because we first listened to our wrong-mindedness? Yes. Does seeking assiduously for these more harmonious ways of living make more sense than engaging in endless battles? Yes.

When I was younger and learning that there was no way to truly gain when there was a loser to go along with the "winner" (and this applies to slander, arguments, and schemes just as much as it does to fighting), this is the truth I began to discover: every time I bullied someone, I felt badly. Every time I allowed myself to be bullied, I felt ashamed. Every time I won a fight, soon after I felt guilty. Every time I lost a fight, I ended up feeling resentful. So where in all this was the winning? In my burgeoning experience, nowhere. This doesn't mean that I became a pacifist or believed it was never right to defend one's interests or country. In a world as troubled as ours, at times, it is. What I was slowly learning, however, is that not fighting against, gossiping about, arguing with, or humiliating others when it can be avoided—and, as with the boy I didn't go back and beat up, it can almost *always* be avoided—is what the rational tell us is the higher road.

For all of us who value the peace of mind that comes only with laying down the senseless shield of pride and the double-edged sword of vanity, the answer to the opposition we encounter in the world is neither force nor conversion. The solution to such situations—be they personal, familial, or national—is to put aside the self-centeredness that lies beyond our demands and expectations *before* we come to the conclusion that we know what others should do. From that place of greater respect, we can view the situation with a recognition of equal rights among the participants and, therefore, gain a more reasonable perception of it. That more reasonable perception, in turn, will show us that since our previous approaches to one another have accomplished little beyond keeping us in the separating and unrelenting war of conflicting opinions, they are deeply suspect—meaning it is certainly possible that, up to now, *we may all have been wrong.*

Making a Different Choice

As Kenneth Wapnick points out, regarding the responsibility I bear in my relationships with others, while there may be times when I am helpless about what someone is doing, this doesn't mean that I am helpless in how I think about what they are doing. In one place in his book *Form versus Content,* he responds to a student's question about a difficult relationship as follows:

> When you are having trouble, you need to recognize first [i.e., not deny] that you are having trouble. Second, try to get past the temptation to attribute the cause of the unpleasantness or discomfort to something external. That attempt is the invitation ... [that] sets into motion the process of [healing]. This means withdrawing the projection of blame from others, placing responsibility for your unhappiness within, then looking at the source of the unhappiness you have chosen, realizing you chose it and so can choose again. *The willingness to attribute the cause of your unhappiness to your mind's decision is the core of forgiveness.*...[49] (italics added)

This also means that, perceived rightly, situations don't have to be pleasant in order for one to remain peaceful. But is this, no matter the severity of the provocation, always true? Another besides Dr. Wapnick who seems to think so is Gregory David Roberts, as expressed in the opening paragraph of his semiautobiographical *Shantaram*:

> It took me a long time and most of the world to learn what I know about love and fate and the choices we make, but the heart of it came to me in an instant, while I was chained to a wall and being tortured. I realized, somehow, through the screaming in my mind, that even in that shackled, bloody helplessness, I was still free: free to hate the men who were torturing me, or to forgive

them. It doesn't sound like much, I know. But in the flinch and the bite of the chain, when it's all you've got, that freedom is a universe of possibility. And the choice you make, between hating and forgiving, can become the story of your life.[50]

This is reminiscent of Victor Frankl's statement in *Man's Search for Meaning* that what he discovered to be true in the concentration camp was that no one could take from anyone "the last of human freedoms—to chose one's attitude in any given set of circumstances."[51] That choice, as Gregory David Roberts put it, really *does* "become the story of your life." For example, how, other than through choosing to forgive, can one become right-minded and unconflicted and remain peaceful in any situation? Therefore, for those who value peace over conflict, forgiveness is always the better choice.

In addition, is it really sensible for me to remain bitter because another failed me in some way or because someone more powerful dominated me in the past? If it is, it must also be "sensible" for me to remain guilty over my own similar mistakes. And if both are so, then what am I left with? A life lived in the shadows of resentment and regret, using distraction as the defense against my loneliness and despair.

On the other hand, what would happen to my view of the world if I chose to accept the idea established in the previous section—that my approaches to others may have often been wrong? Might not this lead to other liberating concepts? For example, since I now know that I deeply regret even the most minor physical or verbal assault I ever made on anyone, and since I'm also convinced that, underneath the roles we've adopted, we are essentially alike, wouldn't that mean that others, whether or not they are ready to acknowledge it, are equally regretful of even their most minor assaults on me?

Another thing I am also now aware of is that despite the arousal of any of my wrong-minded memories to the contrary, deeper than their shallow persuasions and duplicitous witness to my vulnerability, I am completely unhurt by any past mistake made by anyone else.

Therefore, again, if we *are* all alike, then regardless of what others' bad memories may say to them about my past mistakes, in truth, no one is presently hurt by any errors I have made, but only by their decisions to hold onto them.

Lastly, if this is true, then, in effect, whether we are in touch with this truth yet or not, we are already, at some level of the mind, saying to one another, "Hey, I am so sorry for my ignorance in my past relationship to you. What happened that time when I insulted you, or assaulted you, or pretended to be wounded by you wasn't what it appeared to be but was simply the result of my confusion at the time. And to anyone who made such mistakes with me, the absence of any lingering pain on my part has brought me to the place where I can now say, and mean, 'Thank you for helping me understand my past and my power of reevaluation in this healthier light.' "

Whenever we forget that everyone's first responsibility is to look upon everyone else with respect and understanding and compassion, and then unknowingly engage instead in the ugliness of blame and pretend woundedness, we attack ourselves. How? By offering support to the belief that our own past errors were not simply mistakes made in a state of confusion, but crimes that cannot be erased. Now our guilty memories are no longer fading self-accusations, but statements of fact for which, in order to balance the scales of "justice," we will one day be called to account.

To make the conscious choice to begin thinking of others and ourselves in these more intelligent ways has interesting ramifications. What it comes down to is thinking about everyone we meet as an actor in the drama of our lives, and then separating the actor out from his or her actions, which gives rise to the idea that these actions are merely evidence of the actor's mental state—whether he or she is still a captive of the thinking of the guard within or is beginning to (or has) set him or herself free. In this new and much more benign interpretation of reality, the answer to the heartfelt question of Mr. Perkins, the EHM, "How ... did a nice kid from rural New Hampshire ever get into such a dirty business?" is as simple as this: that was where he was in his understanding then and not where he is now.

CHAPTER 4

Joining with Equals

A NOTHER FEW WEEKS PASSED BEFORE I heard from my son again. He was high and not making complete sense, but what I gleaned from our disjointed conversation was that he had been back in the same hospital and then sober for a few days, after which he relapsed, if such a word fits the situation. Then, apparently with the assistance of a doctor from the hospital, he had gained entry into a food stamp program. What was peculiar about this was that the program paid him $470 per month, backdated to the day he arrived in Hawaii, through a debit card he could use at an ATM machine. His first payment was roughly $700, which, as could be expected, he promptly used for the high he was on.

He told me that his new plan was to go to the other side of the island, saying that he was "fed up with being disrespectful" (meaning, to society) and was "going to make it this time." To this, I said, "Good," doing the only thing I could think of as helpful at the moment, which was to listen and be quiet in my responses. I remained aware of our fundamental equality and sameness, determined to keep no thought in my head other than that of wishing him the very best fortune in all matters of his world, his life, and his mind.

Seeing Others as Equals

Earlier, I alluded to the idea that a reasonable perception looks beyond the superficial, recognizing that *everyone* is on the same journey of, to put it one way, returning to the trunk. It should be obvious that speaking about this, and even accepting it, is a far cry from living with it as a premise, with everyone we encounter and on a daily basis. Yet this is the journey we take, going from an intellectual acceptance of the idea of an underlying and shared purpose, onto and through every mental and emotional defense against it, and finally to living it. In my own experience, this meant staying with (or facing directly) every seduction of my pride-driven and beggarly ego over a long period of time.

To cross the desert of ignorance and to stop seeing those who travel with us to the same goal as enemies and strangers requires that we lay aside all of the distorted conceptions we hold about equals, which make up such a large share of what we seem to "know" as reality. When I meet another person in my given role for that occasion, it is hard not to get lost in our roles, as well as in my prejudices and their judgments alike. My perception and our history join to tell me that this person is solely the father, mother, brother, sister, wife, child, friend, enemy, boss, employee, policeman, or waiter that I see. My sight shows me not you, but the image I have made of you, and my wishes and memories bring me the story I hold about who you are and what you mean to me. The point of learning is to see how personally involved I am in making our relationship what it seems to be, and how foolish I am when I, with my limited understanding, believe that I am the one who usually knows better.

If it is true that we are *all* engaged in a process of uncovering the remembrance of our unity in truth, then every condemnation of others for not doing better that I embrace is counterproductive and senseless in regard to my own pursuit of that purpose. My function is not to condemn others, fix others, or correct others, but to learn to give up judgment and accept others as they are. As John Locke, speaking like Plato, put it,

> We should do well to commiserate our mutual igno-
> rance ... and not instantly treat others as obstinate and
> perverse because they will not renounce their own and
> receive our opinions.... For where is the man that has
> incontestable evidence of the truth of all he holds, or
> of the falsehood of all he condemns; or can say that he
> has examined to the bottom all his own or other men's
> opinions? The necessity of believing without knowledge,
> nay, often upon very slight grounds in this fleeting state
> of action and blindness we are in, should make us more
> busy and careful to inform ourselves than to restrain
> others.... There is reason to think that if men were bet-
> ter instructed themselves, they would be less imposing
> on others.[52]

The Declaration of Independence states, "We hold these truths to be self-evident, that all men are created equal." The Gettysburg Address begins, "Four score and seven years ago our fathers brought forth on this great continent a new nation, conceived in liberty, and dedicated to the proposition that all men are created equal." In the *Rights of Man,* Thomas Paine says, "I believe in the equality of man."[53] Yet the entry sign of the Serb-controlled Grand Hotel in Kosovo recently read, "No Dogs—No Albanians."

All this is more important than we may realize. The idea of inequal-ity as factual due to behavior, appearance, breeding, intelligence, or capability contains the suggestion that the inequalities we perceive may be permanent; that, in our collective mind, some of us may forever be different than others. That this thinking is divisive is evident; that it can be wanted, if not demanded, by those who still worship at the reliquary of their own specialness and relish their supposed superiority and favor of fortune, less so. The answer to undoing these dark desires is to expose them for the hatefulness they are by practicing vigilant sensitivity to even the slightest hint of their supposed authenticity. No matter one's current condition, *no one* is superior to another, and everything that seems to prove otherwise, nothing but a veil drawn between our awareness and the truth of our shared reality, which, being true, remains forever unaltered.

In the final analysis, condemning and wanting to hurt others for errors born of a still-retarded development of access to common sense is more like wanting to beat a baby for crying than anything else.

Judgment: Born of Opinion

That we are sometimes in concert with the opinions and actions of others, and sometimes not, is telling. What we believe is correct at any given moment is what we believe is correct at that moment, meaning belief is always changeable and, therefore, not invariably reflective of truth. This means that we should do our best not to let our current beliefs harden into convictions, because once they do, they automatically put us at odds with those of differing views. This leads everyone more deeply into the division of interests, making mistaken beliefs and convictions that much harder to release and undo. In short, looking at others through eyes free of all influence requires that we see our opinions as just that—opinions—and considering the limitations of our understanding, for all we know, most of those opinions could be wrong.

The next thing we must gain is an understanding of how our beliefs and desires influence what we perceive. This is an important step toward recognizing that there is a decision-making power at work in our minds, directing the way we look on and relate to others. As *ACIM* says, "Perception is consistent. What you see reflects your thinking. And your thinking but reflects your choice of what you want to see."[54]

In offering us a more intelligent way of managing our perceptions of others, Marcus Aurelius said,

Whenever you meet someone, ask yourself first this immediate question. "What belief does this person hold about the good and bad in life?" Because if he believes this or that about pleasure and pain or fame and obscurity, then I shall not find it strange if he acts in this or that way and I shall remember that he has no choice but to act as he does.[55]

Obviously, Marcus Aurelius meant "he has no choice but to act as he does" while he believes as he does. Everyone, however, has the power to choose what to believe, as well as the power to reconsider, change his or her mind, and choose again. If that were not true, then there would be no hope, no chance for improvement. What Marcus Aurelius is asking us to accept is the idea that, in all situations, people are responding to their present mindsets. Further, we are to refuse safe harbor to all opinions we hold that condemn others for acting in accordance with what they believe.

To be a reliable witness to anything requires fairness and honesty, and in this case, that means recognizing that it is only our opinions and beliefs that provide our seeming understanding of others, rendering our judgments about them as limited in scope and wisdom as the opinions and beliefs from which they spring. This leaves us each in the position of being an inadequate arbiter of another's reality, which is a position of false authority that we must learn to surrender. To live these words can be trying, because to live them means to respect the other's right to believe as he does, even when he is not at the place of respecting ours. Yet how else could it be? It would be hypocritical, if not paradoxical, to profess a belief in equality while maintaining the conviction that our opinions are right and, therefore, the other's must be wrong. How do we know? Maybe his opinions are as right for him as ours are for us. Or perhaps they are his way of arriving at better opinions. Outside of our duly assigned roles—parent, lawmaker, boss, police officer, judge, etcetera—who are we to say what is right or wrong for another? And all this without losing sight of what is clearly destructive and makes no sense.

A Call for a Greater Understanding

Oscar Wilde said, "We are all in this gutter, but some of us are looking at the stars."[56] To be "in this gutter" in terms of our current topic is to be lost in the darkness of damning others, resisting seeing them as equals, and thus refusing to look beyond their errors and recognize how troubled their minds are.

How troubled are the minds of some of our fellow apples? Well, for example, we have centuries of evidence of different faiths murdering not only strangers, but even neighbors in the name of religion. To compound that viciousness, even today, in some societies, honor killings in response to adultery remain not only acceptable, but insisted upon. And to make this insane response to error even harder to overcome, in many places, fathers who refuse to participate in the madness are literally shunned by their neighbors. Think about this demand for adherence to a bitter ancient code. You are a regular person—a father. You have a young daughter, whom you've raised and loved from infancy. In a moment of passion, your child gets carried away and makes a mistake. She knew the rules of your society, she violated them, and now, according to the code, your only "honorable" choice is to exterminate her.

We in the West wouldn't act in such cruel ways, though, would we? I mean, sure, we lock people up and things like that, but that's much more civilized than killing people, right? Or is it? Let's take a look at the following from *Unlocked*, a book by a man named Louis Ferrante, who spent ten years in one of our prisons.

> Imagine coming home from work at the end of a long day. You turn on the TV to watch the news. Murder, rape, arson, kidnapping, torture, all part of the six o'clock show.
>
> You cringe, might even get a cheap thrill. But you're so far removed from it that it is not real. The following day you might talk about it at work, and then it's done. That's entertainment.

Now, imagine every one of those bastards gets dropped off at your house. You're not allowed to leave your house. You must live with them for years, possibly the remainder of your life. When you're hungry, you go to your kitchen for something to eat. Murderers sit at the table. They stare at your food, asking you if you're done before you've begun. They'd easily kill for your dessert....

When you shower, you must strap a steak knife to your waist because there are naked men in your shower who would love to rape you.

After you shower you decide to watch TV and retire to your den. Over the years, men have been killed in your den. In fact, several murderers have taken control of your TV. They're sprawled on the couch, scratching … cursing and yelling.

You get up and leave, walk past your closet, and from inside you hear the whimpering of a man being raped.

You need to get away from all this. You walk out to your backyard for a breath of fresh air. There are ugly men on your patio who would like to kill you. You think about escape, climb the wall and run away from this madness, but there are sharpshooters in gun towers at the corners of your yard. Nothing would please them more than shooting someone.

You return inside to go to bed, a one-inch thick mattress with no pillow. Your bedroom window is barred, and creepy men stare in at you day and night....

The guards are part of some far-off world you like to remember, the real world. Why not talk to them about all this craziness, let them see that you're not as bad as the rest. They might sympathize with you. Instead they mock you. They're paid for, and express great delight in, keeping you confined to this torture chamber, only adding to the insanity of it all....

This is what a person must get used to to survive in this house, the Big House.[57]

Then there is this trying tale from the past, describing one way in which our "God-fearing" pilgrim forefathers dealt with the "heathen" Indians who stood in their way:

In 1637 war broke out in Connecticut between "settlers" and the Pequot people....

Allied with the Narragansetts ... the colonists attacked at dawn. Surrounding the Pequot village, whose inhabitants were mostly women, children, and old men, the English set it on fire and shot those who tried to escape the flames. William Bradford [an onlooker] described the scene: "It was a fearful sight to see them thus frying in the fire ... and horrible was the stink and scent thereof; but the victory seemed a sweet sacrifice, and [the pilgrims] gave praise thereof to God, who had wrought so wonderfully for them."[58]

Keeping in mind our purpose of looking at such examples of cruelty in order to recognize them as signs, not of evil but of calls for understanding from deeply distressed equals, let's now consider these even more gruesome remembrances from those in concentration camps, as recounted by Terrence des Pres in his book *The Survivor*:

The wagon doors were torn ajar. The shouts were deafening. S. S. men with whips and half-wild Alsatian dogs swarmed all over the place.... Corpses were strewn all over the road. The sound of shots rang in the air continuously. Blazing flames shot into the sky. Starving, emaciated human skeletons stumbled toward us, uttering incoherent sounds....

Entering the tent ... I was completely overcome by what I saw.... It was hard to believe the women on the ground were still human beings. Their rigid bodies were skeletons ... their frozen limbs were covered with wounds and bites to the point of bleeding, and countless lice nestled in the pus.... No stretch of the imagination, no power of the written word can convey the horror of that tent....[59]

Not far from us they were burning little children. Babies! Yes, I saw it with my own eyes. Was I awake? No, none of this could be true. It was a nightmare.[60]

Sweet Are the Uses of Adversity

In *As You Like It,* Shakespeare says, "Sweet are the uses of adversity, which like the toad, ugly and venomous, wears yet a precious jewel in his head."[61] Not sweet is adversity, which is often foul, but sweet are its uses (this being the "precious jewel") if we so determine. Even in the worst of circumstances, people of character have demonstrated that this is possible, exiting torture, childhood abuse, betrayal, and all sorts of forms of unfairness with their minds more balanced for the ordeal. And few have made their exits better than the person who wrote the following, found on a scrap of paper in the liberated Ravensbruck Concentration Camp in 1945:

O Lord
Remember not only the men and women of goodwill,
But all those of ill will.
But do not remember all the suffering
They have inflicted on us.
Remember instead all the fruits we have bought
Thanks to this suffering—
Our comradeship, our loyalty, our humility,

Our courage, our generosity, the greatness of heart
Which has grown out of all this;
And when they come to judgment,
Let all the fruits we have born
Be their forgiveness.[62]

Certainly arriving at such a state of balance and forgiveness is no mean feat. There is a predisposition toward hatred in almost everyone, along with a tendency to believe in the reality of a preordained psychological defeat. "I can't do that, bear with that, forgive that," people regularly proclaim. "No one could do that, bear with that, forgive that." Yet the ten Boom sisters did. As did Socrates, Victor Frankl, the Ravensbruck prisoner, and a number of others. Therefore, who is to say that we too cannot walk through the shadow of accusation, which says that others' decisions and not ours are what are disturbing us, and discover a doorway to equanimity on the other side?

"I Am Alone"

Recently, I was driving with my wife Kathy to a favorite eating place. As we approached the rear of the restaurant, I slowed down to see if the first of its two parking lots was full, momentarily blocking the progress of a car I hadn't noticed behind me. The driver immediately blared his horn, and as I pulled into a spot to let him pass, I looked back and saw that, despite having an older woman as his passenger, he was waving his arms and furiously yelling something at me.

Was it my momentary carelessness that caused this man to become so enraged? Or was he already upset—perhaps unknowingly—and just waiting for someone to make a mistake so he could take it out on him or her? And what about me in this situation? Well, having made similar mistakes in the past—in other words, having gotten greatly upset with others over trivial matters and then realizing later that my upset had come not from these others but from my already disturbed state of mind (which is always the only *real* source of disturbance)—I did not take the man's anger personally and instead waved apologetically.

The reason that seemingly minor matters like this are not so minor is that, seen rightly, they are the very things that can lead us to the recognition that, whatever our problems may appear to be in form, in content they are all the same. Each is an opportunity to choose to think rightly and be of quiet assistance to someone who feels separated and afraid.

To get an idea of how pervasive this feeling of alienation from wholeness, or the trunk, is in most of us, here is what David Foster Wallace, author of *Infinite Jest*, had to say about his experience as a human being:

> There is something particularly sad about it, something that doesn't have very much to do with physical circumstances or the economy, or any of the stuff that gets talked about in the news. It's more like a stomach-level sadness. I see it in myself and my friends in different ways. It manifests itself as a kind of lostness.[63]

Or, as Bertrand Russell describes it in *A History of Western Philosophy*:

> Mary Shelley's Frankenstein ... might almost be regarded as an allegorical prophetic history of [the condition of the separated.] Frankenstein's monster is not, as he has become in proverbial parlance, a *mere* monster: he is, at first, a gentle being, longing for human affection, but he is driven to hatred and violence by the horror which his ugliness inspires in those whose love he attempts to gain. Unseen, he observes a virtuous family of poor cottagers, and surreptitiously assists their labors. At length he decides to make himself known to them.
>
> "The more I saw them, the greater became my desire to claim their protection and kindness; my heart yearned to be known and loved by these amiable creatures, to see their sweet looks directed toward me with affection was

the utmost limit of my ambition! I dared not think that they would turn from me with disdain and horror."

But they did. So first he demanded of his creator the creation of a female like himself. And, when that was refused, devoted himself to murdering, one by one, all whom Frankenstein loved. But even then, when all his murders are accomplished, and while he is gazing upon the dead body of Frankenstein, the monster's *sentiments* remain noble:

"That also is my victim! In his murder are my crimes consummated; the miserable genius of my being is wound to its close! Oh Frankenstein! Generous and self-devoted being! What does it avail that I now ask thee to pardon me? I, who irretrievably destroyed thee by destroying all that thou lovest. Alas, he is cold, he cannot answer me…. When I run over the frightful catalogue of my sins, I cannot believe that I am the same creature whose thoughts were once filled with sublime and transcendent visions of the beauty and the majesty of goodness. But it is even so; the fallen angel becomes the malignant devil. Yet even that enemy of God and man had friends and associates in his desolation. I am alone."[64]

"I am alone"—that is the content behind the noise the screaming man was making in his car. And that is what, no matter the number of our friends and associates, we are all so often feeling in our seemingly separated state. And what makes it even sadder is that some part of us must *want* to be in that condition of isolation and self-centeredness, for otherwise we'd be making a sincere effort to join with everyone around us.

Taking to heart this idea of reaching toward reunification with the trunk calls for our coming to a complete change of mind about almost everything. Either the bad things that happen in our lives have the power to leave behind permanent psychological scars, or they do not.

Either empathy and understanding in the presence of hatred are signs of strength, or they are not. Either generosity benefits the giver as well as the receiver, or it does not. And, finally, either true forgiveness has the power to undo the "unforgivable" emotion about what took place *so completely* it's as though it never happened, or it does not. Simply put, each of us is either as equal in will and as strong in character and potential as the writer of the prayer left on the scrap in Ravensbruck, or we are all forever different from one another, with every thought of unity and oneness being nonsense.

Yet, before we come to any conclusions about our potential, let's do the necessary homework and discover whether we've reached the stage of learning in which we're ready to look with compassion upon *all*, after considering some of the most terrible ways ignorance and its confusion can express itself. For starters, here is the Center for Justice and Accountability's assessment of FRAPH, the far-right paramilitary gang that was established in Haiti in the early 1990s with CIA help to undermine support for Jean-Bertrand Aristide:

> The modus operandi of FRAPH was to team up with members of the Haitian Armed Forces in midnight raids of the poorest neighborhood of Port-au-Prince, Gonaives and other cities. In a typical raid, the attackers would invade a house in search of evidence of pro-democracy activity.... The men of the house would frequently be abducted and subjected to torture, many would be summarily executed. The women would frequently be gang-raped, often in front of the remaining family members. The ages of documented victims range from as young as 10 to as old as 80. According to witness reports, sons were forced at gunpoint to rape their mothers.[65]

Next we have this: in June 2008, the *New York Times* reported that some of Robert Mugabe's supporters in Zimbabwe were searching for an opposition leader. When the opposition leader's wife refused to tell them where he was, they attempted to coerce her. How? They broke her ten-month-old baby's legs.

Further, this ghastliness was matched elsewhere that same month, as reported again in the *Times*:

> DAR ES SALAAM, Tanzania—Samuel Mluge steps outside his office and scans the sidewalk. His pale blue eyes dart back and forth, back and forth, trying to focus.
>
> The sun used to be his main enemy, but now he has others.
>
> Mr. Mluge is an albino, and in Tanzania now there is a price for his pinkish skin…
>
> Many people in Tanzania—and across Africa for that matter—believe albinos have magical powers…. Tanzanian officials say witch doctors are now marketing albino skin, bones and hair as ingredients in potions that are promised to make people rich….
>
> The young are often the targets. In early May, Vumilia Makoye, 17, was eating dinner with her family in their hut … when two men showed up with long knives.
>
> When Vumilia's mother, Jeme, saw the men with the knives, she tried to barricade the door of their hut. But the men overpowered her and burst in….
>
> "They cut my daughter quickly," she said, making hacking motions with her hands.
>
> The men sawed off Vumilia's legs above the knee and ran away with the stumps. Vumilia died."[66]

As we consider such examples of unconscionable brutality, the question of everyone's innocence becomes more than an intellectual exercise.

Is it possible for ordinary people like you and me to learn to rise above our conditioning and look at all this differently, to see it as evidence of madness and, in a kindly way, accept the literal and devastating lostness of the breakers of the baby's legs and Vumilia's two murderers? Can we actually arrive at an interpretation of these attacks that recognizes them as a call for a greater understanding and respond accordingly, without diminishing in the slightest the rights of the preyed upon, or ceasing in any way to enforce our laws and restrain those who do harm? One way we might think of this is, if those who attack are fearful, and we don't want to help them to become unfearful, then *we* must be fearful—of joining.

"Take Them In"

Albert Einstein who said, "Nationalism is an infantile disease, the measles of mankind," in his own Buddha-like way, also said,

> A human being is part of the whole … a part limited in time and space. He experiences himself, his thoughts and feelings, as something separated from the rest, a kind of optical delusion of his consciousness. This delusion is a kind of prison for us, restricting us to our personal desires and to affection for a few persons nearest to us. Our task must be to free ourselves from this prison by widening our circle of compassion to embrace all living creatures….[67]

Using Einstein's thought as a benchmark, we might think of our dilemma as one in which we, the apples, after seemingly coming loose from the tree, didn't really scatter to the ground, but fell into "a kind of optical delusion of [our] consciousness." Why else would we keep attacking each other? If this is the case, our task then becomes to wake up to our shared reality and common purpose through the recognition that self-centeredness is another word for imprisonment, and that escape from it comes from "widening our circle of compassion to embrace all living creatures." It is inclusion, not isolation, that does away with our personal measles, as one quoted in *The Survivor* testified to in the following example:

In our group we shared everything; and the moment one
of the group ate something without sharing it, we knew
it was the beginning of the end for him.[68]

The Golden Rule says, "Do unto others as you would have them
do unto you." And it means to do so regardless of whether the others
reciprocate. Maybe some people's belief in scarcity is so strong at the
moment that they don't understand the value of the Golden Rule to
themselves. Maybe their selfishness is buried so deeply in the bereavement over their seemingly permanent separation from the trunk that
they are blinded by grief. And maybe their mean-spiritedness is nothing less than a valuable opportunity to heal our own minds by refusing
to retaliate in kind. As Shakespeare said through Hamlet,

> Use every man after his deserts, and who shall escape
> whipping?
> Use them after your own honor and dignity. The
> less they deserve the more merit is in your bounty.
> Take them in.[69]

Take them in. How far does one have to go with this directive in
order to complete the journey to the far side of the fear-engendering
nature of unforgiveness, to realize that *nothing* in the world of appearances stands beyond the unlimited nature of true forgiveness and its
greater appreciation of the plight of all lost apples? Using an extreme
example, if I'm Jeme, Vumilia's mother, my deepest responsibility, to
myself and all others, is to set my course on arriving at the place of
having the same degree of compassion for Vumilia's killers as I have for
Vumilia and myself. Not easy to achieve for anyone, to say the least. Yet
if this stage in our learning isn't reached, the belief that forgiveness can
be selective and, therefore, compassion limited will linger on, and there
will be no true salvation for anyone at all. It is holding on to grievances
that retards compassion, turning a giver of mercy into a giver of nothing. And such a giver no right-minded person would ever want to be.

CHAPTER 5

Reform Begins at Home

O VER THREE WEEKS HAD PASSED before I heard from my son again. He told me that in those three short weeks he had gone out and binged, spent five days in a Salvation Army detox facility, gained entry to a sober-living center, and appeared in court on an open container charge. After this, he said, he followed through on a plan to get high again. This, in turn, led to another few days in detox. He then met two people outside a church and, through their kindly patronage, was admitted to a Baptist Rebuilder Addiction Ministry. Having been sober for a few days when he called, he was by now living in a group home with some twenty other recovering addicts, doing landscaping for food and shelter and the $2.50 per hour they were depositing in a savings account for him. He was feeling much better physically and said he thought that this was "the perfect diving board to go forward."

A few weeks later, I heard from him again. He had left the Rebuilder Addiction Ministry due to some unarticulated problems and a professed belief that "their treatment program was inadequate." He then went to a smaller facility that offered "daily treatment help" and also got a "case manager" for assistance programs, which he said he was determined to qualify for. As I wished him the best, I thought, "You know, it's really that simple. I just wish him the best."

Madness Reigns

What is going on with my son and others who keep damaging themselves in different ways? In simple terms, why are some of us most of the time and most of us some of the time acting so destructively? For a possible answer for why we strive to compete and conflict with one another so ferociously, let's look at a central theme in Ernest Becker's *Escape from Evil*:

> From the beginning man … was a peculiarly weak animal … and the only animal conscious of death and decay. And so he engaged in a heightened search for powers of self-perpetuation…. And so [for him] trophies were a major source of protective power; they shielded one from harm…. In addition to this, the trophy was visible proof of survivorship in the contest and thus a demonstration of the favor of the gods…. We see this, of course, in the actual incorporation of parts of the enemy…. An Associated Press dispatch from the "Cambodian Front Lines" quotes a Sgt. Dahn Hun on what he did to his North Vietnamese foes:
>
> > I try to cut them open while they're still dying or soon after they're dead. That way the livers give me the strength of my enemy…. [One day] when they attacked we got about 50 of them and everyone ate liver.
>
> The logic of killing others in order to affirm our own life unlocks much that puzzles us in history, much that with our modern minds we seem unable to com-

prehend, such as the Roman arena games…. The more death you saw unfold before your eyes and the more you thrust your thumbs downward, the more you bought off your own life.[70]

Becker goes on with other ideas that are, as Freud's, quite painful to look at and accept as pertinent to us. Yet, that is Becker's point—that we all, save a few rare exceptions, suffer from this sickness; we need to see it for what it is and deal with it directly to undo its hold on us. He continues:

> The Roman arena games were … a continued staging of victory even in the absence of war; each civilian experienced the same powers that he otherwise had to earn in war. If we are repulsed by the blood thirstiness of those games, it is because we choose to banish from our consciousness what true excitement is. For man, maximum excitement is the confrontation of death, and the skillful defiance of it by watching others fed to it as he survives transfixed with rapture.

Becker then offers some modern-day examples to buttress his point:

> Retreating Germans in Russia and Italy [suspecting they were losing] were especially apt to kill with no apparent motive, just to leave a heap of bodies. It is obvious they were offering last-minute hostages to death, stubbornly affirming in a blind, organismic way, "I will not die, you will—see?" It seems that they wanted some kind of victory over evil, and when it couldn't be the Russians, then it would be the Jews and even other Germans; any substitute scapegoat would have to do. [In another example], in the recent Bengali revolt the Western Pakistanis often killed anyone they saw, and when they didn't see anyone, they would throw

grenades into houses; they piled up a toll of over 3 million despised Bengalis.

Everywhere and anywhere, here and there, then and now, them and us, on and on it goes. And if we are under the apprehension that either denial or patience is going to solve our own portion of this obvious endemic problem, we are mistaken. In order to appreciate the depth of this disease we suffer from as a species, we must first cease underestimating its extent in our own minds. Undeniable proof of its significance and commonality lies in just about *everyone's* penchant to attack others for little or no reason. A careless driver cuts us off and we become angry, as though he or she were doing it directly to us and not everyone else on the road. Someone makes a mistake, and we find ourselves exclaiming, "You didn't do that, did you?" when it is obvious the person did. Our children enter the normally rebellious years, as do all teenagers, and we take their disobedience personally. A politician deceives us, and we feel betrayed, as though politicians had never deceived before. Someone insults us and we go ballistic, acting as if his error lit a match to our fury. And what makes all of it even stranger is that we *willingly* enter into these quasi-deranged states—luxuriate in them you might say—even though we know from experience that we will end the tirade only by feeling depressed later. It's as though we are all secretly saying to one another, "I have a need of you. And I just can't wait until you fail to fulfill it."

Coming to an awareness of what we are doing to ourselves and accepting that there is a serious inner problem that must be addressed requires a seriousness of purpose we are unaccustomed to embrace. It is not easy to put apathy aside or to accept that what we were so sure of before may have been completely wrong. Recognizing this reality of human nature, Schopenhauer said,

> It is quite natural that we should adopt a defensive and negative attitude toward every new opinion concerning something on which we already have an opinion of our

own. For it forces its way as an enemy into the previously closed system of our own convictions, shatters the calm of mind we have attained through this system, demands new efforts of us and declares our former efforts have been in vain.[71]

A different way to approach this is to say that it is clinging to our false beliefs and refusing to consider the new that is the real problem, since belief lacks the power of conviction until given one by us. Assume for a moment that we don't really understand what we perceive, but only think we do. If this is so, and the inconsistency of our behavior born of taking even little things personally certainly shows that it is possible, what should we do? What else but learn what it means to watch our minds taking things personally?

Right now most of us take things very personally. We hear flattering words, and we feel validated, important. We hear critical words, and we feel let down, dismayed. And the closer to us the critical people are, the greater the seeming sting of their criticism, while the farther away the flatterers are, the greater the inflation of pride that seems to come from their praise. None of this makes sense.

Looking at the Worst

What, then, does make sense in such confusion? First, a determination to find a way out. While it may be common, it is not natural to be flustered by the trivial or thrown off balance by the passing. Nor should we allow ourselves to remain under the too-easily-accepted influence of the basically fearful idea that if we just wait here and enjoy our worldly distractions, something otherworldly will appear out of the blue and render our suffering impotent. *We* have to rescue ourselves—by accepting our strength, reining ourselves in and apologizing when we go astray, forgiving others for "making" us choose wrongly (although we are always the ones at fault), picking ourselves up when we stumble and fall, and resolutely leading ourselves forward again every time we falter or retreat. Finding our balance is not accomplished by wishes or good intentions; it is the result of an earnest dedication to leaving all limitations behind.

For many, this begins with positive thinking. I am an advocate of positive thinking as a helpful step in remembering that we always have the power to change our attitudes. I am, however, in no way an advocate of positive thinking as a final solution, there being no real wisdom possible until the mind turns around and examines itself. This leaves positive thinking as a stage we go through on the way to getting in touch with and thus undoing the negative. And to undo the negative in us, we must do nothing more—or less—than look at it without self-criticism or a desire to do anything other than learn from what we see. This is the real journey to the true and unopposed "positive," without which life is little more than a meandering from sorrow to passing satisfaction and back again, in a circle that leads us nowhere.

The following quotes from William James, the early American psychologist and philosopher, and Thomas Hardy, the English novelist and poet, speak directly to this important idea.

> William James: There is no doubt that healthy-mindedness [positive thinking] is inadequate as a philosophical doctrine, because the evil facts which it positively refuses to account for are a genuine portion of reality, and they may after all be the best key to life's significance, and possibly the only openers of our eyes to the deepest levels of truth.

> Thomas Hardy: If a way to the better there be, it lies in taking a full look at the worst.[72]

These quotes underscore the idea that there is a state of wrong-mindedness at work in the unbalanced person—which includes most of us at least some of the time. Choosing not to acknowledge, much less address, this wrong-mindedness is the real sickness that needs to be healed, and it is for this reason that silence of the mind, and not positive thinking, is the answer we seek. The state of wrong-mindedness is nothing without being chosen for; therefore, this choosing, and not negativity, is the only real problem. Right-mindedness simply watches, detecting any temptation to choose wrongly and then responding with an attitude of mind that says, for example, "Thanks, but no thanks," or "I see you, but I no longer want you or what you bring in your wake." It does not fight against these idle persuasions; neither does it cover them with platitudes or "good thoughts." It merely looks in quietness and waits for the seductions to pass. In other words, it reacts in silence, which means it doesn't react at all.

This is why reform begins at "home," or in each of our internal dealings. No matter my good intentions, if I am not steady-minded, how can I be of real assistance to the unstable? And, if I'm not stable, will I even realize what I am up to as I peer about in a world so dimly lit by the flickering lamps of comparison? For instance, if I go to the supermarket and come upon a woman beating her child, and I find myself hating her for what she is doing, am I really all that different from her? Am I now not just beating her with my thoughts as she is beating her child with her hand? Obviously, there is no valid excuse for beating a child, but there is even less excuse for handing someone that small power over one's emotions. This is not to say I should stand idly by if the child is in danger of harm. Yet, at the same time, who am I to condemn the woman because of what she is doing? Will I be able to acknowledge that there is always more than meets the eye when I begin perceiving another through such a dishonest lens? Will I be able to think that the mother might be in a state of great upset because she is feeling disturbed by something happening in her marriage, frightened at the results of a lab test, worried she may have to care for her aging parents, or guilty because of a big mistake she made, all feelings she would be reinforcing through the error of taking her problem out on the child? Is it fair that I look down on someone that distressed just because my own mistakes are, at present, not as apparent as hers?

Everyone makes mistakes. And in our common dilemma, instead of looking to the solution of forgiving ourselves through forgiving others, many of us fall prey to the fallacious idea that escaping the guilt we feel over our own misdeeds means finding others whose mistakes are writ larger.

In my old, not infrequently wild neighborhood in the Bronx, guys who were released for the weekend from the confines of their hard jobs and overcrowded apartments would often cut loose on Friday nights and do the most unbelievable things. One Saturday afternoon, I was in a local bar with a bunch of friends engaged in a common practice: drinking and laughing together over the drunken antics of some of our other friends the night before. The more outrageous the person's actions had been, the more those actions appeared to lessen the foolishness of our own—and, therefore, the greater their misadventures, the louder our peals of laughter. One day, however, in a moment of great lucidity, I looked down the bar at all the laughing faces and realized that, underneath the laughter, everyone was really crying.

So, what is at the heart of *real* positive thinking but to find that quiet place within from which we can watch, without—like the guys in the bar—getting swept away by the exhilarating and separating nature of comparison, refusing to succumb to the enticements of wrong-mindedness no matter how often or how loudly they call? To take "a full look at the worst" is to acknowledge and then expose its shadiness, as well as its inability to prevail over our natural quietness of mind and purpose. This is forgiveness: refusing to engage in meaningless comparisons and feverish accusations in the attempt to secure a foothold in the fraudulent idea that we can find superiority in the failings of others.

Keeping to the Rear of Our Affections

Seeing beyond appearances in such circumstances as the ones described above is important to all of us. It's how we learn that what we see is not fact but our own interpretations of fact. The really good news, however, is that we can cast all of our interpretations in a more benign light.

Along these lines, most of the world's great teachers have, in different ways, agreed with the inscription on the temple to Apollo at Delphi that the first order of business for the aspirant to greater wisdom is as it states, "Know Thyself." As this concept indicates, reform does indeed begin at home; in other words, to attain true wisdom, it is myself and not others that I must work on.

It seems sensible to think that finding the way to right-mindedness is the primary goal of even the partially awake. And since many of us can see the wrong-mindedness of damning mistake-makers, like the lady in the supermarket, we *must* be at least partially awake. Assuming that we want to partake in this process of self-reform, then, let's now take a look at how such a process might begin.

To start with, we must realize that the rift between Republicans and Democrats, conservatives and liberals, evangelicals and agnostics, Muslims and Jews, and so on, is *not* what those on one side or the other of their argument so often insist: a split between right and wrong. These groups, which define equals as inferior in wisdom or as plainly misguided, are merely arbitrary divisions within the same state of wrong-mindedness. To those dedicated to reforming themselves, it makes *no* difference whether another has chosen to be a conservative or a liberal, a Christian, Jew, Buddhist, Hindu, Muslim, or atheist. Their main concern is about themselves, seeking to ensure that their own beliefs about religion, politics, or whatever include a due tolerance for the views of others, no matter how foreign to their own current convictions.

As the Buddhist classic *The Dhammapada* says,

> Greater in combat
> Than a person who conquers
> A thousand times a thousand people
> Is the person who conquers herself.[73]

Seen properly, or right-mindedly, the views anyone holds about anything are recognized as just that—views. Sometimes these views are appropriate and helpful, at least for those who hold them; sometimes they are not. One thing is sure, however: whenever their uncertainty leads those who are married to them into conflict with those who think otherwise, they are inappropriate in their outcomes and, in that way, unhelpful and wrong. Therefore, to go within is to begin to learn that we are not the outcome of our views, our beliefs, or our convictions, but rather what forms them, holds them, protects them, chooses to let them be reduced in importance, or discards them as no longer useful.

A good description of using the power of the mind to stand back from one's wants and beliefs comes in *Hamlet*, where Laertes, warning his sister Ophelia about her susceptibility to her wishes regarding Hamlet, says, "And keep you in the rear of your affections, out of the shot and danger of desire."[74] This is good advice not only for someone like Ophelia, but for all who are liable to be swept away by their emotions, quick to enter the enchantment of inordinate passions or to defend their convictions simply because those convictions are their own.

There Is No "Why"

Do difficulties occur in our world because of the mysterious will of a higher power, or as the result of karma or predestination or chance? Is it that this is the best of all possible worlds, or the product of an evolving consciousness? Or, as some believe, are things the way they are because this is the way we are being taught to shape up? A more reasonable answer, at least insomuch as it offers a different basis for response to what is clearly not understandable, may lie in a story a friend told me he read in a book. I don't remember it exactly, but it went something like this: A group of modern-day "hippies" went to live in a small southern town. They rented some land and began to live in a commune-like setting. Soon after, at the entrance to their campground, they put up a sign that read, "There Is No Why." The townspeople were less than pleased with this invasion of their territory by such strangers, but as time went on, the hippies—since they were law-abiding, orderly, and always pleasant—slowly became accepted by the community.

One day, the sheriff stopped by and, while chatting with the leader of the group, said, "I've been wanting to ask you about your sign. What does it mean?" In response, the young man explained that, as a group, they were trying to learn the lesson of living life as it came to them, as his grandmother had taught him to do. It seems his grandmother had been in a concentration camp and had told him that she learned early on that the healthiest way to survive the great challenges they faced was to begin by accepting that there is no "why."

Suppose with me for a while. Suppose this is true, that there is no "why"—no possible discernment of many an event's cause, no predestination, no karma, no mysterious will, no selective trials, no determinable reason for what so often occurs in this unreasonable world. Suppose, further, that there is no such thing as reward and punishment, or even anyone keeping score. Suppose there is just what shows up, there to be traveled through, at first timidly; then, gradually, more and more certainly; and finally, when we've learned to stay fully "in the rear of our affections and out of the shot and danger of desire," with complete confidence. Suppose the journey we are on is to the end of disbelief in our strength and the dawn of our ability to cope with any ephemeral appearance, no matter how terrible its form. Suppose, just suppose, that our greatest achievement lies not in any accomplishment, but in refusing to be hooked emotionally by *any* fearful—or exciting—apparition, in discovering that we have not lost the wherewithal to remain perfectly calm in the presence of all that comes and flourishes and withers away.

Escaping Punishment

Why does such a picture of total austerity, of unshaken silence in the midst of great noise, of confident authority without need to dominate the ephemeral, of elegant simplicity in being while surrounded by complexity and strife, seem an almost impossible goal? Could it be that part of what blocks the remembrance of our ability to smile at even our greatest challenges—if not at first, then at least in retrospect—is our continuing insistence that for things to be as bad as they sometimes are, there *must* be a "why"? Is it that we, whether knowingly or unknowingly, are interpreting calamitous events as forms of sacrifice asked, believing in guilt's fearful tale of a serious comeuppance for our supposed sinfulness at the hands of an avenging deity? Could this be the underlying cause of our holding onto grievances and the idea of someone keeping score, the primary reason we seek out others to define as "bad guys"? Certainly, many religions have embraced this frightening premise of an often sorely offended god, and just as certainly, people who believe this way often become his self-assigned agents. As Voltaire said,

> The man who says to me, "Believe as I do, or God will damn you," will presently say, "Believe as I do, or I will assassinate you." By what right could a being created free force another to think like himself? A fanaticism composed of superstition and ignorance has been the sickness of all the centuries.[75]

As another example, the powerful American preacher Jonathan Edwards, wrote,

> The God that holds you over the pit of hell much as one holds a spider or some loathsome insect over the fire abhors you, and is dreadfully provoked; his wrath toward you burns like fire; he looks upon you as worthy of nothing else but to be cast into the fire ... you are ten thousand times as abominable in his eyes as the most hateful and venomous serpent is in ours....[76]

I don't know about anyone else, but I don't hold spiders and insects over a fire, or find plausible the idea of a god so moved by my error that he loses his cool and then blames me for his lapse.

To continue with the theme about fanaticism that subsists on finding "bad guys," consider the following:

Elected pope in 1088, Urban ... the French pope stood on a platform [and] summoned Christendom to a crusade, sanctified by God.... He promised them that ... if they died for God's glory, all their sins would be remitted and heaven would await their souls. "God wills it!" he shouted ... and the crowd roared back, "God wills it!"

What was willed by Urban II turned out to be a slaughter.... An eyewitness priest, Raymond of Agiles, wrote delightedly, "Wonderful things were to be seen. Numbers of the Saracens were beheaded ... or forced to jump from the towers, others were tortured for several days and then burned ... one rode about everywhere amid the corpses of men and horses." All seventy thousand Muslim residents of Jerusalem were butchered; Jews were herded into their synagogue and burned alive.[77]

Then there is this from the Koran:

We gave of old the Scriptures ... to the line of Abraham, and we gave them a grand kingdom.

Some of them believe on the *Prophet* and some turn aside from him:—the flame of Hell is their sufficing punishment! Those who disbelieve our signs we will in the end cast into the fire: so oft as their skins shall be well burnt, we will change them for fresh skins, that they may again taste the torment....

And the inmates of the fire shall cry to the inmates of Paradise. "Pour upon us some water, or of the refreshments given you!" They shall say, "Truly God hath forbidden both to unbelievers."[78]

And, finally, the following from a pamphlet that showed up at my front door one day:

THE END OF FALSE RELIGION IS NEAR

What does the future hold for religions that produce rotten fruit?

Picture the scene. A harlot is sitting on the back of a fearsome beast. The beast has seven heads and ten horns (Revelation, 17:14).... This harlot is all religions that produce rotten fruit....

Soon, though, an amazing event will take place. The ten horns that you saw, and the wild beast, these will hate the harlot ... and will eat up her fleshy parts and will completely burn her with fire (Revelation 17:16).... God will call false religion to account for all the despicable acts she has committed in his name....

We urge you to ask us to help you.... Now is the time to act.... The end of false religion is near!

When did all this craziness begin? Was it at the moment some of the apples fell so far from the trunk that they entered into "the great amnesia," believing themselves separated, forgetting their shared origin, and after that, as in a nightmare, only fitfully and fraudulently seeing pieces of their mysterious past? How else but through something like this experience could the idea of the reality of good guys and bad have gained such a hold on us? Where but in blind ignorance and the fear of punishment due could the hatred of equals have had its birth? And why other than this would there be such certitude that we must be better because we can "prove" others worse? Yet, in the same way that my buddies' and my laughter in the bar over our friends' antics was a distraction from our own like mistakes, the convictions that all of us hold regarding the sinfulness of others are a cover over our feelings of little worth. In the words of Kenneth Wapnick,

As long as we are so certain we are right, we must be wrong. Our stubborn insistence is the tip-off, and reflects the ego dynamic of reaction formation, first formulated by Freud a century ago, who described how people act out the opposite of what they unconsciously believe....

[This is why], based on Freud's insight, Jung frequently maintained that religious fanatics were cloaking their own lack of faith; otherwise they would not affirm theirs with such dogmatic tenacity and tenacious dogmatism. [Those] in their right minds would never demonstrate such insistence on being right. Their awareness of truth would simply *be*.[79]

So, to repeat a point made earlier but in a different way, accepting the foregoing means accepting that our "justified" bitterness toward others is not what it seems. Rather, it is proof of self-hatred and wrong-mindedness, a singular and deceptive thought of evil turned inside out and backwards, seemingly fragmented and making its appearance in multiple shadowy forms.

In short, all of our hatred toward others has its roots in self-hatred, protected by projection and a "proof-positive" of escape founded in another being wrong. And it neither makes a difference nor is more sensible when the accuser becomes a self-accuser, expressing the conviction that he, along with everyone else, has missed the mark.

Won't Do and Can't Do

Think about it. Can self-denigration be different from slandering another and, thus, somehow humble and therefore good? Does that make sense? Or are all these strange ideas about how accusation and self-blame will lead to freedom just more signs of confusion in the minds of those who have lost their way? Confusion it is—and the same sort of confusion that holds sway when we forget that in our forgiveness of others lies our own forgiveness, and that, likewise, in withholding forgiveness from others, we demonstrate that we're still withholding it from ourselves.

Let's take a look at another modern-day scandal that might illustrate this confusion. On August 8, 2008, it was disclosed that two years earlier Senator John Edwards had an affair with a young documentary filmmaker covering his presidential campaign. Considering all the other people who had been caught with, so to speak, their pants down, how did this articulate, intelligent, and successful man fall into this age-old trap? Part of the answer can be discovered in a video of the two of them that was shown on the news. In this segment of rough footage for the documentary, that never would have made it into the final cut, Senator Edwards is shown flirting with his paramour on the campaign plane, acting as giddy as a teenager. As the film demonstrates, he had become enthralled, forgetting completely the better choice of remaining "in the rear of [his] affections, out of the shot and danger of desire."

And then, as is often the case, there was the uproar over the obvious "victim" in the tragedy—the betrayed and wounded wife. Or, was that only part of the story with there being, once again, a difference between perception and reality? According to two respected journalists who did hundreds of interviews regarding the scandal, there was a difference. Here's what the book *Game Change*, co-written by the national political correspondent for *New York Magazine* and the editor-at-large and senior political analyst for *Time* magazine, had to say about the "terribly wronged" Elizabeth Edwards and her relationships with her husband and others *prior* to his philandering:

> [After her illness was revealed] no one in the Edwardses'
> political circle felt anything less than complete sympathy for Elizabeth's plight. And yet the romance between
> her and the electorate struck them as ironic nonetheless—because their own relationships with her were
> so unpleasant that they felt like battered spouses. The
> nearly universal assessment among them was that there
> was no one on the national stage for whom the disparity between public image and private reality was vaster

or more disturbing. What the world saw in Elizabeth: a valiant, determined, heroic everywoman. What the Edwards insiders saw: an abusive, intrusive, paranoid, condescending crazy woman....

At times subtly, at times blatantly, she was forever letting John know she regarded him as her intellectual inferior.... She called her spouse a "hick" in front of other people and derided his parents as rednecks....

She [was] prone to irrational outbursts that perplexed and worried John's advisers.... A close friend of the Edwardses from law school informed [them], "She's always been this way ... the sharp manner, the cutting comments, the sudden and inexplicable fulminations."[80]

If we find ourselves looking down on either Senator Edwards or Elizabeth in any way, that should be understood as a sign of an unresolved issue within ourselves. "Yeah, but I don't cheat on or abuse my spouse," we may say. So? Is that justification for condemning those who have? John Edwards made a mistake. Elizabeth Edwards was a disturbed person. So? Is that any reason to look on him or her as inferior? Or, is it only when we wander into the darkness of misperception that we see mistake-makers as less worthy, unaware we are condemning ourselves through the very means that the guard within has told us will exempt us?

We don't get annoyed with those who contract cancer or suffer from heart attacks, even though the cost and the burden of their care can be enormous. And most of us don't become angry at those who get AIDS, even though, for the most part, it's a preventable disease. But the overly stubborn, the foolish, or the ignorant and bad acting—these we easily find in contempt of our personal court, usually without due process or consideration of the possibility that, in our lack of compassion for all, we might be the ones who are wrong. And even when we do grant pardon, too often it is from the vantage point of one who is superior, with the idea of real justice gone in the wind.

In the process of becoming more honest with ourselves about what we are up to with accusation and blame, we should also look at how often we demand that others do what they are unable to do and then become incensed with them afterward for not doing it. "Well, they *can* do it, they just *won't*," we may proclaim, failing to grasp the direct connection between "won't do" and "can't do." "Won't do" is an insistence born of fear that quickly, in the believer's mind, turns into "can't do," and then they don't and we get mad.

Along these same lines, can the case for *everyone* fairly be stated as "until one sees, one does not see"? Is it reasonable to say that when people choose wrongly, it is because at that moment they don't know better? Is it true for everyone that even when they *do* know better and still choose for the worse, they actually *don't* know better—because if they *did* know better, they wouldn't have chosen what was sure to bring them grief later? This is an important line of questioning for all of us, because if others truly *don't* know better, even when it seems almost certain that they *should* know better, then whenever we have made mistakes, we *didn't* know better either.

Perhaps there is much that we, no matter how bright or well-educated or well-intentioned, truly do not understand. Perhaps the reason that we sometimes act in the terrible ways we do is that we are all, save a rare few who did not fall as far into the state of amnesia, in a generalized state of fear, shock, and confusion. Perhaps the purpose of life is not, as we thought, to get ahead, but to seek within for what the kind at heart seem to have discovered: a quietude of mind that is free of conflict and is neither challenged nor moved by all of the ephemeral forms of evil that we've been inculcated into perceiving as so very real up to now.

If we set aside our doubts and fears and thought about what it would mean to have as our birthright the ability to come to the awareness of an absolute power over thought, memory, and emotion, would not all we had sought before pale in comparison to such a possibility? And could it also be as we've been told: that the recognition of such power is not only possible, but *presently* possible, awaiting but the forgiveness of ourselves—for wanting to be separated from sameness and shared interests, and for desiring to be unique unto ourselves—that will lead to the willingness to perceive everyone we meet in a more charitable light?

A Long, Cold Mental Shower

To achieve such peace of mind, the acceptance of equality is what is asked of us; what that acceptance leads to and how it is achieved is not our business. People all over the world are in terrible trouble, some of it material or physical, but much of it stemming from an unknowing subjugation to their own wrong-mindedness. So why *not* try to be of help in this desperate situation? Why *not* learn what the wise tell us they've learned: that the purpose of learning is first to unlearn what we've learned wrongly, that we may learn anew. Then, they say, we will recognize that the greatest danger to ourselves lies not in others and what they say and do, but in our ungenerous interpretations of their fears and defensiveness and deficiencies of pride.

Let me give you yet another example from my teenage years of how minor problems with wounded pride can grow into the more deeply settled problems that plague our world. One afternoon, I was at a party with a bunch of friends in a neighborhood not far from our own. After a while, a particularly tough guy from our neighborhood showed up and soon after began to bully another, but lesser, tough guy from our crowd. A little later, the first guy left, and after some more drinking, the rest of us left too. As we were walking down the sidewalk in broad daylight, the second guy, without a word of warning, picked up a trash can and hurled it through a huge plate-glass store window. We all yelled, "Whoa!" and ran like hell.

What happened in this microcosm of our worldly troubles? It's not hard to figure out. The fellow who had been bullied had such pent-up rage over being humiliated that he temporarily lost his marbles and exploded. He was a disturbed person to begin with, the oldest in a family of six boys, with two alcoholics as parents. And while he could be quite decent on a one-to-one basis, his moods and behavior were wildly inconsistent and even dangerous. His troubled life ended abruptly a decade or so later when he was beaten to death in a drunken brawl.

Is there all that much difference between my young, disturbed, Christian-reared friend, who constantly got into fights and destroyed people's property, and the angry Muslim teenager who decides to take out his personal frustrations by becoming a suicide-bomber? Isn't it all just a matter of degree, with some of us simply in greater control of ourselves than others? Most of us know that Disney song lyric "It's a small world after all." What makes this saying true, as Kenneth Wapnick points out, is that behind the different actors and their varying costumes, everyone is fundamentally the same: right-minded, wrong-minded, and with the power to choose between them. As Mark Twain said in his autobiography,

> The last quarter century of my life has been pretty constantly and faithfully devoted to the study of the human race—that is to say, the study of myself, for, in my individual person, I am the entire human race compacted together. I have found there is no ingredient of the race which I do not possess in either a small or a large way. When it is small compared with the same ingredient in somebody else, there is still enough of it for all the purposes of examination. In my contacts with the species, I find no one who possesses a quality which I do not possess…. Broadly speaking, we are all alike.[81]

Accepting ourselves as alike, but confused, and yet with the power of choice between right- and wrong-mindedness, the questions become these: How do we live up to the ideal of remembering our essential sameness with everyone in a world filled with many who are so deeply disturbed that they must be confined in a secure place for the good of all? How do we properly regard those who tell us that our beliefs offend them or their god? How should we think of those who sit in warm offices and, to suit their idealistic aims or selfish purposes, send boys out into the cold to kill and to maim? And what is the proper perception of the supra-intelligent who play the games of business and finance in ways designed to fleece the less intelligent, their undertakings essentially akin to cheating at cards?

How are we to look upon all of our equals without believing in our judgments of them or being captured by a sense of superiority? And how are we to deal with our own tendencies toward cleverness or our penchants for demanding that others live as we say? How else but through forgiving ourselves for all the hidden self-judgments we may be projecting on these others, seeing how those judgments divide us all in a most unhealthy way, and thus uncovering in ourselves the generosity born of both a greater understanding of everyone's pain and the desire to simply be kind? Perhaps, if we took a long, cold mental shower, we'd come to realize that it is only those who are blinded by ambition who want power without virtue, and then we'd work hard at forgiving ourselves and others every time that we, or they, forgot this was true.

CHAPTER 6

Why Me?

S EVERAL MORE WEEKS PASSED BEFORE my son called. He had left the last place he'd been, used his food stamp money to binge once more, gone through detox yet again, found someone to help him again, and gone back to the Baptist recovery home he'd left just a short while before. We talked for a while about his leaving the past behind and granting himself a fresh start, and I left it at that for the time being. Would this be the time that he changed his mind and headed in the right direction? I suspected not. Did what was important in our relationship come into focus when I accepted that he meant it when he said, "Thanks for not kicking me when I'm down"? I suspected so. Did he presently perceive our relationship as much more than one in which he called me for comfort and the like? I suspected not. Should I willingly remain in the role I was in, perceiving it as beneficial to him but equally so to me? I suspected so.

Most people who reach the place of equanimity and learn to stay there in difficult situations have traveled through their own version of "Why me?" I can remember walking down the street one day, at a time when my three sons were all in trouble. Looking up at the sky, I said to my deceased father, and probably only half-jokingly, "Okay, Pop, are we even yet?" And yet there is no "getting even," no karmic kind of payback in any of this thing we call life. There is only the gift of learning that my mind's shifting, which seems always to be provoked by difficult situations outside myself, comes only from my decisions about how to perceive and react to those situations, and from nowhere else.

Conquering Oneself

"Why me?" is a reasonable question, but only when I see life as an ongoing battle in which I am always dodging bullets (i.e., avoiding difficult situations) and not as a classroom in which I am learning to undo the false convictions I have formed about my inability to *always* remain at peace. To learn to look at the movement of my mind without taking any of it personally—be they calls to excitement or despair, two equally deceptive frauds—is to discover the place of equanimity within from which to perceive intelligently and then act, or not act, effectively. After all, difficult or not, what shows up in life is what shows up, and while it is true that I must deal with it, it is not true that I must accept it as the cause of my feelings. As Epictetus taught,

> It is hard to combine and unite these two qualities, the carefulness of one who is affected by circumstances and the intrepidity of one who heeds them not. But it is not impossible; else were happiness also impossible. We should act [in life] as we do in seafaring.
>
> "What can I do?"—choose the master, the crew, the day, the opportunity. Then comes a sudden storm. What matters it to me? My part has been fully done. The matter is in the hands of another—the master of the ship. The ship is foundering. What then have I to do? To do the only thing that remains to me—to be drowned without fear, without a cry ... knowing what has been born must likewise perish. For I am but a

human being, a part of the whole, and as the hour is
part of the day and passes, I come like the hour, and
like the hour must pass.[82]

Epictetus's example has nothing to do with giving in to circumstance; he is not suggesting an apathetic resignation to fate. His point is that when you've done all that can be done, no matter how grim things may seem, all that's left to do is relax and enjoy the show. This really is at the heart of the "Why me?" question: if we are not dedicated to the arduous work of taking down the defenses we have erected against our ability to deal calmly with every circumstance, then who will be? If we don't understand that, while moments of fear can be a stimulus to action, a fearful state of mind is never a bringer of wisdom, then our actions, no matter how vigorous, will only mirror our inner state and end up confused—which is counterproductive. Thus, unless we begin to have a greater awareness of the power of our minds to remain unmoved by *all* the storms and seeming fascinations of life, we will be constantly unnerved by the unexpected and, in that, lead unexamined lives without meaning or direction.

A good example of this is what I learned with my sons. My cessation of haranguing them about their problems and trading it in for the quiet of reason left me taking all the same actions and doing my very best to help them, but without the emotional distress of taking what they were doing personally, or feeling inadequate whenever my best efforts were not bearing fruit. Through these experiences and others like them, I have come to the conclusion that there can be *nothing* more important to our psychological well-being than our growing confidence in our ability to remain quiet in the midst of the wrong mind's perturbations and all the world's chaos and noise.

The only way to become free of the emotional pull of this drama called life is to grow immunity to our own fearful thoughts as well as to everyone else's. We must come to the understanding that nothing, whether it be the vicious temptation to lash out or lash back, or the puppy love that tells us how wonderful this person is, has a power other than what we've given it. This lesson alone opens the way to a state of emotional and mental balance that is unmoved by all seduction, turmoil, and strife. Along these lines, Epictetus had this to say:

> When you see another man in possession of power, set against this fact that you have not the desire of power; when you see another rich, see what you possess in place of riches, for if you possess nothing in place of them, you are miserable; but if you have not the want of riches, know that you possess more than this man possesses and what is worth much more.[83]

Refusing to Support the Changeable

The overriding message in all of this is that we are far stronger than we are willing to believe. And it is exactly this lack of faith in ourselves, and not the opinions of others, that we need to address. Listening to the guard within, we often foolishly agree with its condemnation of us, without it ever occurring to us that when we turned aside from that brewing argument or invitation to some other form of combat, it wasn't so much because we were afraid of the harm it could have brought us, but of the damage that we, left unchecked, might have done to another. Or, without ever reasoning that we walked out on that relationship or marriage or job because its toxicity was on the rise, and no matter what we or others thought of it, we were actually acting rationally for the good of all.

As in the forgoing examples, any serious investigation of our old assumptions reveals how questionable the premises are on which they rest. For instance, have you ever considered the idea that it is the uneducated, good-hearted garbage collector and not the strict-minded religious leader who can quote Aristotle who is closer to the trunk? Another common assumption that might be questioned: maybe things like great physical strength, extraordinary beauty, or even the possession of a scintillating personality can be, unless one is careful, more of a curse than a blessing. Any "gift" that can so easily lead to self-centeredness is one that you might just as well be without.

Or, might we consider that many people, even while taking care of the basic task of providing for themselves or their families, seek in different ways to be "better than" and to "count" more than others? For example, some want to become famous, while others care more about being well thought of than about doing what is right. Some strive to become powerful, more than a few of those willing to settle for being feared. There are those who yearn above all else to be wealthy, while others make great sacrifices to achieve status. And then some, burdened by the secret wish to be revered, use the repression of their own desires and forced humility to reach the seeming stage of "holier than thou."

All these attempts at personal advancement are understandable when viewed in the light of how uncertain we are of what we are. Yet since all of these "achievements" are just glitter that fades, they are inconsequential in nature and, therefore, of no real significance at all. After all, what value can there be in convincing others to notice me, fear me, serve me, or revere me if, under my driving ambition to be special, I'm still unsure of myself? And if I were not so unsure, would I put such effort into finding fame and fortune or converting others to believe in the wonders of my personality?

Those who seek to eliminate their dissatisfaction with themselves by becoming "more" are missing the point. "More" piled on top of an unbalanced foundation leads only to further instability. All are seeking satisfaction as they define it, more than a few not realizing it can't be found in achievements, possessions, or any form of puffery, be that from oneself or from others. Seeing clearly, the most contented people in the world are not the powerful or the rich or the self-proclaimed holy, but those discovering that peace of mind is possible right where they are, no matter who they are.

Stated another way, to do whatever I can to be more important than others is not the way to find myself, but to lose myself. The attempt to replace an unsatisfactory self-image with a better one, without working to undo the first, is like painting over rust, just another form of layering positive thinking over negative thinking—the resulting ineffective solution to my perceived inadequacy leaving me wandering about in uncertainty. The escape from such uncertainty, then, is not found in inventing new myths about myself, but in learning what it means to set all self-myths—positive and negative—aside.

Images change. Truth does not. Image-making, then, brings nothing in its wake except the conviction of impermanence and the fear of disappearance at death. Therefore, unless I see some sort of promise in a perpetual becoming, I'd better learn to turn away from my desire to be grander than most and accept that, under all my notions of otherwise, I am what I am. And if this shedding of the undue ambition of the "me" to be more than others results in the discovery that I was really nobody special in the first place, but only vainly pretending that I was, even that realization would be more fulfilling than all my wearying prior efforts to gain power or elicit applause.

To settle for enticing others to praise me, or for finding ways to outdo them in the war of images, is to confuse my reality with an image. To put it another way, everyone caught up in the pursuit of inventing a better self to take the place of the one he or she has condemned as inadequate is chasing an ideal that can never be found. We who invented an unsatisfactory self that does not exist must learn to give it up, not fix it up, if we want to remember the unchangeable and true. If, in essence, we are anything at all, that anything we are would have to be real, it being impossible to be something that is made up and at the same time have the permanence possible only for reality. The natural conclusion to this line of reasoning is that spending our time improving our changeable images would be time better spent forgiving ourselves for worshipping idols and then uncovering what remains when we undo the image we've made.

It is this willingness to forgive, and not time, that will do away with our fealty to self-importance. Thus, learning to consistently apply forgiveness to all our forms of self-aggrandizement is the way to return the power of proper perception to ourselves. "A foolish consistency [in rigid thinking may be] the hobgoblin of little minds,"[84] but a sensible consistency in remaining open-minded is the hallmark of stable ones. And only a stable mind is capable of going beyond the devotion to image-making and finding the freedom that comes with learning to forgive ourselves. It's not that complicated. If we want understanding, even if from no one but ourselves, we must be understanding of others. If we want self-respect, we must be respectful.

The Mental Prosperity of Generosity

To become respectful in our thinking, egalitarian in our outlook, and fair in our dealings does not call for self-sacrifice. It does, however, require an appreciation of the complicated problem of the inequalities inherent in our society and a spirit of generosity toward all, which currently may lay somewhat dormant.

For example, is it fair that those who have "arrived" should say to those who have not, "Go and get an education and then come and work for us, and if you work really, really hard, *and* if we need you, we'll help you do better"? This statement may reflect the reality of life today, and for some even a steppingstone toward a better future, but what about those uninterested in continuing in school, who are willing to work, and hard, but not necessarily under the strict rules of the powerful? What is the reasonable thing to say to them? "Take the minimum wages we offer, which you cannot live on, and get yourself a second or third job"? And, even if we were to find our way to a response that was just, such as a much greater appreciation for *all* hard work, how would we deal fairly with everyone involved in situations like the one that follows?

In a *CBS Evening News* segment, correspondent Steve Hartman reported on a young Mexican woman and her fifteen-year-old daughter who were planning to cross the border illegally.

Mr. Hartman said to the daughter, "You know, there are people in America who don't want you there, don't you?"

As her mother wept, the girl replied with a shrug, "We're all equal, aren't we?"

Assuming we are neither bleeding hearts nor cold-hearted bigots, how do we respond to that kind of naiveté? How do we answer that "correctly incorrect" rhetorical question with a kindness toward her that at the same time respects completely the rights of *all*?

To answer such questions, let's look at the inherent quandary. Here are two impoverished people seeking to build a better life for themselves. Are they, or the numerous others like them, aware that their willingness to work for exceedingly low wages has negatively affected both job opportunities and pay rates for millions of the poorest Americans? Of course not. All they see is that their willingness to work at almost any job for close to nothing is their entry card into the American dream, as, like almost everyone else, they are thinking of themselves first. And since they have so little and, where they come from, such a lack of opportunity to gain more, it is hard to find justification to condemn them or turn them away.

Yet there *is* the very real problem of those many Americans whose jobs have been lost or wages lowered in what is euphemistically called the free market. The problem is then compounded by increased costs, borne mainly by the middle class, caused by the added social services these newcomers and their families require. So, ultimately, who is responsible? Everyone. Each of us who wants more for less, which includes every business employing people at subsistence wages instead of paying them what they deserve.

As a result, so far, we have mainly losers: people from other countries working here at the lowest-level jobs, with only a few really getting ahead; already impoverished Americans making less than required to take care of their families, and taking on second jobs to survive; other Americans, who barely have enough, paying taxes for services they don't benefit from; a girl and a mother wanting to be welcomed, who see no damage in what they are doing; and business owners and higher-level managers losing touch with all positive self-regard through egregious actions selfishly taken because they can get away with it.

How does a greater awareness of all this translate into some form of personal growth and helpful social action for people without great power in the marketplace—people like you and me? We certainly can't force those wrapped in the corporate banner of "higher wages will destroy my business" to treat their employees better. So what *can* we do? One thing that could, at least for us, turn out to be everything: we can change our minds about serving our own interests first and dedicate ourselves to dealing with every equal fairly, respecting them completely, even when they are disrespecting us and themselves. We can make a firm commitment to shun sharp practices, every form of cleverness, and all unreasonable bargaining. And we can practice being kind in all situations, slowly realizing that *any* achievement other than this is inconsequential in comparison. This is what we can do, and, reasonably speaking, unless we enter the foolishness of becoming revolutionaries, this solution, while not solving the general problem, will solve the specific dilemma as it relates to us, and just maybe that, for us, will be enough.

Let's consider for a moment the thinking of Immanuel Kant, author of *Critique of Pure Reason*. His idea was that our mental starting point in all relationships should be the following:

> Every man is to be respected as an absolute end in him-
> self; and it is a crime against the dignity that belongs to
> him as a human being, to use him as a mere means for
> some external purpose.[85]

That sounds like Kenneth Wapnick when he says, "The love of [truth] is reflected here by seeing everyone as the same; not using others to meet our needs or glorify our egos."[86]

Why is a dedication to such high-minded principles necessary? Because it is only when we determine to always think rightly and act justly that it is possible to feel better about ourselves. This is not to say that once we make that decision we won't continue to make mistakes, because for quite a while we will. But it does mean the beginning of the acceptance of shared interests and the end of the selfish life as we've known it, something so threatening to the personal notion of special-ness we're entranced with, you might think we were being asked to give up an inheritance.

A Different Way of Living

Epictetus said this about growing up out of impoverished values:

> When I hear any man called fortunate because he is honored by Caesar, I say, "What does he happen to get? The government of a province? Does he also obtain an opinion such as he ought?" A man scatters dried figs and nuts: the children seize them, and fight with one another over them. Men do not, for they think them to be a small matter. Provinces are distributed, let the children look to that. Consulships are distributed, let the children scramble after them, let them kiss the hand of the giver. To me these are only dried figs and nuts.[87]

To everyone committed to getting ahead of the next guy, such sentiments are merely foolish prattle; to those who value being at ease with whatever shows up, the sounds of reason in an unreasonable world. To find equanimity, we must cease searching for it where it is not. Where it is not is in things, titles, achievements, acknowledge-ments, and rewards. Where, then, is it? In the realization that a quiet reconciliation with fate is far superior to the stormiest defiance of its unpredictability. As Nietzsche put it, "[The] formula for greatness in a human being is *amor fati*: that one wants nothing to be other than it is."[88] For us, this shouldn't mean that we don't want things to improve, but only that we want to remain unmoved even if we come to the end of our days before they do.

If we are willing to pay attention, we will find that a number of people have given time and effort to inform us of the importance of what they've discovered, each telling us that it is neither notice nor acquisition but peace of mind that is the grand prize. In the introduction to *Arthur Schopenhauer—Essays and Aphorisms,* there is a brief synopsis of Schopenhauer's views that may help explain at least part of our difficulty with keeping this idea foremost in our minds:

> Every individual is embodied will, and the nature of will is to strive to live—will is "will to live." This means that fundamentally every individual is an ego whose interest in staying alive overrides every other, including of course the life-interest of every other individual. The outcome is universal conflict. The suffering engendered by this conflict is the ... inescapable condition of life, and happiness means merely the diminution of suffering; i.e., happiness is negative. The way out of this circle of suffering lies in the denial of the will, refusal to enter the contest: the power to do so provided by the conscious intellect, which is capable of understanding the nature of the will and its effects, and thus of striving to set them aside.[89]

Later in the book, Schopenhauer says,

> Unjust or wicked actions are in regard to him who performs them, signs of the strength of the will to live, and thus of how far he still is from true salvation, which is the denial of this will, and from redemption from the world; they are also signs of how long a schooling in knowledge and suffering he still has to go before he can attain it....
>
> The value of the [selfish] life lies precisely in this, that [its suffering] teaches him not to want it. For this supreme initiation life itself must prepare him.[90]

So Epictetus warns us to beware of chasing after things that should excite only children, Nietzsche claims that greatness lies in accepting life as it comes, and Schopenhauer says that a selfish will becomes a gift when we let it teach us not to want it. But do we believe them? In honesty, do we respect the teachings of those who have sought to remind us of our strength and worth and called us to a different way of living? What would we really hear if we paid attention? A message as simple as this one, found in the Eastern classic, the *Bhagavad Gita*:

> Perform actions ... relinquishing attachment, be impartial to failure and success ... [showing] no preference in fortune and misfortune.... The higher self of a ... man is perfectly poised in ... honor or contempt.[91]

One after the other we hear them saying to us, "Open your eyes and take a look at your instability, your false desires, and all the pain the love of self has led you into, and quit wasting time waiting for someone else to come along and lead you home. Refuse to succumb to the siren-like calls of wrong-mindedness, which tempt you to become engaged in unnecessary conflicts, entangled in regret over your failings, or imprisoned by expectations of others you have no right to at all. Above all, surrender your need to have things be different by recognizing that need as a choice—and, with that, you'll never be at the mercy of appearances again."

"Why you?" Because you should, and because you can. Why me? Because I'm just like you.

CHAPTER 7

Responsibility and Perception

MY NEXT CALL FROM MY son was from the lockdown section of the same psychiatric hospital, where, according to him, he ended up after deliberately stepping in front of a car. Though he had no broken bones, just bruises, he said they were going to keep him there for four or five days. As usual, I spoke to him as though this were one of our first conversations since he'd reached adulthood, stressing the need for him to reconsider his self-destructive behaviors and to be kinder to himself and the world. What was next on the horizon for him? Another recovery home after his discharge from the hospital. But once he felt better and the next food stamp payment arrived, would he sign it over to the recovery home as he was obliged to? We'd just have to wait and see.

What's worth noting about my conversations with my son is that while he always seemed to understand what I was saying at a superficial level, it didn't ever appear to permeate to the deeper level where he made his now habitual self-destructive decisions. Just as any argument or dogma-driven dialogue between two people, which could be likened to two television sets blaring their form of propaganda at each other without listening in return, so too were my quiet conversations with my son at this point; they were without much substance or meaning. Yet, the tone and tenor of the fact that I still cared for him did seem to register and, perhaps, for now, was all that could be expected. After all, if he really couldn't hear me, he really couldn't hear me, and since, by definition, this meant that, at the moment, he was not just hard of hearing but deaf, shouting to get my point across the gap in our understanding was not going to change that in any way.

One of the things I've learned in dealing with people who are acting unreasonably is that if I get bothered because they won't listen to my appeals to reason, I'm forgetting that it's only because they are refusing to listen to the voice of reason in their own minds as well. I don't have a patent on good sense, and even if I'm more sensible than another at a given moment—and that is often far from assured—I still don't possess something that's not equally theirs. What I want to bear in mind is that if reason, remaining completely reasonable, isn't disturbed in the slightest over another's unwillingness to listen, and I am disturbed because I'm not being heard, then there are two of us who are refusing to listen to reason—the other person *and* I. And if right-mindedness, being forever gracious and completely patient with the confused, is willing to wait quietly until it is heard, if I want to be reasonable, then I must grow in my ability to do exactly the same.

I must also remember that in the same way that there is a blind spot in the retina, there are gaps in my understanding of the world. To a certain degree, this leaves me shrouded in an uncorroborated, somewhat contaminated, and quite suspect version of what I think of as reality. In relationships, this means that when I perceive others from the viewpoint of a feigned superiority because of the severity of their missteps, I have forgotten that in the state of right-mindedness, no one assumes the position of another equal's judge.

Shrouded in confusion, the world is grim in its undertakings and, simply put, not a very nice place. As Schopenhauer said about it,

> If we should bring clearly to a man's sight the terrible
> sufferings and miseries to which his life is constantly

exposed, he would be seized with horror; and if we were to conduct the confirmed optimist through the hospitals, infirmaries, and surgical operating rooms, through the prisons, torture-chambers, and slave kennels, over battlefields and places of execution; if we were to open to him all the dark abodes of misery, where it hides itself from the glance of cold curiosity, and, finally, allow him to look into the starving dungeons of Ugolino, he too would understand at last the [real] nature of this [place Leibnitz termed the] "best of all possible worlds."[92]

While daily life wasn't anywhere near as grim as those examples in the world I lived in while growing up in the Bronx, and while a number of people there lived quiet and religious lives, parts of it were, in their own way, as bizarre as could be. In the bars of my neighborhood, jaws were broken, eyes blackened, faces cut, noses smashed, and teeth knocked out on a regular basis. Inside, and sometimes outside, the distorted world of those seeming refuges from the persistent sting of poverty and the unrelenting monotony of hard labor, young men often acted in the strangest ways. There were guys who would get drunk and then head-butt each other with a force sufficient to send a sober person to the doctor. There were "pile on" football games right in the bars, where bones were occasionally broken. There was the guy who shot the clock one night because he didn't want closing time to arrive. In the twenty bars open twenty hours a day in the few blocks from where I lived, there were bookies and shylocks, degenerate gamblers, cops on the take and other cops drinking on duty, a fair sprinkling of crooks, and always someone to drink with while trying to chase away the goblins of loneliness. I recognized the starkness of this practice of drinking to escape early one Saturday afternoon when I went into one place we hung around in and found seven of my friends drinking at the bar, with eight more sleeping off an all-nighter on the floor of the small pool room that abutted it.

Another example was the time the city decided to plant a skinny, inconsequential tree in the sidewalk outside a friend's bar. We put the word out that there was to be a "tree-planting celebration" (i.e., another excuse for drinking) on Saturday, and by mid-afternoon, there were over a hundred guys in the bar, with more streaming in every moment, many of whom stayed for the rest of the day and night.

To us, and there were hundreds of us, drinking to get drunk was the main idea of drinking. Guys would drink until they fell asleep at the bar, and when they woke up an hour or two later, they would raise their heads and order another. The trained and unvarying response of the bartenders to girlfriends or wives calling was either "he hasn't been in" or "he just left."

The actions of some of the more serious drinkers often touched upon the truly weird. For instance, a couple of the regulars from a popular place nicknamed The Jungle—because all the "animals" in the neighborhood ended up there—were hired by a woman in a wheelchair to paint her house. What did these two beauties do? They painted the parts of the house she could see from her wheelchair and then, because they wanted to get back to their drinking, left the rest undone. Not long after, this same duo, along with one of their brothers, was spotted on a Sunday morning with a moving van, dutifully relocating the goods from a local supermarket while people walked around them on their way to church. It was so brazen, it took the police a while to figure out that they were actually robbing it!

Then there was the day The Jungle had a boat outing. Thirty-one people met at the bar early in the morning for drinks before boarding a chartered bus for a drinking trip to the boat for a day's fishing (really more drinking). They had a wonderful time on the water, getting totally smashed, while a few people actually caught a couple of fish. After returning to the bar late that afternoon for more drinks and chemically infused laughter, they made a sobering discovery: while thirty-one people had embarked on the trip, only thirty had returned. Somehow, Jake had fallen overboard, and everyone was so drunk that no one had even noticed. Jake was never heard from again.

Then there was the young man, a brother of one of the head-butters, whom *Life Magazine* put on its cover under the cruel heading "The Dumbest Marine." There were guys who died in accidents from being drunk and even more who drank themselves to death while still in their twenties. There were some who just disappeared, more than one murdered for sure. There were those who went to prison more than once, construction workers who went directly from work to the bar, numbers runners, "bagmen" (cops who picked up bribe money from the bars and bookies and others), and guys with ulcers who drank their scotch with milk or cream. There was restlessness, despair, a somewhat resentful acceptance of one's lot, and riotous party after party, all to dull the pain, for any or no reason at all.

The point of all this? To illustrate that, to one degree or another, many, many people are, to put it nicely, somewhat touched. Whether one keeps this reality from his or her awareness through excessive intake of drugs and alcohol; praying without ceasing; killing "bad guys"; proudly doing good deeds; overindulging in self-justified righteousness, asceticism, avaricious pursuits, or other "acceptable" distractions; or putting energy into becoming tougher, smarter, wealthier, more attractive, or more powerful than others—it's all the same.

Leaving the Maze

One problem with all the duplicity and aggressiveness we encounter in the world on a larger scale is that it often embodies taking advantage of the weak by the strong under the rubric "for the common good," which really means "for my good." Then, when moral standards have been lowered sufficiently and everywhere, everyone—even those who are not "strong"—acts on selfish motives and does whatever it takes to get a bigger share of the pie. From there, it's just a short journey to all of us becoming so calloused that it's nothing to be completely careless of another's rights, even, in some cases, to the point of savagery. Is this hyperbole? Consider the following terrible tale of selfishness, which is only one among many in Misha Glenny's *McMafia: A Journey through the Global Criminal Underworld.*

This story begins with a waitress in Israel named Victoria, who—with a gun to her head—calls her old friend Ludmila in Moldova to invite her to Israel for a new job, where "the work's easy, the pay's good, and it's real fun." To Ludmila's shock, once she starts on this journey, she is kidnapped and held captive by the Russian mob, being shuttled first through Odessa, Moscow, and then Cairo, and then finally smuggled across the Egyptian-Israeli border by Bedouins in the middle of the night. After her arrival in the Negev capital, Beer-Sheba, she is purchased for a brothel in Tel-Aviv where

> She was forced to work for twelve hours [daily] on the high-volume second shift. "I worked seven days a week and had to service up to twenty clients per session," she explained. That is a euphemism. Ludmila was raped twenty times a night.
>
> In Israel, as in most Western countries, it is the trafficked woman and not the client who is the object of law enforcement procedures. When Ludmila first succeeded in escaping, she was handed back to her pimp by the duty sergeant, who happened to be a client of the brothel. In response, she was beaten senseless by her "owner." The second time she got away, she handed herself in to a police station in another part of town. As is habitual, she was charged with being an illegal immigrant and thrown into a detention center for several months as her deportation order was processed.
>
> When she finally arrived back in Chisinau, destitute and traumatized ... Ludmila could not return to her home, partly for reasons of shame, but above all for fear of being found by her traffickers....
>
> Ludmila is now HIV positive. Unsurprisingly, combination therapy is not readily available in a country such as Moldova.[93]

Seeing this, yet another, terrible tale of cruelty, we must ask what's next for us. Depression? Resignation? Distraction? Apathy? Anger at those who are the most lost? Buying into the argument of the apathetic that says even if we could get back to consistent generosity toward all, what good would it do, since all of these evil-doers continue to listen to their wrong-mindedness and keep overrunning the world? Or, simply refusing to give in to such puerile and self-defeating thinking?

Is it possible to be a real adult, even in the midst of the temptation to be a "justifiably" angry child, in this chaos called the world? For the unseeing and the unforgiving, who are currently, in effect, the unknowing, no. For those beginning to wake up to how they've been denying themselves access to their own higher natures, while slandering everyone else's, and for those who can forgive themselves and everyone else for their ignorance, the answer is yes. There is little doubt that, at times, most of us have had thoughts, and therefore perceptions and behaviors, that have been far less than generous. This fact demonstrates how often we've followed the lead of our wrong-mindedness and how confused we've been about what we want.

And that is the question: what is it that we want? To struggle on, in a diminished capacity, in our misconstrued versions of reality—those unreal stories in which the main character strives to get his or her own way more and more often? Or do we want to awaken to the reality that we are the authors of all stories as they relate to ourselves and to others? The first option leaves us chasing after the evanescent and fretting over whether things will turn out as we want; the second with power over perception and feeling alike. Seen in this light, growing out of a childish subjugation to thought, emotion, and memory, and becoming fully responsible adults has great appeal. To use a metaphor, it would be as if we were walking, downtrodden, around and around in circles, in a seven-foot-high cornfield (our beliefs), led by the nose by our own dismal convictions, until one day we climbed up on a ladder and saw that, beyond the limitations of the cornfield, there were fields of grass, and trees, and towns we never knew existed. Would our miasma evaporate with this new understanding of our limited perception? Yes

SILENCE IS THE ANSWER

and no. Yes, in that we could not have been able to perceive the bigger picture unless we had already made the decision to look beyond all that we were so sure we understood before. No, in that our habituation to the old is so firmly fixed, it would take time to fully "recover" from the shock of our newfound realization and accept ourselves as the sole meaning-givers in every situation we enter.

As the warmth of the sun slowly clears away the dense morning fog, so too does our commitment to being responsible for how we perceive and feel gradually dissolve the murky air of judgment that envelops our minds. It is in the realization that such fog is self-made and founded on a desire to be both irresponsible and special that our motivation to escape its reflexive results grows in power and scope. This is what draws us up to a higher level of awareness, what brings to light the possibility of finding freedom from the maze of the "maize" that heretofore seemed forever without end.

Finding the Road to Real Safety

As our attention shifts from getting ahead to improving our outlook, the guard within will tell us that we're fools to set aside self-interest while so many others are engaged in thinking first of themselves. But the ill will of the ego is just something to get used to, since wrong-mindedness will always tell us that we're wrong when we're right, just as it will tell us we're right when we're wrong, and then condemn us for being wrong later. It is the very need for vigilance against such deceptiveness and against all similar assaults on our character, however, that reminds us that it is we, and not society, who possess the power to discern what is worthy of our striving.

What is it that inspires some people to be kind, not for the sake of the inflation of their egos, but with everyone, always, regardless of circumstance? What is the source of the gentleness of the ten Boom sisters or of the wisdom of Socrates? Are these people and the ones like them different from the rest of us? If so, were they always that way? Or are they simply the ones who recognized that they retained the power of choice and, with that recognition to sustain them, became the rulers of their minds instead of the subjects of their thoughts?

As we've discussed, to rule one's mind is simply to refuse to buy into the petty arguments that arise within it to proclaim us the pawns of circumstance, and to embrace, instead, the idea that everything we experience begins not with external events but with internal decisions about how to perceive them. Yet, how many recognize this? A person like my son feels bereft and decides he wants the pleasure that comes from getting high. It's a poorly chosen respite from the burdens of life, which only invites consequences that later add to the burdens, but in a delusion of the benefits of instant gratification, he decides that he wants what he wants when he wants it, stifling all awareness of its eventual cost. And thus, willingly, but unwittingly, he becomes the victim of his own wrong choice.

In a sense, leaving the limitations of our misinformed beliefs behind is like setting blame and worry aside and entering the present. Yet telling people that the answer to their lingering grievances and anticipatory anxieties is to "live in the present" and leaving it at that is about as effective as telling a curious teenager that the answer to pot or alcohol is to "just say no." Learning to live in the present is not just a matter of being dedicated to it and then training the mind to focus on it; it is a matter of forgiving ourselves and others as well. To escape from the confinement of the past and the future imposed by those dragons of regret, hate, and fear requires trust in the reality of goodness, and no one who holds grievances and believes in enemies can reach the condition of defenselessness required for that trust. Therefore, forgiveness is the necessary key to the doorway of a new life.

Forgiveness is usually a process with stages. It begins when we experience the unsatisfying results of blaming others, along with a dimly lit recognition that something else might serve us better. But since holding on to grievances and perceiving ourselves as beings who are unfairly treated have such powerful attraction as supposed defenses of the pitiful and separated self, we do not readily accept that our letting these defenses go would be a step toward safety and not greater danger. Accepting their release as possible and even desirable starts us on our way, often at first by misusing even forgiveness—falsely forgiving others for what we believe they've done to bring pain to our minds. At this point, we may even pray for those whom we still see as hurtful and beneath us.

The next step is the realization that such "forgiveness" is an ineffective solution, because even though it may allow us to feel more righteous, it doesn't bring us peace. Then, as discussed earlier, we slowly gain the understanding that forgiveness, to be genuine, must be of the mind and about the mind—our forgiving ourselves for having chosen wrongly and blaming others for what they did *not*, emotionally speaking, do to us at all. What follows this stage is the growing realization that forgiveness is ultimately only of ourselves, for all of our past unwillingness to listen to reason and to perceive others' mistakes, as well as our own, as mistakes and not as unforgivable crimes.

At last comes our natural entry into the final stage of the recovery of sense, which is gratitude to everyone who ever seemed to offend us. Why, of all things, would we feel gratitude toward those who have abused our physical or psychological bodies in so many ways? Because they, through the difficult situations that helped pull the covers off of our mind's belief in our weakness, were the ones who gave us opportunities to reconsider and meet such malicious nonsense with that remarkably healthier attitude of a quiet "Says who?"

The idea mentioned earlier, of becoming aware of our absolute power over thought, memory, and emotion as our birthright, finds its fulfillment in forgiveness. Forgiveness, in this context, is no more or less than watching our minds for the vassals of unforgiveness—such as accusation, envy, blame, hatred—to arise and then, when they do, stepping back and offering them no support or respect. It is, as I said, about forgiving myself when I choose to engage in madness, in addition to recognizing that real faith is faith in the goodness of my brother, despite all appearances to the contrary.

For the willing learner, it comes down to accepting that perception and emotion are the results, not of the external, but of choice and the predisposition of thought, an interpretation *we* lay on circumstances, people, and events. In simple terms, when we learn that what we perceive reflects what we believe, and that what we believe comes from what we desire to believe, then, and only then, can we cease accusing others for causing something that has its source solely in us. *ACIM* addresses the responsibility for perception this way:

> Projection makes perception. The world you see is what you gave it, nothing more than that. But though it is no more than that, it is not less. Therefore, to you it is important. It is the witness to your state of mind, the outside picture of an inward condition. As a man thinketh, so does he perceive. Therefore, seek not to change the world, but choose to change your mind about the world. Perception is a result and not a cause.[94]

"Certainty Can Be Murderous"

One way to test our progress in this process of forgiveness is to carefully watch our reactions. Do we examine, or do we avoid (because it makes us uncomfortable), the depths to which the expressions of ignorance can sink in this world, recalling what Thomas Hardy said: "If a way to the better there be, it lies in taking a full look at the worst."[95] As we continue with our looking, let's try to better understand what these overviews make plainer—that we are passing through a world filled with uncertainty and violence, not just here or there or then, but everywhere and always. Perhaps difficulty is not now present in our lives, but it surely exists in the lives of some of our relatives and neighbors and friends, and possibly, one day, like an uninvited bad guest, it will come into our own.

As I said in the beginning of the book, the reality of life is that we can drop from a place of peace into a horror show in an instant, with much of what we believed to be our protection or comfort disappearing in a gust of ill-wind. The ever-flaring monstrousness of evil incidents brought on by man or Mother Nature or even the inexplicable are gross and presumptuous familiars of this world. Therefore, other than denial, which is never helpful, the only successful defense is to learn in advance how to remain right-minded, while the often impertinent world does what it does and the wrong mind blusters, bellows, or begs it be different.

There is no other logical answer to the instability we find here but mental preparedness. Hope is not an answer; it is a wish. Good deeds have done nothing to keep the winds of uncertainty from many good people. Prayer may be comforting, but bad things do happen to a vast number of prayerful people. However, the strength of right-minded-ness seems to have carried even the beleaguered a long way. Therefore, let's try to remain as balanced as they while continuing to take "a full look at the worst."

One place for such looking might be the Inquisition, which began in the thirteenth century. Its avowed purpose was to rid the world of "the heresy" of Catharism, the last remnant of the Gnostic religion of Manichaeism, but it quickly spread to include others who were branded as being among the unfaithful. What made it worse than the usual inhumanity to man was that the megalomaniacal accusers, torturers, and, frequently, executioners of these innocent people unknowingly thought of themselves as "holy men," doing what they were doing to defend the one true faith. In some countries, this persecution, and that of the witch hunts, lasted well into the nineteenth century, with countless victims condemned as guilty and consigned to eternal punishment.

For hundreds of years in America and Europe alike, people who believed or acted differently from the ones in power were tormented or even murdered. A telling example was the longstanding persecution of the Jewish people. How utterly perverse were some of the beliefs spawned by this particular form of fear not that many years back? Consider the following from *The End of Faith* by Sam Harris.

RESPONSIBILITY AND PERCEPTION

Throughout the Middle Ages, Jews were regularly accused of murdering Christian infants, a crime for which they were duly despised. It was well-known that all Jews menstruated, male and female alike, and required the blood of a Christian to replenish their lost stores.... It was common knowledge, too, that all Jews were born blind and that, when smeared upon their eyes, Christian blood granted them the faculty of sight. Jewish boys were frequently born with their fingers attached to their fore-heads, and only the blood of a Christian could allow this pensive gesture to be broken without risk to the child.[96]

Harris then neatly summed up the problem born of prejudice married to an unexamined blind faith by quoting Will Durant, who said, "Intolerance is the natural concomitant of strong faith, tolerance grows only when faith loses certainty; certainty is murderous."[97]

Tolstoy's take on the same issue was stated this way:

Nothing results in bad deeds ... more than belonging to a group of people; a family, a club, [a faith], or society, who think they are better than others. The most astonishing fact is that belonging to such a closed society is considered by some to be virtue.[98]

Tolstoy was speaking about a problem that is in no way limited to a few. While over the centuries, numerous people of one "certain" faith or another have expressed their self-hatred and deeply buried uncertainties by acting terribly toward their neighbors, so too have many others who appeared normal until they were handed the reins by some person or circumstance. This normally powerless individual then hands over the reins to his own baser instincts. Finally, in the name of protecting his family, sect, race, or country, he acts with what is now "justified" cruelty toward one who is, seen properly, no less than a brother under the skin. Consider the following:

> [The corporal took his whip] and then he began to lash
> me across and across with all his might [with] this thing
> which wrapped itself like flaming wire about my body.
> At the instant of each stroke ... the whip fell more and
> more upon existing weals, biting blacker or more wet,
> till my flesh quivered with accumulated pain, and with
> terror of the next blow coming! From the first they hurt
> more horribly than I had dreamed of and, as always
> before the agony of one had fully reached me another
> used to fall, the torture of a series, worked up to an intol-
> erable height.[99]

Who was being tortured? (T. E.) Lawrence of Arabia, tormented
beyond measure at the hands of the Turks who, likely to his greater
benefit, had no idea who they had in their hands. And what about Lawrence's own responses to his and his country's "enemies," as described
in some of his other wartime experiences—his elsewhere romanticized
adventures? Here is how the twisted ideas of reason lost, agony remembered, revenge glorified, and unforgiveness wanted played out in his
life a little while later:

> I said [to the Arabs], "The best of you brings me the most
> Turkish dead," and we turned and rode after the fading
> enemy, on our way shooting down those who had fallen
> out by the road-side and came imploring our pity.
> The Arabs were fighting like devils, the sweat blur-
> ring their eyes, dust parching their throats; while the
> flame of cruelty and revenge, which was burning in
> their bodies so twisted them about that their hands
> could hardly shoot. By my orders we took no prison-
> ers....
> There lay on us a madness ... so that we killed and
> killed, even blowing in the heads of the fallen and of

the animals as though their death and running blood could slake the agony in our brains.[100]

Now consider the actions of these two disparate groups of people, as described in *Boone—A Biography* by Robert Morgan, and let's see if we can find a fundamental difference in the content of their behaviors.

> [The year] 1782 [was] one of the deadliest in frontier history.... In March a party of Pennsylvania militia crossed the Ohio [River] in retaliation for Indian raids [and killed] ninety to a hundred unarmed men, women, and children. Those Indians had been converted by the Moravians and were pacifists.... The Mission Indians were taken out three-at-a-time and executed with mallets or clubs. Twenty-nine men, twenty-seven women, and thirty-four children were killed.... After ... more Indians were brought from the village of Salem and executed.[101]

Morgan then gives the other side of the coin, describing the retaliation by Indians against ten white men they captured nearby.

> Crawford, Dr. Knight, and eight other prisoners were taken to Half King's Town on the upper Sandusky on June 10, 1782.... On June 11 all the captives were painted black ... and four were tomahawked and scalped. The rest ... all but Dr. Knight and Colonel Crawford were killed by women and boys.
>
> At four in the afternoon a fire was made and Dr. Knight and Colonel Crawford were beaten and bound to separate posts. Speeches were made, reminding those present of the massacre and Crawford's ears were cut off. Then the Indians took turns prodding Crawford over his naked body with burning poles....

> After two hours Crawford was pushed face down into
> embers and scalped…. After Crawford … could not be
> revived for more torture, he was roasted over the fire.[102]

Sporadic brutality, bigotry, bestiality—everywhere the expressions of hatred in the world by individual and separate interest groups seem endless, as shown later in the book where Morgan writes of a court case in which "one neighbor had bitten off the ear of another in a fight," recounting, "In frontier fighting, eyes were gouged out and noses or ears bitten off, or pulled out by the roots."[103]

Are things more civilized in today's world than they were back then? When we consider the devastating effects to people and families from things like roadside bombs, criminal activities, fake medications, financial fraud, collateral damage, and the like, it doesn't seem so. Yet many, perceiving life as they wish it to be and not as it is, do believe things are better now. At the same time, they watch young people, taken in by propaganda and their own so-called patriotic spirit, march off to liberate "those poor people" in this or that country from what we, in our superior wisdom, have defined as the yoke of tyranny. While justified indeed in World War II, and probably, at least to the 38th parallel in Korea, such actions were certainly questionable at best and perhaps ignorant at worst in Vietnam, Iraq, and—aside from containing Al Qaeda—Afghanistan. And what about our youthful heroes, the too-young saviors of the downtrodden we so freely send into the arena? What is it *really* like for some of them after the stirring speeches and the beat of the drums have died away? On those days when it is not just hot or cold or boring? Let's return to Sergeant Bellavia's *House to House* for a firsthand look at those we send off to do our "righteous" duty.

Early in his book, Bellavia provides the reader with graphic depictions of the fighting in Iraq, with vivid descriptions of the sound of bullets ripping into flesh and of battles raging day and night. He describes knocking enemy combatants "right out of their shoes … [with] well-placed shots." He writes of enemies being killed in front of their children; of people screaming from wounds; of feral dogs eating the dead; of the fear, insanity, and euphoria that sometimes comes with battle, saying,

> I scream at the top of my lungs. It is a victory cry.... I have killed the enemy and survived. Infantrymen live on the edge. We are hyperalert, hyperaware of our own mortality. It makes us feel more alive, more powerful.... There is no room for Chaplain Brown out here. I scream again. Battle madness grips me. I embrace the battle.... I am the madness.[104]

Later in the book, Bellavia describes an incredible battle with an enemy combatant in a dimly lit house. It is graphic, horrifying, and comes with a surprise ending. We enter the story after they have been fighting for a short while.

> The wounded boogeyman stirs.... He grunts and suddenly swings his AK up. Its barrel slams into my jaw and I feel a tooth break.... His leg flies up from the floor and slams into my crotch. I stagger back, pain radiating from my groin. The pain drives me into a fury. I leap at my enemy. Before he can respond I land right on top of his chest.
>
> His head snaps back against the floor. In an instant his fists are pummeling me. I rock from his counterblows. He lands one on my injured jaw and the pain nearly blinds me. He connects with my nose, and blood and snot pour down my throat. I spit blood between my teeth and scream with him. The two of us sound like caged dogs locked in a death match....
>
> Like a claw my right hand clutches his throat. I squeeze, squeeze, squeeze.... He opens his mouth under my hand. For a moment I think it is over. He's going to surrender. Then a raging pain sears through my arm.

He's clamped his teeth on the side of my thumb near the knuckle, and now he tears at it trying to pull meat from the bone....

We share a single question of survival. Which of us has the stronger will to live?

I gouge his left eye with my right index finger. I am astonished to discover that the human eye is not so much a firm ball, as a soft, pliable sack. I try with all my might to send my finger all the way through. He wails like a child. It unnerves me and I lose the stomach for this dirty trick. I withdraw my finger.

The fight continues, the insurgent biting Bellavia in the crotch, Bellavia smashing him with his helmet, and on and on. Finally, Bellavia pulls a knife and stabs his enemy again and again, until finally he hits an artery.

I keep my weight on the knife and push down on the wound in staccato waves, like Satan's version of CPR. His eyes show nothing but fear now. He knows he's going to die. His face is inches from mine, and I see him regard me for a split second. At the end he says, "Please."

"Surrender," I cry. I'm almost in tears. "No," he manages weakly.

His face goes slack. His right hand slips from my hair. It hangs in the air for a moment, then with one last spasm of strength, he brings it to my cheek. It lingers there, and as I look into his dying eyes, he caresses the side of my face. His hand runs gently from my cheek to jaw, then falls to the floor. He takes a last ragged breath, and his eyes go dim, still staring into mine.

Tears blur my vision. I can hardly see him now, but he looks peaceful. Why did he touch me like that at the end?

He was forgiving me. He was no boogeyman.

I do nothing but lie there, shivering uncontrollably.[105]

How can we read such an account and not be moved by the pathos of it, or end up with anything less than compassion for both young men? Can a tale like this be in any way construed as a story about good guys and bad, and the victory of good over evil? Is it not more accurately a tale of sorrow and redemption? If Sergeant Bellavia had lost the fight, would he, perhaps, have been the one saying "please" and "no" and caressing his killer's face in forgiveness? If the man who had died had instead lived, would he, perhaps, have been the one to write such a moving story? Were these two young warriors for different causes all that different from each other once they entered the house and then remained there, struggling so desperately to survive? And did where they came from and what they were taught to believe in any way have the power to make one of them good and the other evil? Are we, "the free and the brave," always in the right? Or could we, too, at times be just as caught up as anyone in the villainy of it all?

Here's another tragedy of war, this one involving American troops in Vietnam in 1968 at My Lai. As we read it, let's think not only of the victims, but also of all the young men who lived for years afterward with terrible memories of what they had done.

> Early in the morning the soldiers were landed in the village by helicopter. Many were firing as they spread out, killing both people and animals. There was no sign of the Vietcong Battalion and no shot was fired at Charlie Company all day, but they carried on. They burnt down every house. They raped women and girls and then killed them. They stabbed some women in the vagina and disemboweled others, or cut off their hands or scalps. Pregnant women had their stomachs slashed open and were left to die. There were

gang rapes and killings by shooting or with bayonets. There were mass executions. Dozens of people at a time, including old men, women and children, were machine gunned in a ditch. In four hours nearly 500 villagers were killed.[106]

Now there is no possible way those young men in Vietnam got up that morning and said, "I just can't wait to shoot a child, or a grandmother or grandfather, or to be part of a gang rape of a teenage villager today." But that's what they did. Likewise, we, upon our arising do not say, "I just can't wait to tell off my spouse or child or employee this afternoon or to demonstrate in cold anger just how much they have disappointed me." But there are times when we do.

Why? Has the glorification of self led us into such a dark corner of the mind that we are left blinded, thinking we are serving our group's best interests when, in fact, we're unknowingly serving our egos? Plato seemed not only to think so, but also to assert that this was our greatest problem. He said,

> Of all the faults ... the gravest one is one which is inborn in most men, one which all excuse in themselves and none therefore attempts to avoid—that conveyed in the maxim that "everyone is his own friend," and that it is only right and proper that he should be so, whereas, in truth, this same violent attachment to self is the constant source of all manner of misdeeds in every one of us.... From this same fault springs also that universal conviction that one's own folly is wisdom, with its consequence that we fancy we know everything when we know as good as nothing.... Every man, then, must shun self-love and follow ever in the steps of his better [nature], undeterred by any shame for his case.[107]

To really seal this idea about how ignorance and confusion in values can play itself out in the pursuit of personal glory and nationalistic interests, let's look at just two final examples.

The first is a pronouncement by Marine Corps General Smedley Butler in 1931, as quoted in James W. Loewen's *Lies My Teacher Told Me*:

> I helped make Mexico safe for American oil interests in 1914. I helped make Haiti and Cuba a decent place for the National City Bank boys to collect revenue in. I helped purify Nicaragua for the international banking house of Brown Brothers.... I brought light to the Dominican Republic for American sugar interests in 1916. I helped make Honduras "right" for American fruit companies in 1905. Looking back on it, I might have given Al Capone a few hints.[108]

The second example comes from the same book, in the following tale of our storybook hero, Christopher Columbus:

> On his first voyage, Columbus kidnapped some ... twenty-five American Indians and took them back with him to Spain.... They caused quite a stir in Seville. Ferdinand and Isabella [then] provided Columbus with seventeen ships, 1,200 to 1,500 hundred men, cannons, crossbows, guns, cavalry, and attack dogs for a second voyage....
>
> When Columbus and his men returned to Haiti in 1493 ... Columbus ... set up a tribute system....
>
> Ferdinand Columbus described how it worked: "[The Indians] all promised to pay tribute ... every three months.... Whenever an Indian delivered his tribute, he was to receive a ... token which he must wear about his neck as proof he had made his payment. Any Indian found without such a token was to be punished." ... Columbus's son neglected to mention how the Spanish

punished those whose tokens had expired: they cut off
their hands....

Estimates of Haiti's pre-Columbian native Indian
population range as high as eight million.... By 1516,
thanks to the sinister Indian slave trade and labor policies
initiated by Columbus, only some 12,000 remained.[109]

When we really look at what we've just read, it's startling. What
it comes down to is that we can't trust the enemy, we can't trust the
government, we can't trust the corporations, we can't trust the history
books we read in school, and we can't even trust what we had come to
believe and were fairly sure we understood. What, then, can we trust?
Our ability to learn anew if we're willing to look, even when the looking discloses things we'd rather not see.

Paying Attention

To summarize, Epictetus issued this important caution for us in regard
to our responsibility to ourselves and others:

If you would improve, submit to be considered without
sense, and foolish with respect to externals. Wish to be
considered to know nothing; and if you seem to some
to be a person of importance, distrust yourself.... The
mark of one who is making progress is this: in a word,
he watches himself as if he were an enemy and lying in
ambush.[110]

Any honest assessment of what we have been reading and of our
own disturbed thinking and improper behavior, whether it occurs
frequently or infrequently, says that to watch ourselves as if we were
enemies "lying in ambush" is good advice indeed. There certainly
is in most of us, at least at times, a strange submission to the wiles
of wrong-mindedness at work, and denying this will never make it
go away. It may appear unreasonable at first to be told that paying

attention to the ego's predilection toward divisiveness, its guilt, and its litany of complaints about others is our most important function, and that setting forth to fulfill that function every day is our greatest responsibility, but it is.

To accept taking complete responsibility for thought and emotion as our goal is to accept that anything less is not only unsatisfactory, but ultimately irresponsible. Since it is evident that even ordinary young American men can go temporarily insane in places like My Lai, it seems reasonable to believe that learning to stand back from our "violent attachment to self"—the cause of our problems and the reason for our need for self-forgiveness—and watching ourselves as if we were enemies "lying in ambush" are not only endeavors in the direction of a more kindly aspiration, but definitions of our highest present ideals.

CHAPTER 8

Who Really Understands?

T
HE NEXT CALL FROM MY son came from a sober-living facility he had gained access to after leaving the hospital. He said that his plan was to remain there until a slot opened up at the Salvation Army's six-month drug-treatment program, a program he had been promised entry into while in the hospital. He sounded nervous, saying he wished that he had been able to stay in the hospital longer, but also seemed hopeful about the program. Would he make it there? We'd see.

There is a process of growing in understanding, which I have engaged in with, among others, all my sons and daughters. Like almost everyone else, I have a mold for behavior or a program in my mind that says, "I approve of people when they do *A*" (typically something that suits my purposes), "and I disapprove of them when they do *B*" (whatever doesn't suit my purposes). This self-constructed dysfunctional program is most unhelpful because it places me in the stressful position of either fervently trying to convince others to do *A*, or becoming upset whenever they decide for *B*. What is the answer to this frequently encountered conundrum? What else but, as we've been talking about, removing my focus from the behaviors of others and putting it instead on reprogramming myself. Not to reprogram myself to give up my preference that another does *A*, but to adopt a state of awareness in which I watch myself take it personally until I get over it whenever the person does *B*.

It took a while, but this is what brought me to the full acceptance I reached with my eldest son years before he finished drinking and drugging himself to death. I sat down with him one afternoon and drew a map with two roads, one leading to sobriety—perhaps returning to school, work, marriage, and a family—and the other leading to continued self-destruction, possibly prison, and eventually death. As we talked quietly, I told him that if he chose the right road, I would help him, and that if he did not, I couldn't. But what counted most in all I said to him that afternoon was that if he took the right road, I wouldn't love him any more than I did, and if he continued on the wrong road, I wouldn't love him any less. And that is exactly what happened, right up to the day I held his hand as he died.

Was it a tragedy that my son's life ended in his twenties? Or, was it a blessing that someone struggling and making no progress left at such an early age? I guess that depends on your perspective and how you consider life over the long term. Do you believe, as many, that you come into the world or begin here, live a reasonably decent life, and then end up in a place in the sky; or perhaps, instead, in a place of torment, because you were bad; or, at best, in the slums of heaven, because you failed someone's standard of what it means to be good? My son was a good person—gentle, funny, and essentially decent, living a life of self-imposed loneliness, hardship, and despair. Yes, he lived at the beach and got high every day, and, yes, in its own perverse way that was attractive to him. But when he measured that frivolousness against his potential and against all his failed responsibilities to himself and others, under the covers of his almost constant buzz, I'm sure he felt sorely disappointed in himself and his life.

Living up to Our Real Potential

How about people like you and me? We may not have fallen into the straits experienced by my son and others like him, but are we living up to our potential? We may believe we are, and, by the usual standards of society, we may be. But what if the accepted definition of our potential is so shabby at best that it is insulting in fact? What if our potential is far, far greater than we have been led to believe or ever conceived? Not potential in the sense of our bodies and brains doing things they are incapable of, but in the sense of our minds going beyond all assumed limitations of selfishness and self, remaining quiet and reasonable and decent to all in everything we do. What if it really *is* possible to reach the state of trust required to live in consistent harmony in the present? To strive daily toward the ideal of absolute goodness? To face hate-filled memories, tragedy, suffering, pain, and even death with an impersonal resolution that silently says, "You no longer threaten me, because I've taken back all the power to disturb that I previously handed over to you"?

As we set upon a course of observing the thoughts that support our idea of limited self-potential, it becomes more apparent that the self-image we've constructed, cling to, and cherish is that of a victim combined with a hero. A victim, because of all that has been thrust upon us without our permission, and a hero, for withstanding all of those epochal events and even functioning under the circumstances at all. This is what Nietzsche was referring to when he said, "All human-kind wants to be ... pitied";[111] as the self is constantly in need of both pity and praise, wanting to be regarded highly no matter how lowly it lives. This is the childlike image that the maturing mind can learn to lay aside as one would an outgrown toy.

The Excitement of Conflict

Yet becoming mature enough to set aside this dual image of self is another thing easier said than done. It takes mindful practice and time to discover that our selfishness and self-pity are not the natural defense of interests they pretend to be and to realize that what the world holds as unerring truth is often mere confusion born of the acceptance of nonsensical premises. According to what many believe, it makes sense to strike first, strike back, take advantage, win no matter how, forgive but not forget, condemn, compare, and give as little as possible to gain as much as one can. But does any of this make sense? Not if these actions foster guilt and reinforce the fear of retribution, which is exactly what they do.

Take, for example, "strike first" and "strike back"—common themes of the "civilized" world. How many wars have been fought to slake these egoistic thirsts? Too many to count. And *that* is really crazy. To go to war, as we have, killing off our own along with the young enemies of the day and innocent civilians, because our national pride has been offended; to ensure there will be no interference with our larger corporations' interests; to gain a territorial advantage; or to in any way force others to adhere to our norms is irrational. Even when war is unavoidable, it remains a terrible and inglorious endeavor for all concerned. And yet, like other reckless pursuits, time after time, we engage in it.

What is the weird attraction here? Consider what the respected journalist Sebastian Junger had to say about it in his book *War*:

> War is a lot of things and it is useless to pretend that exciting isn't one of them. It's insanely exciting…. Soldiers discuss that fact with each other … but the public will never hear about it…. War is supposed to feel bad because undeniably bad things happen in it, but for a nineteen-year-old at the working end of a .50 cal during a firefight … war is life multiplied by a number that no one has ever heard of…. Don't underestimate the power of that revelation [or] the things young men will wager in order to play that game one more time….

> As for a sense of purpose, combat is it.... It's the ultimate test, and some of the men worry ... that they may have been ruined for anything else ... [coming] home to find themselves desperately missing what should have been the worst experience of their lives....[112]

Or this, from the *New York Times* bestselling author of *Jarhead*, Anthony Swofford:

> There are days I still fantasize about combat ... [believing] there is no grander test for a man than combat. Every other pursuit is pure, unimportant leisure when compared to a firefight....
>
> Like many other combat veterans I know ... I lived with the wickedly exciting and doggedly exhausting knowledge that we had once, for a short period of time, flirted with death, and won. This knowledge is like a drug, the purest cocaine: ... once you have had some, it alters your understanding of the world and of other people and of consequences.[113]

These accounts and others raise an interesting question about other dangerous pursuits as well. Does the bullfighter or the big game hunter or the racecar driver get a secret rush in playing with fire, which they don't tell us about? Do generals get a vicarious thrill in moving their men and equipment around the battlefields? The psychological aspect of all this appears to have been dismissed, considered unimportant. Yet, the *New York Times* war correspondent Chris Hodges proclaimed that the "rush of battle is often a potent and lethal addiction, for war is a drug." If we'll recall, David Bellavia said he thought he'd "pass out from excitement" when he heard he was being called back to Iraq to get "back in the game," calling adrenaline "better than any pain killer." Sergeant O'Byrne's take on it was, "I like firefights—the high point of our day is killing someone else." Chris Kyle called sniping "fun," and Karl Malantes said he "felt exhilaration" when fighting. Then there was

Ernest Becker's statement that, "For man, maximum excitement is the confrontation of death and the skillful defiance of it."

Before I started running into these different examples, I didn't think much about the subject. But now I wonder how much of what motivates people to their many feats of daring is simply being in the grasp of another kind of addiction. Consider the following cases as further possible evidence. The first account is from an undercover policeman who rode with the Hells Angels:

> After being shot, I began the first pangs of invincibility. The rush of near death did something dangerous to me…. I didn't want to get shot ever again, but I wanted to get as close to that flying bullet as I possibly could. Getting cheered [as I often was in a football stadium] by eighty thousand fans was an incredible feeling, but it didn't even register when compared to the rush of walking the line between life and death [even] when no one was watching.[114]

Then we have the experiences of some big-wave surfers, as related to Susan Casey, the author of *The Wave*:

> I'd noticed … that big waves and extreme behavior went hand in hand, and I knew, anecdotally anyway, that dropping onto the likes of a sixty-foot face was a sensation so potent that nothing else—sleeping or eating, for instance—could compete for a rider's attention.
>
> Ricky Grigg, a champion big-wave rider … told me that the risks of riding giant waves were dwarfed by the reward: "Ecstasy beyond words. Mentally, physically, spiritually, it's the highest place I can imagine being." Feeling oneself connected to the ocean at the apex of its power, Grigg emphasized, was utterly addictive…. "That's why these guys are so driven," [he said].

Grigg's friend and contemporary Gregg Noll, a larger-than-life legend ... of big-wave surfing ... described the feeling in more physical terms: "That rush, I can't explain it," he said. "When you blow down the side of a wave and the thing's growling at you and snorting and all that power and fury and you don't know whether you're going to be alive ten seconds from now or not, it's as heavy [as anything]. If you surf, you know. And all the rest of you poor sons of bitches, I feel sorry for you."[115]

Ms. Casey writes about surfers traveling thousands of miles on an instant's notice to meet storms that cause upswells that produce the giant waves they seek to ride. They think nothing of the time and expense involved, because the attraction of the experience is so special that, as far as Gregg Noll is concerned, "If you surf, you know. And all the rest of you poor sons of bitches, I feel sorry for you." What Mr. Noll likely doesn't know is that, like so many other thrill-seekers, he is just, in effect, another kind of addict in a world filled with addicts, and that there are a number of people who believe they have superior addictions, who feel equally sorry for him.

For example, at the higher levels of the game of finance and business, what almost all the participants have in common is the conviction that their game, because it is the one where most of the money is, is the only real game in town. Like the surfer who leaves the sixty-foot wave craving the seventy footer, or the soldier who wants back in the game, the top-level financiers and executives, who may have power and position and wealth beyond counting, still lack one thing—and that is the fulfillment of the hunger for more. And so they chase the satisfaction they hope for but cannot find. And so it is with the boxer who can't quit, or the aging golfer just making ends meet on the senior tour, or the bullfighter who is past his prime, or the sex addict with multiple partners who can't ever find fruition, or the gambler who never wins—or loses—enough, and so on.

Looked at objectively, these people are not much different from alcoholics who drink too much to chase away their depression or drug users who are constantly seeking a rush. It's just that society has deemed some self-hurtful activities as admirable and others as criminal. Yet, is it really meritorious to want to go back to war because you feel more alive in battle, and then to call fighting "patriotism" when often it's not? Or to make billions and give away a little, getting your name on a hospital or university building while hoarding the rest so you can stay in the game? I'm not criticizing any of these people for what they do, any more than I am applauding those who choose more "productive" ways of dealing with their buried grief over their perceived separation from the trunk. What I'm trying to point out is the similarity underneath our differences, raising the question of whether Gregg Noll is really different from the young man who wants the rush that comes from killing "bad guys," believing himself to be a warrior for the good. Or from the financier with $500 million who strives daily for the satisfaction he is sure he'll find when he finally reaches the rarified status of the billionaires club. Or from the bullfighter feeding on the stirring chants of "Olé, Olé!"

What makes this phenomenon even more peculiar than one might expect is that these experiences aren't what they appear to be at all. Excitement over getting what we want or having it our way is a grand deception, leaving the one who reaches its peak sliding down its backside, ever in pursuit of a greater experience. And yet the greater experience—be it surfing the eighty-foot wave, turning the one billion into five, gaining victory over the fearsome enemy, becoming the greatest bullfighter or the heavyweight champion, gaining the worship of the many, or being pronounced king or queen of this or that—is all just a set-up, leading the "conqueror" to the dark side of the moon, only to find out that he or she had been confusing it with the sun all along. And let's not kid ourselves about this. This is exactly what awaits the champions of this or that once they realize they've been focusing their energies on goals so far beneath their own true, higher potential.

Big-wave surfers lose friends to drowning all the time, leaving girlfriends and wives and children staring at the ocean wondering why their loved ones had to die. Some financiers become too big for their britches and end up broke or in prison or both. The best of them almost never quit the game. With the rarest of exceptions, great boxers keep fighting past their prime, bullfighters who stay around long enough often get gored, great football players find themselves suffering from serious physical problems, and a number of financially well-off golfers traipse around the country on the senior tour. Many people with exceptional power, almost as if this power were an uncontrollable force they couldn't handle, end up misusing it in one way or the other. And war, for all its excitement, ends with many not sliding through the winner's slot of the big pinball machine. Further gruesome examples of what is really going on in war come from David Finkel's *The Good Soldiers*.

> [The] magazines [for the troops] had come from an Arkansas Middle School, along with a hand-drawn card that read, "Show dem Arabs Who's Boss. Nuke em. Happy Thanksgiving."
>
> [Colonel] Kauzlarich [the Battalion Commander] flew to San Antonio and was escorted to the fourth floor of the hospital....
>
> He had decided to start with Duncan Crookston. He put on a protective gown, protective boots, and protective gloves and walked toward a nineteen-year-old soldier whose left leg was gone, right leg was gone, right arm was gone, left lower arm was gone, ears were gone, nose was gone, and eyelids were gone, and who was burned over what little remained of him.
>
> "Wow," Kauzlarich said under his breath. And then, taking it all in: "Bastards...."

[A]t the Center for the Intrepid, the Chairman of the Joint Chiefs of Staff was saying in a dedication speech, "There are those who speak about you who say, 'He lost an arm. He lost a leg. She lost her sight.' I object. You *gave* your arm. You *gave* your leg. You *gave* your sight. As gifts to your nation. That we might live in freedom. Thank you."[116]

In France in the 1570s, in the war between the Catholics and the Protestant Huguenots, a provincial lawyer said in a letter to the king that the conflict left the rustic poor in his area as "miserable, martyrized, and abandoned men" who lived off the land. He also reported tales of people …

> buried alive in heaps of manure, thrown into wells and ditches and left to die, howling like dogs; they had been nailed in boxes without air, walled up in towers without food, and garroted upon trees in the depths of the mountains and forests; they had been stretched in front of fires, their feet fricasseed in grease; their women had been raped and those who were pregnant had been aborted; their children had been kidnapped and ransomed, or even roasted alive before the parents.[117]

According to General William Tecumseh Sherman,

> You cannot qualify war in harsher terms than I will. War is cruelty and you cannot refine it. War is at best barbarism…. Its glory is all moonshine. It is only those who have neither fired a shot nor heard the shrieks and groans of the wounded who cry aloud for more blood, more vengeance, more desolation.
> War is hell.[118]

In *A Stillness at Appomattox*, historian Bruce Catton writes about what the Civil War was actually like:

> Riding back to headquarters in the twilight, Grant passed many dead and wounded men from both armies.... [As] men were borne away, Grant and his party rode off. There were so many dead and wounded that the horses were constantly shying nervously, and Grant at last turned to Colonel Webster with the remark: "Let's get away from this dreadful place. I suppose this work is part of the devil that is left in us all."
>
> There were wild flurries of hand-to-hand fighting.... Federals crouched on one side of a log breastwork while Confederates crouched on the other side, not five feet away. Men shot between chinks in the logs, or jabbed through them with bayonets....
>
> The fighting was worst of all at a place ... known as the Bloody Angle. The trenches were knee-deep in mud and rainwater, wounded men drowning there; dead men falling on top of them....
>
> The storm of bullets ... killed and wounded men and then cut up their bodies until they were unrecognizable.... A fresh Union regiment was moving up ... and as the men came out into the open, they heard the uproar of battle—"strange and terrible, a sound that came from a thousand human throats and yells, but rather like a vast mournful roar."[119]

So, war is burned and wounded torsos, the "giving" of limbs, and people being "buried alive in heaps of manure." "War is hell." War is "this work [on the] part of the devil that is left in all of us." War is "wounded men drowning" in trenches that are "knee-deep in mud and rainwater." "War is ... insanely exciting ... life multiplied by a number that no one has even heard of." War is flirting with death. Who can make sense of these multifarious experiences and contradictions? Who can make sense of war? Who can make sense of the motivation behind our engagements in it and in any conflict for that matter? Or, when we become truly honest, who can make sense of the "reasoning" behind much of what we do? To address this question, let's examine a quite different idea and use it as a benchmark to compare what we have accepted without question as true.

An Invention of Our Minds

In early 2010, a movie titled *The Invention of Lying* was released. The movie was just so-so, in my opinion, but parts of it were funny, and the idea behind it was unique. The movie is set in the modern everyday world, with the main difference between it and the real world being that, in the movie, everyone always, and often cold-heartedly, tells the truth exactly as he or she sees it. The hero of the movie is a nebbishy kind of guy who has a job as a TV scriptwriter (which he is about to lose), a mother dying in a nursing home, and a crush on an attractive woman (who, as she tells him straight to his face, is out of his league).

On the day our hero is fired, his landlord comes to collect his eight hundred dollars in rent, but the man has only three hundred dollars in the bank. The landlord tells his tenant he couldn't care less and advises he use the three hundred dollars to rent a truck to move his things elsewhere—by morning. When the man goes to the bank to cash out his savings, the computers are down, so the teller asks him how much he has in his account. Our hero pauses. Something completely out of the ordinary clicks in his brain. He says eight hundred dollars, and thus the first lie ever in this cold, cruel world is told. As he stands at the teller's window, however, the computer system comes back up, and the records show only three hundred dollars in his account. Amusingly, the teller apologizes profusely for the system's error and hands him eight hundred dollars. He takes the money and pays the landlord.

He is beside himself. He goes to the local bar and begins to tell his friends absurd things, saying, for example, that he is an Eskimo, has a prosthetic arm, and invented the bicycle. They instantly believe everything he says, no matter how ludicrous, because no one until now has ever told a lie.

The main character then takes his new technique further. To get his job back, he writes an imaginative and interesting TV script to present to his ex-boss, and because everything written up to this point has been strictly factual and pretty boring, he is begged to return. His script is then turned into the greatest movie ever made, and he becomes rich. Then, while on a date with the attractive girl, whom he is involved with now because he is in a better league, he is told that his mother is dying, so he rushes off to the hospital. When he arrives, a doctor is informing his mother that she is about to die, and that when she does, it will be "lights out" and nothing more.

Our hero, moved by his mother's fear, holds her hand and begins to tell her a story about this wonderful place she will go to after she dies, where she will be reunited with her beloved late husband, reside in a beautiful mansion, always be happy, and live forever. As he tells her this comforting tale, doctors and nurses and aides fill the room to listen, and when he finishes and she dies peacefully, all want to hear more about this incredible new information that has reached the world through him.

Later, at home, as he is grieving over his loss, people begin showing up outside the apartment building where he lives, wanting to hear more about what he had told his mom. His new girlfriend encourages him to tell them all more, and so he sits down that night and works up ten things to tell the people of the world about their future.

The following morning, he addresses the crowd gathered outside the building, telling them that their world is controlled by a "big man in the sky," who wants them to be nice to one another. Among other such stories, he also tells them that everyone can make three big mistakes and still go to the nice place with the mansions. But then people start to ask questions such as, "Does the big man cause earthquakes?"

and "Did he give my mother cancer?" When he says yes, they start to get mad at the big man until someone says, "Did he cure my father's heart problem?" and another asks, "Did he save me from that almost fatal car accident?" And when he replies "Yes," again, they murmur, "Oh, he's a good big man too." Finally, to appease the anxious and confused crowd, our hero says, "Yes, it's true that he does all these bad and good things, but he'll make up for it all later in the land of mansions." Everyone accepts that as good enough and goes away.

What makes this movie worth noting, beyond its entertainment value, is its parallel to this world. And watching it with a curious mind raises interesting questions: What if, like the characters in the movie, we have bought into stories told to us by people possessing nothing other than a self-proclaimed access to the truth? Or by people who claim to be communicating for the "big man in the sky," whom they tell us we should both fear and love (as though that makes sense), while giving him credit for all of the mysterious ills of the world? And what if, as a result, we've been convinced by these doomsayers and the guard within that our tiny errors are actually sins? And then what if, instead of challenging such pitiful notions, we just painted them over with the darkness of fear and, by hiding them under those covers, made them seem permanent? And what if we have done all of this when we could have just as easily exposed these sad notions to reason, questioned their significance, and learned to dismiss them as groundless? Is it thus that we have found ourselves in this world of conflict, struggling with the chaos without and our guilty memories within, unstable, lonely, and flinching at shadows?

The way out of the dismal condition of leading lives designed to cover up the fear we experience is to perceive that we are living in a world of imagination, an invention of our minds founded on misdirected desires and minutely important needs, and then to accept that we have the wherewithal to set ourselves free. The moment we realize that we are the ones supplying the meaning to the world we are traveling through, the bitter complaints that have sapped our confidence begin to lose the hold that we have given them on our minds. It is looking within that will teach us that what we see is all make-believe, with our dual demand to be without problems and treated specially the real cause of our misery.

Here is how the respected Sri Nisargadatta put it,

> Your outer life is unimportant. You can become a night watchman and live happily. It is what you are inwardly that matters. Your inner peace and joy you have to earn. It is much more difficult than earning money. No university can teach you to be yourself. The only way to learn is by practice. Right away begin to be yourself. Discard all that you are not and go ever deeper. Just as a man digging a well discards what is not water until he reaches the water-bearing strata, so must you discard what is not your own, till nothing is left which you can disown....
>
> Without [this discarding, you'll be] consumed by desires and fears, repeating themselves meaninglessly in endless suffering. Most people do not know there can be an end to pain. But once they have heard the good news, obviously going beyond all strife and struggle is the most urgent task that can be. You know that you can be free and now it is up to you.[120]

The Stories We Tell Ourselves

In this impossible-to-understand and far-*less*-than-best of all possible worlds, where we have not yet discarded all we are not, and wherein we are often subject to either the unpredictable whims of others or an uncaring fate, it does seem reasonable at times to condone feeling upset and to give in to anger. Yet what is anger other than the projection of our guilt and the protection of our decision for separation and fear? Therefore, unless we want to remain in the disagreeable condition of being the agreeable host to such unpleasantness, we must first, as mentioned, learn to accept each upset as the result of a wrong-minded choice, recognizing that what we previously chose for, we can now choose against or discard. From here, we can begin to perceive the world, which once seemed to have the power to provoke or excite us, as no more than a story about reality that we've been telling ourselves. This new perception leaves us free to lay down our defenses against a disturber of peace that was never truly there to begin with.

Let's take a look at how others explain our subjective perceptions, or stories, of reality.

> *ACIM*: This is … perception's fundamental law: you see what you believe is there and you believe it there because you want it there…. Seeing adapts to wish, for sight is always secondary to desire.[121]

> William James: What we say about reality depends on the perspective into which we throw it. The *that* of it is its own; but the *what* depends on the *which*; and the which depends on *us*….
>
> By our inclusions and omissions we trace the field's extent; by our emphasis we mark its foreground and its background; by our order we read it in this direction or that. We receive in short the block of marble, but we carve the statue ourselves….
>
> As a matter of fact we can hardly take in an impression … in the absence of a preconception….
>
> [Therefore] when we talk of reality "independent" of human thinking … it seems a thing very hard to find…. We may glimpse it, but … what we grasp is always some substitute for it which previous human thinking has peptonized and cooked for our consumption.[122]

> Emerson: The world is his who can see through its pretensions. What deafness, what stone blind custom,

what overgrown error you behold is there only by your sufferance. See it to be a lie and you have already dealt it its mortal blow.[123]

Schiller: "An individual claims his belief to be true. But what does he mean by true? And how does he establish the claim?" … To be true, it appears, means, *for that individual*, to work satisfactorily for him; and the working and the satisfaction, since they vary from case to case, admit of no universal description.[124]

Thackeray: Ah sir, — a distinct universe walks about under your hat and under mine—all things in nature are different to each—the woman we look at has not the same features, the dish we eat from has not the same taste to the one and the other—you and I are but a pair of infinite isolations, with some fellow islands a little more or less near to us.

What are they all saying in different ways except that each of us is making life to be as we want it? That is, we, the makers of our personal worlds, give our daily affairs the meaning that they hold for us. The problem with this phenomenon comes when rationalization serves as a buffer and as the justifier of our reactions, and thus makes perception the fulfillment of misguided aims.

This tendency not to be open-eyed about what we perceive is clearly never more true than in war. For example, I once heard the evening news report that eighty-six civilians were killed in a missile attack in Afghanistan. That means eighty-six civilians were killed in the furtherance of a grand design, the response to which, later, was a regretful "oops." Yet how is that different in content from blowing up a bus filled with women and children to further some group's outlandish and self-justified aim? Or from obliterating an entire section of a city because some who live there have acted badly? I'm not taking sides here. I understand that *all* these varying groups have convinced themselves they're doing the right thing. The problem is that in their certainty, in the unquestioned righteousness behind their ferocious acts, they never pause long enough to ask themselves whether their interpretations of reality could be wrong.

How often has this happened to the rest of us? How often, due to our mass confusion—and clearly we are in a state of mass confusion about our values—have we become unaware pawns of the guard within, advocates of the lies we tell ourselves without any real cognition of what we are up to? At the opposite of the extreme presented in the movie *The Invention of Lying*, in our world, companies lie, politicians lie, advertising lies, parents and children lie, and we lie to one another and to ourselves. Just about everyone twists the facts and shaves corners and rearranges memories to carve out a version of reality that suits him or herself. On Wall Street, before financial reform was forced on them, while some companies were selling massive amounts of insurance for risks they had no wherewithal to cover, others were placing bets on things that did not even exist. It may be hard to comprehend the audacity of it, but in essence what they did was create a virtual reality. They made up a casino in the sky wherein they gambled heavily with ordinary people's money in hopes of making a killing, not primarily for their investors, but for themselves.

Here's another example. I once asked a well-known and kindly religious leader how he could reconcile the idea of a wholly loving god and his religion's belief in the terrible concept of hell. His reply, illuminating the power of rationalization, was, "Well, I don't have to believe there is anyone in there, do I?"

Being required, as a member in good-standing of his faith, to believe there is a hell, but disliking the idea of it, he came up with his own belief that it is there, but empty. This is the weird kind of "sense" we all seem to make about reality on a regular basis. We take a position and then adjust our thinking to support it, instead of examining the premise we began with to verify its validity. This often leaves us in the position of defending false notions—the stories we've created—without any real awareness we are doing so.

Close Enough

What is up to us in terms of freedom from the world of appearances is to learn to stand aside from the old sad song of the guard within about our cares and woes, and hear instead the message that we, not as bodies but as decision-making minds, *can* free ourselves—not later and somewhere else, but here and soon. As mentioned before, this requires first accepting the idea that how we feel about anyone or anything begins with an inner choice for right- or wrong-mindedness, with the outside "reality" being that we are responding to the reflection or the shadow of that choice. And nothing more or less. This is a difficult lesson to learn well enough to apply it to all people in all situations. It requires a balance righted after much practice, dismissing the worry that becoming so impersonal will lead us to a functional quietude in which emotion plays no part at all—as if that were bad. But it is not. A good example of how finding our balance can play out positively in the difficulties of an active life comes from the following story by emergency room doctor Paul Austin:

> The ER is changing me. When I started out I was emotionally engaged and eager to help. I was afraid I'd never know enough to be useful in an emergency. But I'm proud of the competence I've acquired, and grateful to the people who trained me. And I've come to think that compassion isn't an emotion. It's an action. A discipline.
>
> I'm still trying to decide how emotionally porous I should be…. Like the aperture of a camera that opens and closes, I'm learning to vary my emotional permeability. Sometimes, a hard glaze is needed to squeak a patient through a tight spot.
>
> Imagine a floppy three-month old who will die without intravenous medications and fluids. The most skillful nurses in the department have tried, and failed, to establish an IV. The "life-saving" intervention is to

hold the chubby little leg in your left hand, and with your right hand, force a needle the size of a sixpenny nail down through the skin and muscles and into the bone itself…. You feel a crunchy little "pop" as the needle breaks through the cortex, and into the bone…. It's brutal, but it works. I've had to do it, and I focused exclusively on the spike and the bone I was driving it down into. No emotion. No hesitation. But [later] when I talked to the mother, her face colored by fear, I needed to soften the edge I'd brought forward to help me resuscitate her child….

If my only response was clinical detachment, I'd lose connection with my family, coworkers and patients. If I remained fully open to the pain and risk around me, I'd be paralyzed. I dig into people's lives for brief but important slivers of time. Most shifts, I bring some order into the chaos…. I'm learning to call that close enough.[125]

And "close enough" it should be for the rest of us as well, as we do our best to "bring some order" into personal worlds so obviously fraught with confusion. In this respect, there is much to be learned—meaning, really, unlearned—beginning with the notion that we can somehow come to understand what no one, including the wise, has understood before. For example, can we comprehend the need to jam a large needle into the bone of a three-month old? I don't mean the medical necessity. I mean the *source* from which such a necessity springs. Can we really find a logical cause *behind* that need—not a scientific cause but an understandable reason—or for that of war, or cancer, or Alzheimer's, or famine, or any of the other traumatic events of our chaotic world?

The world is often a difficult place to cope with, and those who think otherwise are either presently sheltered or naive. For most of us, like Dr. Austin in the ER, one moment, the situation calls for discipline and even clinical detachment, while the next requires relaxing the rules and putting simple generosity foremost. No formula exists that tells us what to do in response to all our shifting circumstances, other than to be decent and kind. And that is why Dr. Austin's conclusion that it was enough to do his best to bring some order to the chaos is so important. It points out that this is all that is really possible in any given situation and, therefore, "close enough" for everyone trying to go beyond selfishness.

Dr. Austin's definition of compassion as "an action, a discipline" is equally important, otherwise compassion becomes just a form of pity, an emotional outreach to some people during some times, rather than a way of living that can return order to our minds and meaning to our lives. The dictionary's definition of compassion is "a sympathetic consciousness of other's distress."[126] My version includes respecting others' power to choose the way they regard distress.

Using these definitions, we must ask, how far we, who are lost in specialness and its belief in separate interests, are from having compassion for all who are caught in humanity's common plight? I remember a TV documentary a few years back that showed a tall, clean-cut, good-looking young Israeli border guard describing the Palestinians who regularly passed by his post as "animals." He was probably too young or, at the time, too dense to realize that this was exactly the way the Nazis used to think of people like his beloved grandparents. Yet the reality is that this problem is so pervasive, this is how we think whenever we assume ourselves fit to look down on another in such dark-minded and prejudicial nonsense, forgetting that our true purpose is to be respectful of equals and have compassion for all.

Undoing the "Dark Side"

Is there a "dark side" of the mind to be dealt with in almost everyone, even in most of the seeming saintly? You bet. This dark side, however, is but an apparition, active only because of our hidden desire that it be so. Yet, since we far too often respond to the dictates of the dark side as if it were authoritative and real, we must deal with it as such until we realize differently. Once we perceive our hidden desires and acknowledge this dark mindedness for the mirage it is, however, our grievances, feelings of hurt, judgments, superciliousness, and anger must be seen for the defenses they are, and thus recognized as unworthy of further support. In other words, adjustments to the thought systems of the dark side are not the answer to the dark side. Undoing it is.

As to the uprising of anger, how common is the ego's use of it to protect the pseudo-reality of guilt and the dark side? Very common indeed. And is that sign of irrationality any different even when anger is cold and lies dormant? Here is a short story that explains what I mean. Once, sitting in a bar in my old neighborhood, I was talking to a big, tough merchant marine. As we were speaking quietly in the crowded bar, another large-enough fellow we knew well began bumping into him. Guys who were half-drunk were always doing things like that; bored, I guess, with the fundamentally boring dark world of the bars, they'd strike a match, if you will, to get some action started. The third time the other fellow bumped into him, the guy I was talking to turned to him and, without raising his voice in the slightest, said, "If you bump into me one more time, I am going to get up off this stool and knock you out. Then I am going to take you by the heels and drag you outside. Then I am going to turn you over and I'm going to drag you back and forth on the pavement until the skin is off your face." And without blinking, he turned back to face me and continued our conversation as if we had never been interrupted.

That was a demonstration of cold anger in its preparation stage, as dangerous and ready to strike as a poisonous snake. And the guy doing the bumping, seeing it as such, turned around and left the bar. But does such angry self-defensiveness ever solve anything? A week after that episode, in another altercation, a friend who ended up as the best man at my wedding decked the merchant marine. Two weeks later, I watched the merchant marine's younger brother and another guy fight over nothing for close to twenty minutes. And on and on went the violent expressions of insulted pride and its contemptuous valuation of peace in my old neighborhood, as they do without cessation in our overly prideful world.

Proving what? No more than who was the biggest, toughest, or most skilled in victories without meaning—other than to show the uselessness of violence to those with eyes to see. These are the eyes that recognize that war, for the most part, is about as sensible as a bar fight, and see that politely spoken leaders, sitting in paneled conference rooms, plotting to tear apart towns and lives for their own or their country's benefit, are just as irrational in their own cold anger as was my friend, the merchant marine, in his.

The idea that we, whether that be as a nation or as individuals, must defend what we perceive as our interests at all costs is as wrong-minded as the idea that we must maintain our position as number one in the race to nowhere. "We have a math and science crisis," a number of noted people say. No, we don't. We have a "learning to be reasonable with everyone because we shun responsibility for how we think and perceive and feel" crisis—and increased adroitness in that crisis, and not in the worldwide contest to gain nothing of lasting value, is where our focus really belongs.

Out of the Trap

Now, while some of the ideas that follow have been discussed before, the fact that we all have erected strong defenses against their full acceptance calls for a further review. The concept that our problems with others begin and end in our minds is the key to unlocking our potential to go beyond our old, fixed beliefs of our unworthiness; it is what offers us a way out of the trap of mundane pursuits and belief in the mendacious proclamations that we have labored in for so long. For only when we reach the cornerstone of our wrong-minded thought system—the idea that separate interests can serve us well or, really, even at all—can we go beyond it, helping us see that all of our previous efforts to improve the system were merely like moving shadows of the problem from here to there.

Let me give you an example from my younger days about being responsible for oneself. In the seventh grade, I had a cruel teacher. Unable to control her class by other means, she tormented many children, and because I fought back, as the year went on, she made a particular target of me. In the eighth grade, I was greatly relieved to find a gentle and pleasant nun as my new teacher. Six weeks later, she became ill, and my nemesis took her place. This was a truly disturbed woman, and in my youthful ignorance, combined with a festering authority problem, I did not understand the situation as a whole—and so I did my best to stand up to her. Yet, she had the power and I did not, so although I won a few skirmishes, I lost every battle. I left the school hating that nun.

A number of years later, reflecting on my lingering grievances against her, I began to realize that my continuing resentment really wasn't about her; it was about me. I was just using her as a scapegoat for my own unwillingness to forgive and let go. Yes, she had bullied me, and yes, she had at times acted sadistically toward other students. But what did any of that have to do with my power to see her in the light of a more generous interpretation now? Was it not more likely that she had acted as she had because she was struggling internally than because she was an evil person? And was it not also possible, if not probable, that I had used her lapses into nastiness as excuses to be mean to her in return?

Now older and more aware of how easy it is to have a convenient memory, I wondered how many of the difficulties I'd had with her might well have been instigated by me. I was smart enough in school to be challenging, and also, at that age, rapidly turning into a smartass. Therefore, was I, perhaps, more often than not the inappropriate student, pretending to myself, then and later, that I was just an innocent victim of her unfounded wrath? And, again, in either case, what did any of it have to do with my ability to perceive those difficulties with greater understanding now?

As I was meditating on these ideas one day, a picture of her appeared in my mind. She had a dark cloud in the center of her body. I suddenly became aware that the darkness I was perceiving in her, however, didn't come from her at all, but was being projected onto her by me. Just as I had realized with my boxer friend, I didn't hate this person because of her mistakes; rather, I hated myself for my own ungenerous spirit and was just using her errors as a defense against that recognition—as a means to excuse myself. And in that insight, my unforgiveness of her began to disappear, and the fog of accusation was lifted from my mind.

This was not the first time I had pardoned someone for what they had *not* done to my mind. But because my hatred of this teacher had been so powerful, so excusatory, and so protected, this instance was the most significant. I had played this scenario out in a different way with my father, going through the same process and coming to the same conclusion. Yet, as intense as that was, for some reason, I had gotten to the bottom of it far earlier. In both cases, and in fact, in all other cases, people with power had symbolized my confusion about and resistance to authority, which included my childish notion that it was unfair that they had rights which I did not.

All this, and other similar realizations, helped me enormously in coming to the understanding that whenever I had a problem with another, it was, in fact, always *my* problem to keep, and keep it I would, until I decided I wanted it no longer. In every case, no matter the form of the difficulty with the other person, the moment I accepted that what I had to forgive in the other was a projection of what I had not yet forgiven in myself, my hold on the grievance and its hold on me quickly disappeared. This doesn't mean that my mind never again presented a memory of the problem, or that there was never again the pull of negative emotion about it, but only that I no longer believed that someone else was responsible for choosing what was going on within me.

In this context of learning to live more peacefully, you might say that our first responsibility is to always pay attention, be on guard, and be alert and vigilant against the seemingly persuasive arguments of wrong-mindedness, which insist that the distress we are experiencing in every difficult situation comes from the hostile (read: fearful) actions of someone else in our world. While it is true that we, at times, encounter fearful (read: hostile) people in our lives, it is *not* true that *their* words or actions sweep us away from right-mindedness and generate the upset we feel.

The reason it is so important to stay aware of the activity of our wrong minds is that whatever is within us will always be projected out, *unless we first look at what is within and own it.* When someone says or does something we don't like and we get upset about it, accepting authorship for how we think and feel about it is what will save us from believing that the problem is "out there." If we do not accept authorship, we'll attempt to—either sweetly because we're "good," or nastily because "he asked for it"—deal with the difficulty we have with another as if it were real and not merely our interpretation. This is not to deny whatever the other person improperly said or did. But it is to say that only once we recognize our feelings as coming from a decision within us, and not from the event outside, can we ask ourselves whether there might be a more intelligent way of looking at the other, such as thinking, "If he knew what he was doing, he would never act or speak that way."

Seeing things from this different perspective helped me begin to depersonalize, in a positive sense, my relationships with my relatives and others, whether those relationships were blameful or comforting. All of our interactions, seen rightly, are actually this impersonal. If my mother, to use a close relationship as an example, was upset with me on a given day, no matter what I had done or not done, her acting up had *nothing* to do with me, and *everything* to do with her. After all, if the neighbor's son had been her son instead, and in my shoes at that moment she chose for wrong-mindedness, she would have done *exactly* the same thing with him that she did with me. In the same vein, if on a given day, she was only loving and encouraging, her actions would equally have had *nothing* to do with me or my behavior, and *only* to do with her and her choice for right-mindedness. And, again, the neighbor's child standing in my shoes would have done just as nicely.

To summarize, it is *never* about the other person when we are upset or reasonable, but only about the often unrecognized decision we make to be in one frame of mind or another. And while we may fall again and again into the trap of believing that we feel as we do because of a person or event external to us, the truth is that the feelings we experience are a result of our choice, coming to us not really *because,* but *regardless.*

CHAPTER 9

Questioning Thought and Belief

T HE NEXT TIME MY SON called, it was from the same sober-living facility where he was still awaiting entry into the Salvation Army's drug-treatment program. In our conversation, he informed me that shortly before his release from prison, he had traded his personal effects for four Vicodin tablets, which he had then used to get high. He said that he now realized it hadn't been Hawaii that he'd been looking forward to upon his release, but getting his hands on drugs. And while he also said that he believed this had been "foolish," I didn't hear him say, "and I'll never do it again." He was due to receive more money from the food stamp program in a few days. Would that lead to yet another party?

If I looked at my son's current dilemma in the grander sense of his life's pattern to that point, could I say I knew enough to draw a conclusion about what he was learning through this obviously difficult process? How could I know what would lead him to say, at last, "This has been foolish in the extreme, and I'll never do it again"?

It seems doubtful, within the confused-in-values system in which we've been educated and in which we participate daily, that really knowing what others should do or how they should arrive at their goals is possible. Therefore, perhaps the only thing in relationships that we should consider to know for certain is that, even when we are being necessarily firm, we are less likely to be of harm if we maintain one thought in the forefront of our minds, and that is simply to be kind.

The Musings of Fear

Another apparent case in which the admission of ignorance is the beginning of wisdom lies in realizing what we've done not just to others, but to ourselves. Think of the deceptions that we have, over the years, agreed to be subject to. First, there were those foisted on us by our parents who, depending on their needs, outlooks, and moods, either "nurtured" us with the dangerous notion that we were special, fed us the poison that insisted we were worthless, or, perhaps, to make it even less understandable, asked us to believe that sometimes we were one and sometimes the other. Then there were the similar packages of nonsense purveyed by the uncertain, who, through striving, raised themselves to positions of religious leadership, many using dogma to condemn us because they knew no better. To top it off, we often swallowed whole the opinions of our siblings, friends, enemies, lovers, spouses, children, and teachers, who also knew nothing and were, therefore, generally speaking, wrong.

How terrible—and, to the vulnerable, terrifying—can the wrong-minded opinions and actions of some of the more fearful and dogmatic among us be? Let's spend a moment with a few of the more unexamined and overlooked splenetic outpourings of viciousness by some of the "knowing" ones of the past, and not with the aim of looking down in criticism upon our equals, but of recognizing, as we ponder these examples from our collective heritage, what we might be unconsciously conditioned by.

From the Koran: Among the Jews are those who ... [are] wounding the faith by their reviling....

God hath cursed them for their unbelief.... O ye ...
we efface your features and twist your head around back-
ward.... The flame of hell is [your] suffering punishment.[127]

From Deuteronomy in the Old Testament: If your
brother, the son of your mother, or your son, or your
daughter, or the wife of your bosom, or your friend
who is as your soul, entices you ... saying, "Let us go
and serve other gods" ... you shall stone him to death
with stones.[128]

From *Under the Banner of Heaven* by Jon Krakauer:
Shortly after the resurrection of Christ, according to
The Book of Mormon, Jesus visited North America to
share his new gospel with the Nephites [the good ones]
and the Lamanites [the bad ones] who were engaged in
a war that eventually destroyed both sides.

The leader of the Nephites during their final battles had been a figure of uncommon wisdom named
Mormon [whose son Moroni] ... would return fourteen
centuries later to deliver the [sacred text written on]
golden plates to be shared ... and thereby effect the
salvation of the world.

Suitably awed that God had chosen Joseph [Smith]
to receive the gold plates, converts had no trouble
believing his assertion that his new religion was "the
only true and living church on the face of the earth"
[divulging the] blunder of the "Great apostasy" [which
showed] that virtually all Christian doctrine ... was
a whopping lie. [According to] *The Book of Mormon*
"There are two churches only; the one is [theirs] the
church of the Lamb of God, and the other ... the
Mother of abominations."[129]

From *Letter to a Christian Nation* by Sam Harris: It was even possible for the most venerated patriarchs of the Church, like St. Augustine and St. Thomas Aquinas, to conclude that heretics should be tortured (Augustine) or killed (Aquinas). [Likewise] Martin Luther and John Calvin advocated the wholesale murder of heretics, apostates, Jews, and witches.[130]

And, finally, we have the grand prize winner in this portion of the Contest of the Absurd, this greatly abridged anecdotal evidence of a frantic common impairment, from James Joyce's semiautobiographical *A Portrait of the Artist as a Young Man*:

The preacher's voice sank. He paused … then he resumed:

Now let us try for a moment to realize, as far as we can, the nature of that abode of the damned which the justice of an offended God has called into existence for the eternal punishment of sinners. Hell is a strait and dark and foulsmelling prison…. In earthly prisons the poor captive has at least some liberty of movement…. Not so in hell. There, by reason of the great number of the damned, the prisoners are heaped together in their awful prison, the walls of which are said to be four thousand miles thick….

They lie in exterior darkness…. It is a never-ending storm of darkness … the horror of [which] is increased by its awful stench….

But this stench is not … the greatest physical torment to which the damned are subjected…. The sulphurous brimstone which burns in hell is a substance which is specially designed to burn forever and forever with unspeakable fury … with incredible intensity it rages forever….

Yet [this] is nothing ... when compared in its intensity ... [to the] fire which proceeds from the ire of God, ... cruel tongues of flame, ... the immortal soul tortured eternally ... by the offended majesty of the omnipotent God.[131]

Whether Joyce was taught this in school or church or invented it is not the point. The point is that someone, maybe even Joyce himself, was able to imagine it—as others have obviously done as well. For example, ask yourself what kind of thinking could have led to not only the invention of the following practices, but also the acceptance that these practices would be desired by, let alone acceptable, to someone's version of "the Lord."

It was not until the eleventh century that a monastic reformer, the Italian Benedictine Peter Damian, established voluntary self-flagellation as a central ascetic practice acceptable to the church....

"The body has to be shaped like a piece of wood," explained one of the many texts that followed in Damian's wake, "with beating and whippings, with canes, scourges, and discipline. The body has to be tortured and starved so that it submits to the spirit and takes perfect shape."[132]

Further, here is a description of the Dominican nuns of Colmar, penned at the turn of the fourteenth century by a sister named Catherine von Gebersweiler, who had lived in the convent since childhood:

At Advent and during the whole of Lent, the sisters would make their way after matins into the main hall or some other place devoted to their purpose. There they abused their bodies in the most acute fashion with all manner of scourging instruments until their blood flowed, so that the sound of the blows of the whip rang through the entire convent and rose more sweetly than any other melody to the ears of the Lord.[133]

Striking the Match

Returning now to our examination of what it actually means to learn, let's consider the following idea, widely attributed to Yeats: "Education is not the filling of a pail, but the lighting of a fire." To educate in a proper sense is, as Socrates taught, to "educe," which means "to bring out something latent."[134] For most of us, not having the benefit of someone like Yeats as a mentor, much of our education has been little more than the filling of a pail by those who were also filled like pails. Unfortunately, this education often included force-feeding the very young with ideological pap, laced with stern admonishments against questioning what they were assured was certainly not just the assertions of a few and the ruminations of the herd. The unfortunate result of this strict training was numerous people so terrified into an inflexible fixation on faulty beliefs that, to this day, they remain unamenable to healthy doubt and impervious to reason, determining that in believing what they were taught lies their salvation and safety.

Once so conditioned, is it not likely that if I deeply desired that my group (whether that be a religion or a country or something else) be more important than another's, I would then be highly prone to delude myself into believing that my wishes had come true? Would it not also be probable that, once having placed my faith in what I wanted to be true, I would permit into my awareness only evidence that supported my position and, consequently, end up perceiving my world according to my own hidden dictates? Depending on my fear and my stubbornness, from this point forward, whatever I was inclined to believe, I would likely believe, and whatever I was not desirous of believing, I might not perceive at all. As a boy living in a polyglot neighborhood, for example, I had concluded at one time, without evidence, that those who spoke

English were more intelligent than those who did not—an out-picture of a wish for specialness made up by my unnoticed wrong mind.

Listen to how Pulitzer Prize winner Daniel Kahneman describes the phenomenon:

> The trader-philosopher-statistician Nassim Taleb could also be considered a psychologist. In *The Black Swan*, Taleb introduced the notion of *narrative fallacy* to describe how flawed stories of the past shape our views of the world and our expectations for the future. Narrative fallacies arise inevitably from our continuous attempt to make sense of the world. The explanatory stories that people find compelling are simple, are concrete rather than abstract, … and focus on a few striking events that happened rather than on countless events that failed to happen…. Taleb suggests that we constantly fool ourselves by constructing flimsy accounts of the past and believing they are true….
>
> Our comforting conviction that the world makes sense rests on a secure foundation: our almost unlimited ability to ignore our ignorance.[135]

When people resign themselves to bowing to authority without question, they lose sight of their ability to regard the questionable with that helpful attitude of "Wait a minute, says who?" At that point, groups large and small seem bound in a shared mental servility, without the wherewithal to decide for themselves, and thus easily swayed in one direction or another by religious propaganda or political threat. Here is the case made for the latter by one of Hitler's henchman, Herman Goering, at the Nuremberg Trials:

> Naturally, the common people don't want war, but after all, it is the leaders of the country who determine the policy, and it is always a simple matter to drag the people along, whether it is a democracy, or a fascist dictatorship,

or a parliament, or a communist dictatorship. Voice or no voice the people can always be brought to the bidding of the leaders. This is easy. All you have to do is tell them they are being attacked, and denounce the pacifists for lack of patriotism and exposing the country to danger. It works the same in every country.[136]

As we reflect on this, a good question would be, "If education is the lighting of a fire, then regardless of who hands us the matches, who but we are in charge of striking them?" After all, if we find ourselves lulled into stupidity by the gobbledygook of prior ages, who has agreed to that but us? The foolishness of another's thoughts is nothing to us without our acceptance and consent.

A good example of how that can carry down was the attitude of my parents and teachers to the Protestant church across the street from where I grew up, the grounds of which church we Catholic kids were admonished never to enter. What were they afraid of? That we would find it more attractive than our own church down the street? And did any of them understand how this teaching was fostering our belief in the significance of the separation between "us" and "them"? Of course not.

A pertinent example of what I mean by being taken in—and often willingly when it suits us—comes in the following quote by Aristotle:

> One who is a human being belonging by nature not to himself but another is by nature a slave ... an article of property [or] an instrument. A slave is a living tool, just as a tool is an inanimate slave.... Bodily service for the necessities of life [for us] is forthcoming, from slaves and domestic animals alike.[137]

Now if Aristotle could have been so easily deceived by what is, as expressed, little more than a belief in an inherited right to be catered to, surely the rest of us are in some danger of being fooled by hidden wishes to think ourselves more important than others. When we look with honesty at our own heightened tendencies toward selfishness, it becomes apparent that many of us are, at least at times, the delusional minions of an inner choice for specialness: something untrue made true for us by our wanting it. In one sense, it is almost as if we were stumbling about in the darkness of a spell woven from shadowy threads of self-aggrandizement, our selfishness itself proof we are the now unwitting captives of a narcissistic narcosis we have induced in ourselves.

The problem with escaping from such a deviously conceived state of enchantment, which we cast on ourselves, is that it would be one in which our faculties could do little to inform us about, and as such, we could not identify the true nature of our problem. In a condition such as this, even our power to reach to reason would be infected by our self-hypnosis, placing us in a position of great difficulty in accepting that only our self-centeredness and its unkindness are the causes of our distress.

Now, let's close the chapter by taking a brief look at what some who have tried to hand us matches have said about returning to sense in how we perceive and react to the world.

> From *The Journey Home* by Kenneth Wapnick: The idea that the choice of what we are going to perceive in the world is ours contains the only hope for peace. As long as we continue to perceive enemies, whether in China, Central America, Iraq, or anywhere else, or perceive fear in any form, there is no hope of ending conflict among nations. Peace can come only when individual people change how they perceive this world and accept responsibility for what they perceive....
>
> The undoing of the world of fear cannot be accomplished simply through the dismantling of nuclear weapons, because all that would happen is that other weapons would rise to take their place. That could be a helpful place to begin certainly, but the real shift,

once again, is not made in the world. The only hope of undoing fear in the world lies in the *minds* of people who make up this world of fear—this is the only place in which a meaningful shift can occur....[138]

From an address by Ralph Waldo Emerson to the Harvard Divinity School: Truly speaking, it is not instruction, but provocation, that I can receive from another soul. What he announces, I must find true ... or wholly reject, and on his word ... I can accept nothing. On the contrary, the absence of this primary faith [in oneself] is the presence of degradation.... The doctrine of the divine nature being forgotten, a sickness infects and dwarfs the constitution.... [T]he base doctrine of the majority ... usurps the place of the doctrine of the soul.... The high ends of being fade out of sight, and man becomes nearsighted, and can only attend to what addresses the senses....

That popular fable of the sot who was picked up dead drunk in the street, carried to the duke's house, washed and dressed and laid in the duke's bed, and, on his waking, treated with all the obsequious ceremony like the duke, and assured that he had been insane, owes its popularity to the fact that it symbolizes so well the state of man, who is in the world a sort of sot, but now and then wakes up, exercises his reason, and finds himself a true prince.[139]

From *Thus Spoke Zarathustra* by Friedrich Nietzsche: Physician, heal thyself: thus will you heal your patient too. May this be ... [the patient's] best remedy, that he might see with his own eyes one who makes himself whole.[140]

From *The First and Last Freedom* by J. Krishnamurti: To understand anything ... what is essential? A quiet mind, is it not? ... So long as the mind is in conflict, blaming, resisting, condemning, there can be no understanding....

When the mind is still, tranquil, not seeking, ... neither resisting nor avoiding—it is only then there can be regeneration, because then the mind is capable of receiving what is true; and it is truth that liberates, not your effort to be free....[141]

From *The Myth of Sisyphus* by Albert Camus: Knowing whether or not one can live *without appeal* is all that interests me.... Everything begins with lucid indifference.[142]

From Kenneth Wapnick's *From Futility to Happiness*: We [want to learn to] make every relationship, situation, and world event the same in terms of our response: a quiet calm.... If we truly desire peace, we will see everything that happens—regardless of how the world judges it—as a means of helping us achieve our goal. We will have learned that neither salvation nor distress comes from outside—only from the mind's decision....

Only the mind's decision for separation is the cause of suffering.... Thus if we do not undo ... the belief in separate interests, nothing will ever change; or if it does, some other problem will inevitably rise to take its place. Since we are seeking in the wrong place for the answer, no matter how well-meaning our solution, it will be wrong.[143]

CHAPTER 10

Compassion for All

O VER A PERIOD OF SEVERAL months, my son's disturbed life continued to unravel. First, he was arrested for attempting to shoplift two sweaters from a department store. He then went to jail for a few months, after which he was sentenced to three years' probation, with the proviso that he complete a state-run, state-funded live-in drug-treatment program. Hating jail and frightened of a three-year prison sentence, he gladly entered the program.

Vowing to succeed this time, he did well at first. He lost thirty pounds, did everything that was asked of him, struggled somewhat with the therapy while still speaking positively of it, and seemed to be settling down. Then he began dating a woman in the program and, soon after, ran off with her and went back to drugs. He came out of that episode and entered detox, but had to go before a judge for violating probation. The judge gave him a break and let him re-enter the program. He called to tell me how relieved he was to be back in it; yet, a week later he took off again on another flight into fantasy. Eight days after that, he was re-arrested and was now back in jail awaiting the court's decision on what to do with him next. His life in its current state was reminiscent of this little poem:

> I want to go on the wagon. Really
> I want to, but I like it,
> I like it, and I can't, really,
> I mean I can, but
> I won't.[144]

Why "won't" people like my son, who love drugs or alcohol so dearly that they would do anything for them, open their eyes to the evident danger to their lives and "go on the wagon"? Obviously, they are attracted to self-punishment, but what else is it about crack, for instance, that draws its feverish fans like moths to a flame? Here is what David Carr, who traveled from addict to regular columnist for the *New York Times,* had to say about it:

> [Smoked] coke calls its own frantic tune, with all the amps turned up to eleven. [It] releases dopamine, the lingua franca of the pleasure impulse. In a neat trick, it attaches to the dopamine transporter, and so the dopamine hangs around instead of reabsorbing, creating a lingering sensation of extreme euphoria. Dopamine rides between the nerve endings for ten to fifteen minutes, cycling the user through a range of pleasurable feelings.
>
> It is, for want of a better metaphor, akin to scoring the winning touchdown in the final game of a championship season, and then reliving that moment of crossing the goal line over and over until the rush ebbs. And rather than the gradual ride up from powdered cocaine, crack makes it happen immediately and profoundly.... You feel like the lord of all you survey....
>
> Many normal people get a sense of its lurid ambush and walk away. Others take another hit....

> With nerve endings and dopamine levels in a natural state, inhaled cocaine vapor is the mallet that hits the spot and sends the ringer straight to the bell. Every time thereafter, it goes up a little less quickly, rises not so much. But it still feels better than not.
>
> [Yet] higher doses lead to diminishing returns.... What seemed like a way to leave the gravitational pull of this ball of earth becomes a shovel repetitively deployed to dig a hole the user cannot crawl out of....
>
> The synapses ... making a fuss—a head full of baby birds with their beaks open, crying out for more....[145]

The inconsistencies and dissociation in thought that remove our awareness of the ending from the beginning in such scenarios border on the ridiculous. For example, my son is making good progress in a well-formulated recovery program, when an opportunity for a party presents itself. Not unintelligent, at some level he recognizes it as an invitation to another life-wreck. Despite this, he elects to drive head-on into the impenetrable wall. This makes no sense. Especially when the price of a few days of such gratification is the possibility of a three-year prison sentence for this not-very-cheap thrill.

True Mercy

As I look upon my son and anyone else making mistakes, whether those mistakes seem large or small, I try to keep in mind the edict of the sane: innocent of all charges! If I want compassion to be seen as fully deserved by me, then, like Betsy ten Boom, I must recognize it as deserved by everyone. After all, *all good things are shared.* There is no exception, no exclusion, and no compromise. Either the evil actions we see are the result of ignorance or mental illness and are justifiably pardonable, or they are not pardonable at all. Either all of us are the same in truth and deserving of a plenary indulgence and general amnesty for all of our misthoughts and misdeeds, or none of us are.

True mercy, uncontaminated and incapable of judgment, should not be confused with what the world calls mercy, with its harsh conceptions of balancing the scales of justice. For instance, can it be merciful and "just" to punish the ignorant or mentally ill—and I mean to *punish* them, not to keep them segregated so they don't do further harm—closing our ears to their pleas for clemency, while trying to hurt them because they listened to their wrong-mindedness and acted maliciously? If we embrace this vengeful version of justice, which is not too different from the version used to justify the "honor killing" and stoning of "wayward" daughters, then how can we escape the belief that such vicious standards not also be applied to us? We can't, at least until we change our minds about what others deserve. So what do we do with that fearful thought of punishment due? We convert it into the notion that some will be saved while others will not, and then hide from our awareness the fear that we'll be among the ones who won't.

Fulfilling Our Wish for Specialness

ACIM says that the real challenge of acting fairly toward all is our vaunted self-importance, which tries to make us believe we are special, while separating and secretly frightening us in the process. In one passage, it explains,

> No belief is neutral. Everyone has the power to dictate each decision you make. For a decision is a conclusion based on everything that you believe. It is the outcome of belief....
> All that is ever cherished as a hidden belief, to be defended though unrecognized, is faith in specialness.... Only the special ... have enemies, for they are different and not the same. And difference of any kind imposes ... a need to judge that cannot be escaped....
> For specialness not only sets apart, but serves as grounds

from which attack on those who seem "beneath" the special one is "natural" and "just"....

The fear of ... your brother comes from each unrecognized belief in specialness. For you demand your brother bow to it against his will.... Every twinge of malice, or stab of hate, or wish to separate arises here....

You love your brother not while it is this you would defend against him. This is what he attacks, and you protect. Here is the ground of battle which you wage against him. Here must he be your enemy and not your friend. Never can there be peace among the different. [146]

Is love of specialness a problem for most of us? Here is what another troubled apple, actor and singer Rick Springfield, thought about it:

Honestly, I think that we're all—every one of us—constantly and hungrily searching for signs that we are singular, unique, chosen, and that an equally singular, unique, choice future awaits us. Actors are the neediest bastards in this way; don't ever let us pretend otherwise. Maybe we artist-performers need this kind of affirmation more than most, hence our career choice. I know that a strong defining element of my character is the five-year-old inside me jumping up and down, demanding, "Hey, ... look at me!!!" This need to be noticed and thought of as "special" has, to a large degree, charted my unholy course through adulthood. Dammit.[147]

Don't most people, that is, until they learn the cost, want to be special? Rick Springfield, like so many other rock stars, sports celebrities, and actors, had all kinds of trouble with sex and drugs. Sugar Ray Leonard, who also struggled, noted the early beginnings of his journey into painful consequences when he wrote,

When I was fifteen, I was asked by a local reporter who I wanted to be when I grew up. I did not hesitate. "I want to be special," I said.[148]

The problem with this is that, when I buy into the idea that I'm special, it makes me seem different; seeming different implies that I'm separated; being separated means that I'm alone; being alone makes me feel frightened; and being frightened gives rise to accusation and defensiveness. Thus, defensiveness and accusation are the hallmarks of the seemingly special, who are really the self-alienated and afraid. So where is my core problem in difficult relationships? In the other's unkind acts or dismissive behavior? Or in my need to feed and protect my specialness and its so easily wounded pride?

According to William Blake, "As the air to a bird, or the sea to a fish, so is contempt to the contemptible."[149] The disrespectful, being uncharitable, support their convictions of specialness by wielding self-crafted swords of comparison in their make-believe worlds. They are without the understanding that perceives the panhandler as equal in worth to the president or the pope or the prime minister. And so they render ineffective the right-mindedness that calls them to return to equality and peace. In contrast, those who respect themselves are respectful toward all, rejecting the notion that because they possess some quality not commonly held, this somehow makes them superior.

To examine how egalitarianism versus specialness plays out on the global stage, we should wonder why, if it is somehow weirdly permissible for some nations to possess nuclear weapons, is it impermissible for others? Is it because we who possess them are more enlightened and trustworthy than others? Yet, if we who possess them were truly enlightened, would we have them at all? This leads to the question of whether it is possible to sit down and have a nonpaternalistic and rewarding dialogue with equals if the conversation begins with the premise that *you people* are less trustworthy than *we*. Without being foolish about militaristic and so-called rogue nations, would it not be more honest to state that, to date, none of us have been proven all that trustworthy?

In one sense we could liken the way some stronger countries talk down to weaker ones, whose interests they see as interfering with their own, to a larger twenty-five-year-old bully saying to a smaller sixteen-year-old something like, "Boy, I have a stick, and if you refuse to offer me the respect I demand, or don't follow my instructions, I am going to beat you with it. And just so we're clear about who's in charge here, I also, on threat of serious punishment, forbid you to acquire a stick of your own." Just imagine how that sixteen-year-old would feel and what he probably would think. Would it be likely that the younger one would find reason for trust and respect when his older counterpart was offering him none? What are the odds that he would believe in the existence of equality and fairness when the stronger one either kept picking his pocket or slapping his hands?

As we've discovered, in our ambitious and divided humanity, shrouded in the misaligned persuasion that "my self, nation, religion, or group is more important than yours," there is neither true compassion nor hope of peace, but only the occasional truce and selective spates of largesse. In such confused group mindsets, those who are considered worthy and those who are not depends strictly on where one's identification lies. "I'm a Catholic, Protestant, Muslim, Jew, Hindu, or Buddhist," for example, or, "I'm American, French, Chinese, or Iranian," added to "I just *know* that my side is right, which means, since you are different, your side is wrong."

The rarely considered question in all this is "*Why* am I Catholic, Protestant, Jewish, Muslim, American, French, Iranian," or whatever? For most, the answer is because that is the religion or nationality into which they were born. For how many are thoughtfully convinced members of their particular group and not just accepting, conditioned ones? Fewer, I suspect, than we might ordinarily think.

Yet if *compassion* is, as Webster's defines it, "A sympathetic consciousness of another's distress, together with a desire to alleviate it," and if it must be unrestricted—meaning without excluding anyone—in order to bring us back to an awareness of our safe inclusion in the whole, then it's reasonable to say that anyone who doesn't believe in compassion for all, and the tolerance that goes along with it, has a lot of learning yet to do.

The Carelessness of the Unaware

This idea of full inclusion easily slips away when we allow ourselves to drift into judgment of *anyone*. In this vein, and keeping in full awareness the bewildered condition of so many lost apples, let's consider again, without condemnation, what can happen to some people when they are caught up in the rush of war. The following is from noncombatant Pulitzer Prize-winning author Steve Fainaru's *Big Boy Rules*. The book is a compilation of real-life accounts about the independent contractors, or mercenaries, in Iraq—young men who had once served as soldiers or Marines and returned to war for the money. The title refers to the lack of rules that these mercenaries were subject to, being granted almost unlimited power in Iraq.

> Josh Munns was serious business; in 2004 he had fought his way into Fallujah with a Marine sniper platoon. A year later, he found himself installing swimming pools in Redding, California, bored out of his mind. "I needed something to shock my system to remind myself I'm still alive," he explained. That was one of the reasons he came back to Iraq.
>
> The mercs had a saying, which I [Steve Fainaru] heard, in some variation, all over Iraq: "Come for the money, stay for the life."
>
> For many Americans, it was their first taste of combat, and what stayed with them—more than the figures falling in the dark, the tracers that passed before them like red comets, and the jackhammer sounds of their

weapons—was the floating intoxication, the seconds of pure joy that seemed to lift them from their bodies and the places they had come from....

In college, [John] Cote had always felt old. Not even his relationships with his fraternity brothers had come close to the bonds he had forged in the military. It was America's post-millennial war that had infused his life with meaning and given him the adrenaline rush he craved. Cote had come back to Iraq to chase that feeling....

"[I] had driven straight into the ambush...." [Cote said, "There were] streams of red glaring rounds passing in front of us. All I could think was that there was no way around it.... So I held my breath, dropped the Humvee in first gear, floored it, and then pushed it into second. I drove straight through the cross-fire yelling *fuck yeaaaaah* with the guys in the back yelling *fuck youuuuu*. This is by far the coolest thing I have ever experienced in my life," he concluded, "and these are the kinds of [cool] things that are going on in Iraq."

And then there is the callousness toward others that grows around one like a shell, denying the urgings of equal rights and common decency:

One day Horner was driving north of Baghdad when the convoy approached Al Afem, a small town where [his group, the independent contractor called] Crescent had been hit by a roadside bomb. Horner said the Crescent team leader quickly devised a strategy: blast everything in sight. As the convoy roared through Al Afem, the operators aimed their automatic weapons out the windows and emptied magazine after magazine into the town, pausing only to reload....

Horner said that became Crescent's permanent posture toward Al Afem: "Shoot and don't ask questions." "We never stopped to see what damage was done: it was just blaze through the town. But the thing was, I never saw anybody actually shooting *at* us. Not one time."

And then, the psychological aftermath:

Correa … [found that] the shooting had forced him to confront not just his actions but his presence in Iraq, the reasons why he was there. It wasn't a pretty picture. He thought about his hollow life … and how he was using another country, another people, to satisfy, what, a primal urge?

And finally, this to Fainaru from one young man who had not yet reached where Correa found himself:

"I am so thankful for this war," one of them said to me one night.[150]

Thankful for what? For the chance to make more money than they could at home, and, at least for some, for the opportunity to engage in the legalized violence that brought such excitement into their otherwise mundane lives? Pondering this, there are a few questions to consider: Are we unknowing "pushers" of a different sort, making adrenaline junkies out of some of these kids we agree to send into battle? Is *patriotism*, for some, just a cover, a nice-sounding codename for a desire to kill the "bad guys" whose own patriotism, or perhaps religiosity, are also simply codenames for their desires to kill us? And, lastly, is all this just what it appears to be to the analytical eye—prejudice and hatred directing the show from under the covers? Or, is there a deeper singular cause for this continually blossoming murderousness on the parts of nations and men?

Make It about Them

In the novel *Horn*, written in the late 1960s, D. Keith Mano, a Kellet Fellow at Cambridge, has his protagonist, Mr. Smith, a black man, speaking with Mr. Pratt, a Caucasian priest, as to the source of hatred. The setting is an abandoned church during a race riot, which swirls and rages outside:

> I [Mr. Pratt] heard Jimmy's satisfied laughter. Then Smith's fist struck the hard wood of the pew bench....
> "Nine," he said. "Nine. And it's my fault. I killed them."
>
> "It's not you," I said. "It's this dammed hatred and bigotry. I pray every day that it will end. I pray for love, so many of us pray for love. I—"
>
> "Please, Mr. Pratt. Please." He stood up. "You know nothing about it. Love…"
>
> "Love, you said," he pointed at me. "Love. Are you really so stupid? What is your God, Mr. Pratt—*The New York Times?*… Use your brains, Mr. White Priest. There is no such thing as prejudice. He slapped the side of the pew. These are all stories that you tell little children. Sometimes … sometimes. I even think there is no such thing as love."
>
> "I don't understand you." As I spoke, I moved farther away from him, for his vehemence was terrible.
>
> "No," he exhaled. Then he bent down and picked up his hat. "No one understands me. That's why we have come to this—whole cities burning in the summer. You—all of you—you are too proud or too stupid to admit the truth."
>
> "What is it then? Tell me. What is the truth?"
>
> "That there is no hatred. No hatred. Only fear. That there is no bigotry. Only fear." He cursed. "You,

Mr. Pratt, what do you care for truth? You get up in the pulpit and you say, 'We must love the black man.' We must love him? And you are surprised when there is no love. How can there be? How? There still is fear. You haven't taken away the fear.... [Y]ou have failed...."

"I am sorry," he said at last. "This is not the time."

"Even so," I said sullenly. "I can't just let this go.... I don't often hear black men say that there is no prejudice. If you meant that, then I want you to explain it. Seems to me, for years we've treated you like an inferior race. We've —"

"No!" he said. "You see. You see. That's wrong." He came quickly back across the aisle. "Listen to me. If I think you are inferior, Mr. Pratt—I don't hate you. No. I feel sorry for you. Maybe I just don't think about you at all. But I don't hate you, because I don't fear you. Cats and dogs are inferior yet we love them. Children are inferior and we love them best of all. But snakes. Oh, yes. Snakes. They are inferior, but they bite too. I hate snakes...!"

"White racism." He laughed without enjoyment. "What a stupid thing to say. Does it help? Does it teach us anything? Does it explain why you hate the black man? No."

"So explain. Why do I—we—why do we hate the black man?"

"For a very good reason, Mr. Pratt. You are afraid of us...."

"Think a minute. You are a smart man.... When last did someone say to you, 'I hate Indians?' " he sneered. "Not lately, I think. Not since Mr. Custer made his last stand. We don't fear them. [And since we don't,] we don't hate them…. It is fear that fills us full of hate."[151]

Therefore, if, as Mr. Smith was propounding, hatred is the outcome of fear, and fear arises when we perceive ourselves and our interests as separate and threatened, then it is that sense of separateness that needs healing first. Otherwise, as Mr. Smith was making clear to Mr. Pratt, we will profess to love while hiding from ourselves that we still fear, seemingly joining with some while excluding others. Therefore, we will have accomplished nothing, because we will not "have taken away the fear."

It is the seeming separation from the trunk and one another that is the source of the fields of mists and myths in which we labor, leading to the alienating and ultimately distressing wish that life be about *me* and not others. Yet, if our separation from the trunk is just a myth, if we are not really separate from the trunk and, therefore, the interests of the whole, then we must begin to set aside our overvaluation of our personal interests. In other words, if we want to experience the benefits of generosity, we must, as Kenneth Wapnick put it, begin to live so as to "make it about them." This is the meaning behind Dostoevsky's statement, "It's somehow indecent to love only well-being."[152] Or, as Dr. Wapnick was quoted as saying earlier,

> Only the mind's decision for separation is the cause of suffering…. Thus if we do not undo … the belief in separate interests, nothing will ever change.[153]

Not Two

To conclude this chapter, let's look at how Aldous Huxley, in his own unique way, looked at the problem of misidentification we suffer from:

> If I only knew who in fact I am, I should cease to behave as what I think I am, and if I stopped behaving as what I think I am, I should know who I am.

What in fact I am, if only the Manichee (read: ego) I think I am would allow me to know it, is the reconciliation of yes and no lived out in total acceptance, and the blessed experience of Not Two....

[It] is not by pretending to be somebody else, even somebody supremely good and wise, that we can pass from insulated Manichee-hood to Good Being.

Good Being is knowing who in fact we are; and in order to know who in fact we are, we must first know, moment by moment who we think we are and what this bad habit of thought compels us to feel and do....

So be aware—aware in every context at all times and whatever, creditable or discreditable, pleasant or unpleasant, you may be doing or suffering. This is the only creditable yoga, the only spiritual exercise worth practicing....

Faith is something very different from belief.... For Faith is the empirically justified confidence in our capacity to know who in fact we are, to forget the belief-intoxicated Manichee in Good Being. Give us this day our daily Faith, but deliver us, dear God, from Belief.[154]

And now to Kenneth Wapnick for a description of what functioning in "Good Being" would be like. But first, let me elaborate a bit about the quote above as well as the one to follow. Earlier, I said that faith really means having faith in your brother's goodness, despite all appearances to the contrary. What Aldous Huxley and Kenneth Wapnick and others are saying is that our shared reality lies beyond the body and the ego and the world of clashing and separate forms. They are all also saying that while love, being one, cannot truly be experienced in a state of separation or duality, its reflection (forgiveness) and its product (kindness) can and must be if we are to remember that truth, which we both share and are.

If [truth] is perfect Oneness, so is love, which is why love is impossible here [in a state of duality]. Yet, its reflection is possible, in the sense that we can love everyone in *content*—meaning we do not make significant distinctions among the different.... The world obviously makes such distinctions, as do our brains and eyes, but these are all based on form, having nothing to do with the underlying content. We are the same because we share the same delusional thought system ... as we also share the same need to escape from it.... We are thus the same in sharing the one problem of believing in separation, and the need to undo it through forgiveness.

[True vision] makes no distinctions among the seemingly different.... Once again, love, being Oneness [i.e., "Not Two"] does not exclude because it sees nothing other than itself. Even when people act in unloving ways—often hateful, cruel, and vicious—one can nonetheless see beyond the external sights of evil, and hear beyond the sounds of battle the call for love. [True] perception recognizes that everyone in the world either expresses love or calls for it. In the end it makes no difference which it is, because [Good Being's] response would be the same—love....[155]

CHAPTER 11

Above the Chaos

MY SON CONTINUED TO LANGUISH in jail, awaiting the court's decision regarding where he would go next. There, he lingered, a deeply divided man with above-average charm and intelligence, who had yet to consistently put either to any good use. Was his, then, another one of those wasted lives that, for all intents and purposes, was over? Not if he didn't want it to be. Even though he refused to acknowledge its presence, the truth and all its accompanying wisdom still abided deep in his mind, as it does in everyone's. When would he choose to listen to it and its ever-present messenger, common sense? On the day he would finally realize that following the advice of his wrong-mindedness had *never* brought him anything more than momentary pleasure, followed *always* by extraordinary guilt and pain.

Standing up in the Sandbox

Is difficulty living quietly and reasonably limited to the foundering and lost, who, like my son, end up in prisons, in asylums, or on the streets?

Not really. Consider the rise and fall of so many of the mighty—the devastation that has besmirched the reputations of so many mistake-making politicians, religious leaders, entertainment figures, and sports stars, among others. And then consider, as we've seen, the lack of compassion with which so many of them are greeted when the rest of us decide to join the righteous.

What is happening here? Why is it that sometimes we become so defensive and strictly principled that we find ourselves with no recourse but to look down our noses at one of our own simply because he has erred? Just think of the dissociation involved when any self-proclaimed (and thus secretly guilty) moralist hectors an equal about a purism he himself does not possess. Why is it that those who think in terms of "rotten apples" are convinced that the only mitigation for their own deep sense of impropriety is to attack another?

To borrow one of Kenneth Wapnick's metaphors, imagine our condition as if we are children playing in a very large sandbox, throwing sand at others, who keep throwing sand right back at us. The sand is blinding, and it stings when it hits us, but we keep at it because we are afraid that if we stop, they'll all just gang up and throw their sand at us, and we'll be infinitely worse off than we are now. Then, after a long while, becoming truly fed up with what was supposed to be pleasurable and clearly is not, we begin to think outside the box, saying to ourselves, "There must be a better game than this." Not long after, it starts to dawn on us that the reason we find ourselves with such distressing feelings of littleness and so caught up in our tirades is not because we were made to be that way, but because, in our deep engrossment in protecting ourselves, we had forgotten that the price of admission we had agreed to pay was to kneel down to play the purportedly fun game.

Imagine further that, in realizing this, we say to ourselves, "What nonsense!" and begin to rise up from our self-imposed childishness, accepting ourselves as the grownups we are. Having knelt for so long in the game of Let's Pretend We're Limited, Small-Minded, and Competitive, the first part of the journey upward would certainly seem foreign. Yet, after a while, this more natural position would become stable and familiar. From there, looking down at those still throwing sand and screaming foul in the bad bargain, we'd realize that any sand still being thrown at us would, at most, reach our waists and thus cause us distress no longer. And how would we now, from our place above, think of those who continued to play the spiteful games of I Hate You for Making Me So Little and Let's Be Friends until We Get Those Others? Would we not begin to perceive them as merely those who had not yet realized that to become "king of the sandbox" is to conquer a barren realm indeed? And I say "begin to perceive them" because learning to do so happens not overnight, but only in a process that takes quite some time. It takes practice and commitment to stay alert to the promptings of our vanity and a sincere desire to grow beyond our childishness to meet its demands with "Thank you, but no thank you," without excuse or exception. Yet, what better use could we have for our time?

What follows is an excerpt from *ACIM* that speaks to the subject from a psychological and much more sophisticated and metaphysical viewpoint. Its message: it is senseless to remain mired in unrewarding conflict—and *all* conflict is unrewarding—when there is a way of rising up and finding our way out.

> Mistake not truce for peace, nor compromise for the escape from conflict! To be released from conflict means that it is over. The door is open; you have left the battleground. You have not lingered there in cowering hope that it will not return because the guns are stilled an instant, and the fear that haunts the place of death is not apparent. There is no safety in a battleground. You can look down on it in safety from above and not be touched. But from within it you can find no safety. Not one tree left standing will shelter you. Not one illusion of protection stands against the faith in murder....
>
> Be lifted up and from a higher place look down on it. From there will your perspective be quite different.

Here in the midst of it, it does seem real. Here you have chosen to be part of it. Yet from above the choice is miracles instead of murder....

The senselessness of conquest is quite apparent from the quiet sphere above the battleground. What can conflict with everything? And what is there that offers less, yet could be wanted more?[156]

These are powerful words, as they are meant to be. Underlying them is the idea that if we really want to wake up to what we are doing to ourselves in our attempts to harm others, we must rise above every flimsy excuse that says, "I wouldn't be the—for example, bereft, wounded, vengeful, unforgiving—person I am, if he or she hadn't made me this way." It is as foreign to our *true* natures to listen to our egos and march off to war after war for the childish reasons of "We have to get them first" or "Well, they started it" and "We'll show them," as it is alien to reason that we should remain angry at a family member, friend, teacher, coworker, or boss because he or she made a mistake we choose to remain wounded by. In all cases, what we are refusing to accept is that what hurts us is our initial decision to kneel down and play the children's game of spite, and *not* the sand, which, from that lower level, inevitably ends up in our mind's eyes.

Now, this reasoning is not meant to dismiss the very real experience of pain we can feel after a tragedy or a great disappointment, which should not be denied. What it does mean is learning that the misunderstandings and errors of others, while perhaps causing distress to my body and even great inconvenience in my life, have no real power to influence my ability to interpret or perceive things as I will. Another's mistakes are, in fact, no more personal for me than when my mother had a bad day and took it out on me. Therefore, again, seen properly, human error and tragedy are actually calls for a greater understanding, and not poisoned lances that have pierced my heart.

So the other guy—wife, husband, sibling, child, parent, friend, boss, teacher—screwed up. Big time. And that screw-up, in one way or another, changed my life and seemed, without question, the cause of my emotional distress. Yet, here I am now, stronger and wiser for all my experiences, among which this one event played a most helpful and significant part. Was I hurt by it then? I had thought I was. But when I remember my power of choice to see and experience what I will, I begin to doubt the reality of those memories and feelings, just as much as I did my old belief that I had been hurt by the actions of that disturbed nun.

People try to hurt me because they do not understand. And I feel wounded for the same reason: because I do not understand. But then I see something most important—that not a bit of it was or is, then or now, personal at all.

Watching Our Resistance to Change

In the Kalahari Desert in southern Africa, Bushmen have learned to find their way to water in the dry season. First, they hollow out a small opening in a tree, and then they carve out a deeper pocket within it. Into this pocket they place sweet nuts. Monkeys, who know where secret caches of water are among the nearby caves, are attracted to the smell of the nuts. When one finally comes and reaches into the tree to gather the nuts, he finds that his then closed fist is too large to remove from the tree.

The Bushman quietly approaches the monkey who, being a monkey, refuses to let go of the nuts, even while screaming in fear. The Bushman then ties a noose around the monkey's neck, after which he pours salt down its throat. Finally, while keeping the monkey secured by a long tether, the Bushman waits for the animal's thirst to overpower its desire for the nuts. When it does, while holding on to the tether, he follows it to the cave with the water, where it goes to slake its thirst.

Who is the monkey in the desert of our lives? We are, every time we choose to kneel down and cling to the "nutty" idea that playing wounded and better than others is more important to our welfare than standing up and letting such hateful treats go. How hard is letting go? Because we're so unaccustomed to it, hard, but not as hard as the alternative—wanting to be separate and special and have it be someone else's fault. But until we grow out of this desire for specialness and its consequent sense of incompletion, we will remain the slaves of that secret wish.

Sigmund Freud, who taught that the goal of psychoanalysis is to get to the root of the problem and bring it to conscious awareness, had the following to say about the difference between palliative and truly effective therapy, and our resistance to learning just how much of this is actually up to us.

> In the light of the knowledge we have gained from psy-cho-analysis we can describe the difference between hypnotic and psycho-analytic suggestion as follows. Hypnotic treatment seeks to cover up and gloss over something in mental life; analytic treatment seeks to expose and get rid of something. The former acts like a cosmetic; the latter like surgery. The former makes use of suggestions in order to forbid the symptoms, it strengthens the repressions, but, apart from that, leaves all the processes that have led to the formations of the symptoms unaltered. Analytic treatment makes its impact further back toward the roots, where the conflicts are which gave rise to the symptoms, and uses suggestion in order to alter the outcome of those conflicts....
>
> An analytic treatment demands ... serious work, which is employed in lifting internal resistances. Through the overcoming of these resistances the patient's mental life is permanently changed, is raised to a high level of development and remains protected against fresh possibilities of falling ill. This work of overcoming resistances is the essential function of anal-ysis treatment, the patient has to accomplish it [learning

to know himself] in what has justly been described as a kind of *after-education*.[157]

Freud continues:

> This involves some psychological preparation of the patient. We must aim at bringing about two changes in him: an increase in the attention he pays to his own psychical perceptions, and the elimination of the criticism by which he normally sifts the thoughts that occur to him.... It is necessary to insist explicitly on his renouncing all criticism of the thoughts that he perceives.... He must adopt a completely impartial attitude to what occurs to him, since it is precisely his critical attitude which is responsible for his being unable, in the ordinary course of things, to achieve the desired unraveling of his ... obsessional idea or whatever it may be.[158]

In describing how one uses this process of self-observation to trace our choices for self-centeredness back to their source, and then to forgive ourselves, Kenneth Wapnick says,

> As you go through your day, pay careful attention to the way you perceive others. This will reveal [the right- or wrong-mindedness] you have chosen. If you find yourself indulging in specialness, becoming bored, depressed, or critical of others, it is only because you first chose to see yourself as hateful. Rather than accept responsibility for that choice, you projected it and saw the hate in someone else. Yet when you understand that what you see in this other person is a projection of what you see in yourself, your ... reaction becomes a reminder that you made the wrong choice. This allows you to return to the mind where the mistake was made and choose again. *It*

is thus not the other you forgive, but yourself for having chosen wrongly.[159]

As we've seen here and elsewhere, wrong-mindedness says that another's mistake with me is the cause of my fierce response. Right-mindedness says that my defensiveness is the result of the guilt I experience and deny and project when I make the decision to protect my image instead of protecting the other from further harm. Wrong-mindedness hides the fact that when I deign to put a cover over my justified wrath and "forgive" the attacker, I am doing nothing but offering one, whom I perceive as being less than I am, something that I believe he or she does not deserve. Right-mindedness gently corrects my misunderstanding of whose wrong choice it is that needs forgiveness, teaching me that my real problem comes from my resistance and my refusal to be reasonable, and not from the other's actions at all.

Looking at Our Conditioned Minds

Speaking to the underlying systems of thought that maintain not only relationships but even the functioning of everything from motorcycles to government institutions, *Zen and the Art of Motorcycle Maintenance* says,

> To speak of certain government and establishment institutions as "the system" is to speak correctly, since these organizations are founded upon the same structural conceptual relationships as a motorcycle. They are sustained by structural relationships even when they have lost all other meaning and purpose. People arrive at a factory and perform a totally meaningless task from eight to five without question because the structure demands that it be that way. There's no villain, no "mean guy" who wants them to live meaningless lives, it's just that the structure, the system demands it and no one is willing

to take on the formidable task of changing the structure just because it is meaningless.

> But to … revolt against a government … because it is a system is to attack effects rather than causes; and as long as the attack is upon effects only, no change is possible. The true system, the real system, is our present [conditioning, our] construction of systematic thought itself, rationality itself, and if a … revolution destroys a systematic government, but the systematic patterns of thought that produced that government are left intact, then those patterns will repeat themselves in the succeeding government. There is so much talk about the system. And so little understanding.[160]

Experientially, this means that when our minds awaken enough to watch themselves in action all the time, which is, again, what "silence is the answer" really means, we have the dawning realization that the world we see has no meaning beyond what our own systematic patterns of thought have postulated, but it also has no meaning that we cannot as easily remove. Only when we recognize that the events we perceive and react to get their "juice" from our plugging into them and offering them power can there be escape from the perturbations of emotions born of choosing wrongly and the equanimity necessary to learn anew. As Krishnamurti said, "If there is not [the] stillness which is the outcome of a total understanding of [your] conditioning, your search for truth has no meaning at all, it is merely a trap."[161]

It "has no meaning at all" and "is merely a trap" because all the learning before the understanding will have taken place within the conditioning. Therefore, it will have led only to modifications in the conditioning, and not to the silence that allows for the possibility of something completely new. Freedom means escape from the bondage of conditioning, not improvements within it. This translates into the idea that if we don't pay attention to our conditioning and its systematic patterns of thought, we'll be living in a world made of projections of the past, which we'll confuse with reality.

The lesson here is that while one can always shift things around in meaningless patterns, no one can actually improve a thought system based on false premises. And, if we think about it, what could be falser than a system of thought that gives such honor to specialness and war, and such undue seriousness to the ephemeral? In contradiction to the world's fixation on opposition and all its sorrows, Nietzsche once said, "[Only] he who climbs upon the highest mountain [can] laugh at all tragedies, real or imaginary."[162] This doesn't mean laughing at our suffering or at the suffering of others, but it does mean laughing at the idea that such tragedies could be real, or that sorrow over suffering is somehow respectful and should be seen as such.

Rather, what we should be serious about is desiring to reach a place of balance so perfect it would see an inner smile as the appropriate response to "all tragedies, real or imaginary." The value in dealing directly with so-called conditionally acceptable problems, such as sorrow, is that it helps us return quickly to that great question "Says who?" In other words, who says sorrow is acceptable? Allowing sorrow to fall like a veil over facts is like making a mental sacrifice to the gods, who we just know want us to take everything seriously. Smiling at this idea, no matter the fixed beliefs of the wrong mind to the contrary, the suffering *behind* the suffering would be seen for the fraud that it is. Yet, this process can be perceived as possible only by a mind that has begun to free itself from its conditioning, because its conditioning *is* sorrow. Describing the inherent challenge in this journey, Krishnamurti said,

> Because [most teachers of the world] have never ... gone into themselves and examined, explored, searched out, looked and watched, they have always conformed to a pattern. And they are trying to teach me how to live within that pattern....
>
> So as nobody is going to help me to educate myself inwardly, how shall I begin?

What shall I do? How shall I face all this [inward ambition, sorrow, envy, and violence], look at it, listen to all the terrible noise in the world? Shall I choose a particular noise that appeals to me and follow that noise for the rest of my life? What shall I do? This is a tremendous problem, it is not a simple problem.[163]

Since this *is* a tremendous problem, and since functioning within the confines of our conditioning and fixed beliefs is not far from mindlessness, let's see what some others have had to say on the subject. In the introduction to *The Zen Reader*, it says,

Zen is traditionally called the School of the Awakened Mind.... The premise of Zen is that our personality, culture, and beliefs are not an inherent part of [us], but "guests" of a recondite [or concealed] "host".... We are not limited in our essence or mode of being to what we happen to believe we are, or what we happen to believe the world is....

This realization may not seem to have ... significance at first, until it is remembered how much anger, antagonism, and grief arises from the ideas of "them" and "us" based on historically conditioned factors like culture, customs, and habits of thought. Any reasonable person knows these things are not absolute, and yet the force of conditioning creates seemingly insurmountable barriers of communication [not only with others, but with our own good sense].[164]

Along the same lines, the Jesuit philosopher, Anthony de Mello, says this about our mind's conditioning:

Take a look at the world and see the unhappiness around you and in you. Do you know what causes this unhappiness? You will probably say loneliness or oppression or war or hatred. And you will be wrong. There is only one cause of unhappiness: the false beliefs you have in your head, beliefs so widespread, so commonly held, that it never occurs to you to question them. Because of these false beliefs you see the world and yourself in a false way. Your programming is so strong and the pressure of society so intense that you are literally trapped…. There is no way out, because you do not even have a suspicion that your perception is distorted, your thinking is wrong and your beliefs are false.[165]

How awake to the promptings of these false beliefs and our conditioning are we? Do we realize that many of the conclusions we reach are based on assumptions of a questionable nature? Further, are we aware of how often not examining our presumptions for validity, or even sense, can lead to difficulty for others, even in the mildest of cases? *Newsweek* found occasion to publish a humorous, yet educational, article headed "Thou Shalt Not Turn Me into a False Idol" that spoke to this. What follows is a condensed version of it:

Because I'm a pastor's wife, everyone thinks my life is perfect and they have me figured out. Not so fast.

I married a banker. I like to remind my banker-turned-pastor husband of this when we are having a particularly difficult time in the ministry. Although I wouldn't trade his occupation … , my husband's career choice bestowed on me a title I never bargained for when we walked down the aisle. I am a pastor's wife.

Over the years I have been introduced to others without my first name. Just "the pastor's wife," as though the label alone is sufficient in describing who I am. "I'm Eileen," I gently correct. I usually get the same response. "Oh … nice to meet you." As the conversation progresses, I feel their eyes examining me, as though something about stance, attire or aura might confirm that I am, in fact, married to a pastor.

What they seem to be looking for—and what they'll never find in me—is perfection. It is assumed that my children never fight, my husband and I never disagree, my home is always clean for drop-in visitors and my meals are always nutritionally balanced.... For them, I am a symbol—a projected fantasy of what it means to live a life of faith—not an actual person....

With a title like mine, it is easy to feel pushed into a box with the lid closing fast....

For those who suppose they have me pegged, I'd like to dispel a few stereotypes: ... I applaud those who may not be churchgoers but whose actions and gener- osity reflect Christ.... I don't wear stockings, pumps or flowered dresses. I don't volunteer in the nursery of the children's church.... I don't perform with the music team ... and the only song I know how to play on the piano is "Chopsticks"....

And I bite my tongue if our children complain about going to church. I've vowed to never respond to their complaints with "You have to! You're the pastor's kid!" I know all too well the claustrophobic feelings associated with the label.[166]

The philosopher Will Durant quotes the Romans as saying, "*Initium dimiduim facti*," or "The start is half the deed."[167] This is good advice in business and worldly affairs. In personal relationships, even better, for here, the start or the premise or the programming, until or unless modified, is the *whole* thing. For instance, it was belief and preconcep- tion that caused Eileen to become unrecognizable behind the image of "the pastor's wife," as it is preconception and belief that so often render invisible the reality of what we're so sure we are, at any given moment, perceiving properly. To continue with this important topic, let's take a look at how Kenneth Wapnick understands it:

> You should underline this in multi-colors. "Everything you see is the result of your thoughts." This important sentence needs to be understood on two levels, as it means everything you see in terms of *form*, but also in terms of *interpretation*. Both are the "result of your thoughts."
>
> [It is important] we understand that it is not only *what* we see [that counts] but *how* we see it.... We cannot separate our perception of "objective reality" from our interpretation of it because they are one and the same. Again, it is not only *what* we see, but *how* we see it.
>
> [The purpose of learning this] is to cultivate in us a vigilance in watching how we think....
>
> Any time you see an enemy "out there," or believe someone has the power to victimize, betray, or hurt you [emotionally], you are saying ... you are right because you can see and feel the attack, and have the evidence to prove it. However, you are not aware that *you* planted the evidence so you could find it. What you see is what you *want* to see, and so you put the evidence there and say, "See! My thoughts are *not* the problem. In fact my thoughts are nothing. The problem is out there. That is the problem." And almost always there is some special person that is the focus of your problem....
>
> [Simply put,] The thoughts in our mind are the *cause* and our perceptions are the *effect*![168]

Along the same lines of how preconceptions crowd out objectivity and the importance of awareness, Krishnamurti says,

> It is only when we see without any preconceptions, any image, that we are able to be in direct contact with any-

thing in life. If I have an image about you and you have an image about me, naturally we don't see each other at all as we actually are. What we see is the images we have formed about each other which prevent us from being in contact, and that is why our relationships go wrong....

Investigation into this whole question is meditation.... Meditation is not following any system. It is not constant repetition and imitation. Meditation is not concentration....

Meditation is to be aware of every thought and of every feeling, never to say it is right or wrong but just to watch it.... In that watching you begin to understand the whole movement of thought and feeling. And out of this awareness comes silence.[169]

And from *The Zen Reader*, we find this:

Straightforward mindfulness involves no thought; if you can observe without thought you can be said to be heading [toward] wisdom.

—Han-shan

No matter how bad a state of mind you may get into, if you keep strong and hold out [and simply watch], eventually the floating clouds [of negativity] must vanish and the withering wind [of recrimination] must cease.

—Dogen

If you misunderstand your mind, you are an ordinary mortal; if you understand your mind you are a sage.

—Jakushitsu[170]

As we begin a more careful observation of our mind's activity and its restlessness, the strange and even pitiful nature of some of our thoughts and memories becomes clearer. And while it is true that a number of them will appear pleasant, it is equally true that others will appear shameful or hurtful, making us want to turn away and cringe. Yet, with practice, we will come to understand that pure observation, uncontaminated by judgment, blame, or self-criticism, does not suffer from those dark things that, without an invitation to stay, have no choice but to leave. Pure observation, like simply standing up in the sandbox and leaving the sad game, may seem inactive as it quietly does nothing, but in actuality, it speaks volumes, actively refusing to honor the slightest whisper of doubt that we are anything less than the masters of our inner fate.

And so the mighty struggle to regain our balance is reduced to this: when our watching of the noise of the mind becomes more important than the noise, the noise loses its power to disturb. And even though, for a while, on occasion, it may continue to rear its ugly head, what's that to a mind remembering its power to remain out of the grasp of the baneful, by doing nothing but watching as the noise goes on by?

CHAPTER 12

No Mea, No Culpa

M Y SON WAS ACCEPTED INTO a two-year state-run drug-treatment program on a remote part of Oahu, another attempt on the part of the State of Hawaii to help him straighten out. He was relieved that he was not heading off to prison and seemed to enter the program with a positive attitude. Eight days later, he took off to have another party. A week later, the police picked him up and put him back in jail. A few months after this a judge put him back in the original program he'd run away from. Then, in an inexplicable and complete about-face, he completed the program, stayed sober, found a job, got married, and is now, like his brother, a church-going, tax-paying, calmed-down citizen of the planet. After everything that he'd gone through up to now? Talk about not understanding.

True Wisdom

Success or failure, what do I think of my son? I think that he is, for the moment, another equal; another apple doing his best to come out of his coma; a gentle and essentially decent guy, limitless in his capacity for goodness, but still a lost soul surrounded by dark dreams of a guilty past that make it terribly difficult for him to recognize his bad memories as no more than bad dreams and to accept a fresh start in a present world. I also believe that he is one among many enmeshed in the frightening but captivating web of belief that, without that terrible past, he'd be nothing special and, therefore, perhaps, nothing at all. It's kind of like a sad version of the old Woody Allen joke, "I stand at a crossroads. On the one hand, there is suffering, death, and the possibility of eternal punishment. On the other, likely oblivion. Let us pray that I have the wisdom to make the proper choice!"

Like my son, rather than put the effort into directly facing one's guilt and the tendency to blame, in order to advance in true wisdom, many in the world—those not just scrambling to survive, that is—substitute the easier "solution" of "eat, drink and be merry, for tomorrow we die."[171] Yet what is this way of living really, but a means of temporarily distracting oneself from (and thus not dealing with) the dismal outlook that results from an assumed lack of real worth and fears about death and disappearance?

Assuming Socrates was right when he taught that there is no such thing as evil, but only ignorance, what could the purpose and the goal of a meaningful life be but awakening from our stuporous denial that this is so? "Wake up to what you're doing to yourself," the wise say. Along those lines, in the brief biography that introduces Freud's *Introductory Lectures on Psycho-Analysis,* Peter Gay says, "It was Freud's fate, as he observed not without pride, to 'agitate the sleep of mankind.' "[172] In another example, centuries earlier, Socrates, who, if you read Plato carefully, you'll discover was among the wisest of men, was quoted at his trial as saying,

> It is literally true, even if it sounds rather comical, that [I have been] specially appointed ... to this city, as though it were a large thoroughbred horse which because of its

great size is inclined to be lazy and needs the stimulation of some stinging fly.... All day long I never cease to settle here, there, and everywhere, rousing ... every one of you.

You will not easily find another like me, gentlemen, and if you take my advice, you will spare my life. I suspect, however, that before long you will awake from your drowsing, and in your annoyance you will ... finish me off with a single slap, and then go on sleeping till the end of your days.... For [my crime is that] I spend all my time going about trying to persuade you, young and old, to make your first and chief concern not for your bodies, nor for your possessions, but for the highest welfare of your [minds]....

I set myself to do ... what I hold to be the greatest possible service. I tried to persuade each of you not to think more of practical advantages than of his mental and moral well-being....

Life without this sort of examination is not worth living.[173]

The "examined life" is one that recognizes how filled with questionable and spurious generalizations are our "pails" and then acknowledges our freedom to disbelieve much of what we've believed before; in short, it is a life that we live in recognition of the fact that we truly have limited understanding. Limited understanding, by definition, understands only in part. The point, therefore, to the seeker of wisdom is to grow in understanding, not achievement. In turn, the real purpose of understanding is that it be used in the service of the reunification of the whole, not just for personal advancement. Otherwise, a tool meant to be helpful in our awakening becomes one that takes us further into the dream of fame and fortune, with its attendant strife, confusion, and an unthought-through higher regard for the words of others than for our own ability to reason. Speaking of the danger of this abuse of so-called knowledge, Plato critiques one teacher of rhetoric as follows:

And it is not true wisdom that you offer your disciples, but only its semblance, for by telling them many things without teaching them [how to think for themselves], you make them seem to know much, where for the most part they know nothing, and as men filled not with wisdom, but the conceit of wisdom, they will be a burden to their fellows….[174]

"The Victor Belongs to the Spoils"

All over the world people are seeking better educations for their children, not so much so that they grow in wisdom and goodness, but so they become stronger competitors for the prizes that glitter and shine—prizes that, as Socrates warned, feed the body but never the mind. With rare exception, there is little credit for doing one's best, no high marks to be earned for being peaceful and kind. The result of this so-called education is that, in the end, there is nothing but madness and violence. After thinking about it seriously, can you adequately explain to yourself someone paying $31,000 for John Lennon's tooth or $4.6 million for the dress that Marilyn Monroe wore in *The Seven Year Itch*? Can you find the reasoning behind fairly good-looking people voluntarily engaging in relatively short-lived and sometimes quite painful plastic surgery? Or already pretty good athletes taking steroids and risking their health for fame? Or people going in for big game hunting, swimming with sharks, or cage fighting? Or what about social climbing, that expensive and strenuous pursuit in which life is defined by whether society's desired stratum has been reached? Better yet, what about a different kind of climbing? Consider the following excerpt from a book about people who repeatedly attempted to summit Mount Everest, and ask yourself if you can understand the attraction that would lead anyone to put themselves through such an experience, not once, not twice, but again and again.

Staying healthy is often a greater challenge than the climbing. Some mountain maladies are killers. Pulmonary edema fills the skull with fluid.... Other illnesses are just as uncomfortable.... Acute mountain sickness brings nausea and headaches ... Cheyne-Stokes respiration ... causes climbers to hold their breath when they sleep so they awaken gasping and terrified. Third World sanitation gives others ... illnesses such as giardia and dysentery....

My ... smile faded when I saw my wife upon my return to Advanced Base Camp.... It struck me that she was emaciated. Altitude sickness had her throwing up most of her meals during the previous weeks, leaving her weak with hunger. Eventually, my already slender wife would lose twenty-five pounds. Her hair fell out in clumps, and her teeth ached from the lost enamel...

On April 14, Nils slept only half the night due to "persistent nightmares of suffocation and desperate thirst." He reached Base Camp on April 16 with a GI infection and diarrhea, and on April 17, wrote only "Gastroenteritis terrible. No food. Dehydrated. Weak. Miserable."

Despite his illness and diminishing strength, Nils continued up the mountain ... through the Icefall. "Exhausted, shouldn't have," he wrote....[175]

The rest of the book is about the dog-eat-dog competition to be first up the mountain, along with tales of lost toes, lost fingers, lost legs, and lost climbers, including the sixty-nine-year-old Nils, abandoned by his guide and his Sherpas while still alive but freezing to death on his way down from summiting the world's highest mountain.

What sort of possession causes people to embark on these self-punishing pursuits of personal glory? And is the accomplishment ever really glorious or merely further evidence of an irrational attraction to outdoing others, no matter the cost to achieve it?

F. Scott Fitzgerald said, "The victor belongs to the spoils." That seems an accurate assessment of the ultimate condition of those still possessed by the desire for the treasure of a crooked mirror that will whisper, "You're still the fairest—or fastest, strongest, 'bestest'—of them all."

Kenneth Wapnick, using the Shakespearean tragedy *Macbeth* as his example, speaks to our self-glorification, saying,

> We try to cover over the horror of life here in this world—which the play *Macbeth* depicts in an almost ghoulish way—and make it into something pretty. We take murder and try to justify it…. [In *Macbeth*,] Macbeth's ambition goes beyond itself ("Vaulting ambition, which o'erleaps itself, and falls on the other") and falls on another: [King] Duncan. He does not care, for he is driven…. He was not always like that; and we were not always the way we are: obsessed with specialness. There is a part of our minds that is a doorway back home … but we keep it buried, as did Macbeth.
>
> [Subsequently] we continually try to justify our hate, our specialness and our grandiosity. We seek to justify our attempts to be number one, to be king, to be the most loved, the most highly approved of, the center of attention. We strive always to justify our egos, [delaying] our inevitable confrontation with … the shadowy world of guilt and fear that lies underneath.[176]

The Highest Achievement

As we've seen, according to Plato, the healthy life is the examined life. In Plato's *Phaedrus*, Socrates is quoted as saying that the mind is divided into three parts: two like steeds and the third a "charioteer." He calls one steed "good" and the other "not," teaching that the charioteer's mission is to unite with the good steed in taming the unruly one, defining our real goal as follows:

> And so, if the victory be won by the higher elements of the mind, guiding them into the ordered rule of the philosophical life ... [with] the power of evil in the [mind] subjected, and the power of goodness liberated, they have won self-mastery and inward peace. And when life is over, with burden shed and wings recovered they stand victorious in ... that truly Olympic struggle: nor can any nobler prize be secured ... by man.[177]

"Self-mastery and inward peace"—since this, in the opinion of Socrates, is the pinnacle of achievement (i.e., "nor can any nobler prize be secured ... by man"), let's examine what a few others have said about learning, practice, and arriving there.

> Kenneth Wapnick from *A Tale Told by an Idiot*: We are all different in form.... But we are the same on the level of the mind. We have the same hate-filled ego [or wrong mind] ... the same right-minded love, and the same power to choose between them. No one here is exempt from this structure of the mind....
>
> [This means that] in everything—every hour, minute and second of your life—you make a choice ... to become angry or upset ... and [believe] there are causes outside yourself that are responsible for your misery, [or not].
>
> Thus you are asked—day in and day out—to monitor your mind and be vigilant for those moments when you are tempted to make something ... serious ... by giving it the power to affect you.

Nothing in the world has that power unless you give it to it, which means that all the power in this world is yours—not to do things on the level of the body, but to do things on the level of the mind, which is the only level that matters.[178]

Walt Whitman: I affirm that mind governs, that all depends on the mind ... that refinement [of the mind] is the greatest of all.[179]

Me imperturbe, standing at ease ...
   Master of all, or mistress of all—aplomb in the midst of irrational things....[180]

Epictetus: At each thing that happens to you, remember to turn to *yourself* and ask *yourself* what capacity you have for dealing with it. If you see a beautiful woman, you will find the capacity of self-control in that. If hardship comes to you, you will find endurance. If it is abuse, you will find patience. And if you become used to [thinking this way] you will not be carried away by appearances.[181]

All these quotes affirm the idea that "self-mastery and inward peace" is the real goal, and suggest that *everything* else, being ephemeral, has nothing to do with achieving that permanent state at all. How, then, should we look at the time we've spent on other pursuits? As time well spent if it culminated in showing us that what our egos or the marketplace calls valuable isn't worth much at all. Seen rightly, every disappointment is an aid in demonstrating how greatly we have misunderstood our purpose and underestimated our worth and, if we are to find true happiness, how necessary it is that we turn within.

If we turn away from self-mastery and inward peace because it makes us uncomfortable, we'll be no different than the man in the old story who comes home late at night, drops his key on the doorstep, and then goes and searches for it under the streetlight because he is afraid of the dark. The idea that the only workable answer is to turn within is, admittedly, not easy to accept. To be informed that all our hopes and wishes and even our sincerity and study will not lead to self-mastery, and that only a dedication to kindness and a constant and noncritical observation of our behavior and thinking will, is indeed foreign to what most of us have been taught. Yet, keep in mind that we have been badly taught.

Consider how similarly two teachers from quite different backgrounds address this most important subject of not being afraid to honestly look at ourselves, without ascribing guilt, in order to attain peace. First, from Kenneth Wapnick:

> [Therefore the] theme of mind searching is central to the practice ... of forgiveness. Without this self-honesty of looking within the mind for our buried ego thoughts, forgiveness has no meaning.
>
> If we attack or hate anyone, we are projecting a spot of darkness in our minds, a place of guilt that once projected out is seen in another but never recognized to be in ourselves.... Set up ... to protect ourselves from the fear of confronting our guilt, projection simply reinforces the fear by teaching us that we are indeed guilty; for otherwise we would not be requiring a defense against it....
>
> The [idea] here is that every single last aspect of guilt ... must be brought into awareness, looked at ... and thus let go of completely.[182]

And from J. Krishnamurti:

> Man suffers [and feels guilty] ... and with that comes sorrow. Now when the mind can remain with that, not move away from it, out of that comes a passion ... that is born out of this non-withdrawal from sorrow....

All of this comes down to a sense of deep inward seriousness, and that seriousness itself brings about attention, and ... the observation, the seeing of suffering. Not to go beyond it, refuse it, rationalize it, or run away from it, just to see it. And as you are choicelessly aware of this flowering, it comes naturally to wither away. You don't have to do something about it.[183]

It is incumbent on everyone who wishes to escape from self-centeredness to begin by becoming honest in every sense of the word. Avoiding looking at the possibility of our insincerity and focusing instead on improved behaviors will never make the problem go away, but will only drive it underground. For example, if the hidden desire for self-glorification is the motivation behind our good deeds, then no matter how sweet these deeds may appear, they are nothing other than poison to the mind.

The most salient dishonesty to be faced, however, is that, in relationships, most of us still have a children's "high-horse" we are eager to climb upon, from which, in a pretense of virtue, we look down on others to nourish our self-image. Like Narcissus, we've fallen in love with the reflection we saw in the pond in the moonlight. Yet, in the sunlight—the light of true equality—this idol cannot be seen. Therefore, we remain shrouded in the dark clouds of an assumed inequality, very accusatory, highly excusatory, and deeply engaged with a special self we've invented for ourselves.

Teaching and Learning

Looking at self-centeredness for what it is is the way to recognize how we, too, are contributing to the sense of alienation from sameness that most of us experience but that none of us ever truly left. Rejoining that sameness is to accept, as the Stoics taught, that "all human beings have their own value and importance ... that makes them akin to each other, irrespective of race or status or sex, in the universal brotherhood of humankind."[184] This quote reflects the idea that once we remove the cataracts of bias from our mind's eyes, we'll see that there is a way to be helpful if we want to, and that way is to refuse to believe ourselves different from all who think they are different and, thereby, to learn that, in purpose, we are all the same.

A basic law of the sea is that smaller and more maneuverable crafts are to get out of the way of larger and more ponderous ones. In life, wouldn't that logically translate into the idea that those who are more rational at any given moment are meant to be more flexible with those who are less so? In the same way a good physician begins with the guiding principle of "do no harm," shouldn't anyone who wants to be a good person begin with the goal of doing the same, especially since placing this credo in mind at the beginning of any interaction, and then keeping it in mind throughout, is the way to maintain our equanimity? This mindset may appear to contradict those experiences in which our concluding state of mind seemed dictated by the circumstance, but perhaps that only speaks to the weakness of our dedication to the proper goal.

The solution to the problem of keeping the proper goal in mind necessarily begins with the admission there is a problem. And there is! The grim world of one or the other can never provide us with the shelter we seek, because everything here is in a state of combat, division, and dissolution. How can safety be found in such a condition? And yet if this world can be, for those who want it to be so, changed from a vain meandering in selfishness to a classroom in awakening to our sameness, then using it for that purpose becomes all that makes sense.

To accept sameness alone as reflective of our shared equality, we must be willing to extend the thought to everyone, including those who are the most distressed. What do the self-hateful mistake-makers of the world—be they criminals or otherwise—need, want, and deserve from their more perspicacious equals? Not further condemnation, but rather a friend in the court of their low opinion of themselves, an advocate to plead the case of their self-accusation to a higher court, arguing for a reversal of their conviction on the sound basis that their mistakes, no matter how severe, were not a sign of evil, but of ignorance or mental instability.

For example, if everyone at a candlelight vigil weeping for the slain victim while damning his or her slayer could step back and see themselves as part of the psychological lynch mob they are, they would be mortified at what they were up to. When we have tears in our eyes for the victimized and none left over for the victimizer, we have failed to understand the all-inclusive nature of compassion. And what we have understood even less is the guilt that we engender by limiting love and the fear that follows from our separating ourselves by judgment from *any* part of the whole.

As *ACIM* says in one place,

> You who are not at war must look for brothers and recognize all whom you see as brothers, because only equals are at peace. Because [true equals] ... have everything, they cannot compete. Yet if they perceive any of their brothers as anything other than their perfect equals, the idea of competition has entered their minds. Do not underestimate your need to be vigilant *against* this idea, because all your conflicts come from it. It is the belief that conflicting interests are possible, and therefore you have accepted the impossible as true. Is that different from saying you perceive yourself as unreal?[185]

Nietzsche once said, "One repays a teacher badly if one remains only a pupil."[186] In that same sense, when we insist on remaining punitive in our outlook, we repay the generous at heart—and even the difficult ones, who have helped us so much—badly for their efforts. We owe them, and ourselves, much better. In another place, *ACIM* explains,

> Any concept of punishment involves the projection of blame and reinforces the idea that blame is justified. The

result is a lesson in blame, for all behavior teaches the beliefs that motivate it.[187]

If we follow this logic carefully and also take into consideration the point it makes when it says, "As you teach so will you learn" and "do not forget that what you teach is teaching you,"[188] it becomes apparent that it is in our best interests to resign from our positions as teachers of accusation—and learners of self-accusation—and work on accepting the idea that everyone we meet is doing his or her best.

Nor should we give in to the temptation to worship at the altar of the idol of a personal weakness, wanting others to do for us that which can be done only by ourselves. This is what Nietzsche, speaking as Zarathustra, was warning everyone of when he followed his comment, "One repays a teacher badly if one remains only a pupil," with,

> You respect me; but how [will you fare] if one day your respect should tumble? Take care that a falling [idol] does not strike you dead.
>
> You say that you believe in Zarathustra. But of what importance is Zarathustra? You are my believers: but of what importance are all believers?
>
> You had not yet sought yourself when you found me! Thus do all believers. Therefore all belief is of so little account.
>
> Now I bid you, lose me and find yourselves.[189]

Finding All We Are Not

If somewhere deep within and far beyond the dreary world of Forgetfulness of Our Sameness and True Equality an ultimate fairness is real, then the wisdom that resides within the wise would have to live in everyone—hidden more in some than in others, but still existing the same in all. As Emerson said, "In yourself slumbers the whole of Reason. It is for you to know all, to dare all ... [and not to be] the parrot of other men's thinking."[190] Or, to be one who, as Nietzsche put it, "rebels against a state of things in which he only repeats what he has heard, learns what is already known, imitates what already exists."[191]

If we're fed up enough with our interpretations of reality, the ideas above can help to awaken us to the "whole of Reason" within. The logical start on our ensuing quest would then be to seek, in a sensible manner, not for what we are (for who would there be outside what we are to do such seeking?), but for what we are not. And what is it that we are not? Every selfish idea or belief in a personal specialness we would keep to ourselves and not want to share with the whole forever.

Perhaps it is this diminution of self-interest that is exactly the price we are trying to avoid paying, and, therefore, in our unwillingness to let go, we are unable to let go. Because we fear "*no culpa, no mea*" (translated "no fault, no me"), we can't see the benefits of "*no mea, no culpa*" ("no me, no fault"), and so the concept escapes us completely. We want to let go of the unrelenting memories of our supposed crimes of the past, but, at the same time, we are desperate to hold on to the good parts of this puff of fading vanity called "me." Yet the "me"—with all its so-called good and bad—is not a divisible package, but rather an imaginary and indivisible whole. This, being so, leaves us in the disturbing position of insisting that our safety and happiness rest on what is not and can never be. Yet what if the response to this supposedly terrifying realization of the impermanence of self is simply, "Little loss, big gain"? Is the conundrum in this, as author John Burdett put it, that "the fear of letting go prevents you from letting go of the fear of letting go"? Here is his description of what all who still identify with a "me" and its special interests are afraid to face, much less think of accepting:

> You see, dear reader (speaking frankly, and without any intention to offend) you are a ramshackle collection of coincidences held together by a desperate and irrational clinging, there is no center at all, everything depends on everything else ... and even your best side is a super-

ficial piece of social programming that will fall apart just as soon as your spouse leaves with the kids and the money in the joint account, or the economy starts to fail and you get the sack, or you get conscripted into some idiot's war, or they give you the news about your brain tumor. To name this amorphous morass of self pity, vanity and despair *self* is not only the height of hubris, it is also proof (if any were needed) that we are above all a delusional species, in a trance from birth to death.[192]

"[I]n a trance from birth to death" is similar to Socrates's idea that "Our birth is but a sleep and a forgetting."[193] If we are actually in something like "a trance from birth to death," or "a sleep and a forgetting," then it seems logical that the business we should be pursuing is not to outdo and overcome, or to correct and convert, but to awaken and remember. And if, as the great mystics and teachers of the world have taught over the centuries, things are not as they appear, then what are they? If, upon examination, the answer turns out to be just appearances that come and go, that are impermanent and therefore not everlasting and real, what could be more startling?

I remember my own great puzzlement about life when I was struggling to deal with my children's many problems, along with my failing marriage and the surprising lack of fulfillment I was experiencing with all my success at work. It was then, in my disappointment, that I made the decision to turn to the works of those mystics and teachers. And in the second book I read, I came upon the following quote by Yogananda: "The world is an illusion."[194]

This idea was one I'd heard and read about before, but hadn't paid much attention to. This time, however, I was thunderstruck at the possibility of it actually being true.

"Of all the things I've ever seriously considered," I thought, "this is one that escaped me completely."

Since this is a revolutionary concept for some, it's not one I'm suggesting that anyone should embrace. But I will say that in light of the staggering confusion of the world we abide in, neither is it an idea that we should cavalierly dismiss.

Now, in relation to Yogananda's quote, let's examine what a few others have had to say about not only the world but also the self as an illusion:

> *ACIM*: The self you made is not the [truth]. Therefore, this self does not exist at all. And anything it seems to do and think means nothing. It is neither bad nor good. It is unreal, and nothing more than that.[195]

> Stephen Asma: The "self" is a virtual fiction.... My "self" acts as a meta-physical ... repository of all my memories, personality traits, and core values. It is the essential me. But in reality this self is only a mental construction ... that erroneously groups diverse experiences into a virtual unity.[196]

> Plato: Men without experience of truth and reality hold unsound opinions about many things.... Those who have no experience of wisdom ... deal with the ... forever changing [and illusory], never with the eternal.[197]

> Sri Nisargadatta: The mind is but a set of mental habits, of ways of thinking and feeling, and to change they must be brought to the surface and examined....
>
> The mind must learn that behind the moving mind there is the background of awareness, which does not change.[198]

> J. Krishnamurti: It is only when the mind is free from idea, that there can be experiencing. Ideas are not truth. And truth is something that must be experienced directly, from beyond the bundle of ideas—which is the "me," which is the mind—only when one can go beyond

that, when thought is completely silent, is there a state of experiencing....

Let us be clear. The "door" is the "me" through which I have to go. It is not outside of "me." It is not a factual door as that painted door. It is a door in me through which I have to go. [And the wise man says,] "Do that."[199]

Like most, and for the longest time, I had thought that the purpose of life was advancement—first of the body, and then of the intellect. Yet, these quotes imply that no matter the extent of our advancements in either, they are just stages we pass through on the way to the examination of our thinking and beliefs—where the real journey begins.

Errors Are for Correction

The attempt to scale such heights of aspiration calls for a complete revision of the thinking behind the wrong mind's plaintive cry, "But what about me?" Only a dedicated indifference to such complaints of the mind can free us to "make it about them," and only by making this idea a reigning principle of our daily lives can we leave behind the isolation and agony of the selfishness tied to the idea of *me*. As mentioned, however, considering the abiding love most of us have for self, this is a difficult spell to escape from indeed. *ACIM* describes one form of this clinging to the ego, and all that it entails, as follows:

To the ego [or the guard within] it is kind and right and good to point out errors and "correct" them. This makes perfect sense to the ego, which is unaware of what errors are and what correction is. Errors are of the ego, and correction of errors lies in the relinquishment of the ego....

You cannot correct yourself. Is it possible then for you to correct another? Yet you can see him truly, because it is possible for you to see yourself truly. It is not up to you to change your brother, but merely to accept him as he is. His errors do not come from the truth that is in him, and only this truth is yours. His errors cannot change this, and can have no effect at all on the truth in you.[200]

Shortly after, it follows with, "Accept his errors as real, and you have attacked yourself." In other words, if another's errors are real, then so are mine and so are yours. And if all or our errors are real, then there will be an inevitable price to pay. To the Course, errors are for correction and nothing else. To the ego, however, errors are to be kept in the mind forever as proof of the reality of sin, guilt, and our irreconcilable separation from the trunk. And thus the reason for our fearful attempts to escape imagined penalties by magnifying others' errors and excusing our own is more apparent—another "sorry," and that's a nice word for what is actually a murderous, attempt to maximize his or her guilt in hopes of minimizing our own. Yet, without due regard for the well-being of all, there is no freedom from the belief in retribution, but only unhappy endeavors to escape it, through the other's enslavement to a future of woe. In a call to true equality and a greater generosity toward all, Walt Whitman said,

> With one man or woman … I even pick the lowest…. I
> now illustrate the whole law:
> I say that every right … shall be eligible to that man
> or woman, on the same terms as any other.[201]

More Things in Heaven and Earth

Doesn't it sometimes seem as if we've wandered into a strange and foreign land, a very odd place wherein the answer to our dilemma seems either that we sacrifice in hopes of a future reward or eat, drink, and be merry, for tomorrow we die? What are the odds that we have become mindless pawns in our own strange version of Alice's Wonderland, staggering about in a place of general impairment, a "darkling plain" where "ignorant armies clash by night"?[202] Could Shakespeare have been speaking to everyone when he had Hamlet say, "There are more things in Heaven and Earth, Horatio, than are dreamt of in your philosophy"?[203]

To examine this, let's look at something *not* "dreamt of in [our] philosophy," one among many inexplicable tales that should serve to disturb our complacency and bring doubt to our convictions that we know what's real and how things are. The following is a well-documented paranormal event that people usually gloss over, but one that we can use to question our certitude in a healthy way:

> A remarkable series of [events took place in the life of] Therese Neumann. In addition to her stigmata, Neumann also displayed *inedia*, the supernormal ability to live without food.... In 1927, she gave up both food and water entirely.
>
> The local bishop ... sent a commission into her home to investigate.... Under the supervision of a medical doctor named Seidl, four Franciscan nursing sisters scrutinized her every move [for two weeks]. They watched her day and night, and the water she used for washing and rinsing her mouth was carefully measured and weighed. She never went to the bathroom. She also showed no signs of dehydration, even though the average human body expels about fourteen ounces of water daily in the air he or she exhales, and a like amount through the pores.
>
> Yet this [test] was nothing for Neumann; *she did not eat or drink a thing for the next thirty-five years.*[204]

If this story is true, and based on the long-term documentation, there seems little reason to doubt it is, then what other laws of the world that say such things can't be so aren't laws at all but just commonly held beliefs?

Although, as mentioned, the idea of the world as an illusion is not a particularly new one, the danger to many unfamiliar with the concept is that it may appear as either a quick and simplified answer to our perplexity or, instead, something unreal to be rejected out of hand. I propose we avoid both these approaches, giving consideration to a concept with the potential to leave much of the world's certitude lying lifeless in the dust, which, perhaps, is exactly where it belongs. Therefore, as we are already examining possibilities and perchances, opening up to review some of our previously fixed beliefs about reality, let's take a look at what more thoughtful people have said about the topic. The large number of quotes to follow is reflective of the plethora of such material available, which, in itself, may be a testament to the possibility that the world of one or the other is actually a dream.

> René Descartes: How often, asleep at night, am I convinced that I am here in my dressing gown, sitting by the fire—when in fact I am lying undressed in my bed? … How can I be certain my whole life is not a dream?[205]

> Johann von Goethe: That the life of man is only a dream has already occurred to many, and I am always haunted by this feeling.[206]

> Ramana Maharishi: The world should be considered like a dream…. Waking is long and a dream short; other than this there is no difference.[207]

> Kenneth Wapnick: Since in truth nothing exists outside the mind, anyone we *perceive* must be an illusory figure. Just as in a sleeping dream where, psychologists tell us, all the characters are but projections of split off thoughts in our brains, so too in the waking dreams we call our personal lives….
>
> Thus, again, my relationship with you (from *my* point of view) exists only in my mind.[208]

William Shakespeare:
… We are such stuff
As dreams are made on, and our little life
Is rounded with a sleep.[209]

Rumi:
This place is a dream
Only a sleeper considers it real….

.   .   .   .

A man goes to sleep in the town….
In the dream, he doesn't remember the town he's sleeping in his bed in. He believes the reality of the dream
town.
The world is that kind of sleep.[210]

Robert Powell: Our waking state experiences are the
products of a dream.[211]

Aldous Huxley: Our business is to wake up. We have to
find a way in which to detect the whole of reality in the
one illusory part which our self-centered consciousness
permits us to see.[212]

Sri Nisargadatta: You need not bring your dream to a
definite conclusion … all you need is to realize you are
dreaming.[213]

J. Krishnamurti: One has to be a light to oneself…. then
the mind is … awake.[214]

Walt Whitman: Maybe the things I perceive, the animals, plants, men, hills, shining and flowing waters,
maybe these are … only apparitions, and the real something is yet to be known.[215]

Kary Mullis (Nobel laureate): Time and space don't really count for much in the inferno of the very small things that we now think are fundamental. Nobody who is sane understands what goes on down at the level where the fundamental things like quarks and electrons do not have any volume or any position. If you can understand something with zero volume and no position, then welcome to insanity.[216]

Michael Talbot: Dr. Stanislav Grof, chief of psychiatric research ... at Johns Hopkins, ... not only takes ... paranormal phenomena seriously, but feels that reality is indeed cloud-built.... "The world is not ... as solid as we perceive it," he says.

Physicist William Tiller [of] Stanford University agrees, [and] thinks the universe is a kind of holo-deck....

Indeed if the universe is a holodeck, all things that appear stable and eternal ... would have to be looked on as illusory.[217]

John Keats (dictating his epitaph): "Here lies one whose name is writ in water."[218]

ACIM: The miracle establishes you dream a dream and that its content is not true.[219]

Shankara: Both bondage and liberation are fictions.... [Reality] is infinite, without parts ... serene, stainless, pure.

Who can be called wise? He who can discriminate between the real and the unreal.[220]

Shih-Shuang: If you turn your attention around and look [inward], you will realize your original nature is unborn and imperishable....

The impure elemental body has no ultimate reality at all. It is like a dream, like an illusion, like a reflection, like an echo.

When awakened, there is ... only the ungraspable universal way ... the true religion with no fixations.[221]

Stephen Mitchell: In its true state, mind is immaculate, transparent, timeless ... self-radiant, indivisible, and without qualities. Without beginning or ending, your original wisdom has been shining forever, like the sun. To know whether or not this is true, look inside your own mind.[222]

Edgar Allan Poe:
All that we see or seem
Is but a dream within a dream.[223]

Michel de Montaigne: Those who have compared our life to a dream were right....[224]

Looking Again at the Worst

But what if, in order to undo the accumulated obstacles to the awareness of what is really ours, we necessarily have to, as Becker said, "follow Hardy [and] take a full look at the worst in order to get rid of illusions"? Worst or not, nightmare or no nightmare, how bad could that be? Grab your socks, take a deep breath, and let's take a look at what Becker so graphically had to say about this place so many keep trying to fit into the crooked mold of a beautiful world:

What could we say in the simplest possible way that would "reveal" man to us—show what [we think of as creation and evolution have] all added up to? ... I now see that we must make a clear distinction between man's creatureliness—his appetite—on the one hand and his ingenuity on the other....

The basic human condition [is] that man is first and foremost an animal moving about on a planet shining in the sun, whatever else he is, is built on this…. The only certain thing we know about this planet is that it is a theater for crawling life, organismic life, and at least we know what organisms are and what they are trying to do.

At its most elemental level the human organism, like crawling life, has a mouth, digestive tract, and anus, a skin to keep it intact and appendages with which to acquire food. Existence for all organismic life is a constant struggle to feed—a struggle to incorporate whatever other organisms they can fit into their mouths and press down their gullets without choking. Seen in these stark terms, life on this planet is a gory spectacle, a science-fiction nightmare in which digestive tracts filled with teeth at one end are tearing away at whatever flesh they can reach, and at the other end are piling up the fuming waste excrement as they move along in search of more flesh….[225]

So far, this look at the worst is not an easy read. Yet, how else but by facing the facts without flinching can we leave illusions behind and awaken to reality? Unless we make our way back to the thought of separation from the whole that is producing the world of separate interests, there is no hope—just further mirages of light on the wrong side of darkness. Becker continues with,

Life cannot go on without the mutual devouring of organisms. If at the end of each person's life he were to be presented with the living spectacle of all that he had organismically incorporated to stay alive, he might well feel horrified by the living energy he had ingested. The horizon of a gourmet, or even the average person,

NO MEA, NO CULPA

would be taken up with hundreds of chickens, flocks of lambs and sheep, a small herd of steers, sties full of pigs, and rivers of fish. The din alone would be deafening. To paraphrase Elias Canetti, each organism raises its head over a field of corpses, smiles into the sun, and declares life is good.[226]

Unless you have a pretty good sense of humor, this is hard stuff to swallow. Yet, if Hardy is right, then all who want to go beyond this nightmarish scenario *must* look, not so much at how we eat, which need not be changed, but at how we feed off others to enlarge a sense of personal importance, which we should be starving out of its cannibalistic existence instead.

Innocence Remembered and Shared

Given the ridiculous trash that has filled our "pails," combined with the spite, envy, and malice that intermittently spew forth from our hidden guilt over our desire to be more important than others, it may seem an impossible leap of faith to accept ourselves as completely innocent. Yet, if we've actually been, even at our worst, simply ignorant—and, given that, *have* been doing our best—then on the assurances of the wise about what we've forgotten but have not lost, and not our sad dreams to the contrary, is where our reliance belongs. That is, either we are in fact not as we know ourselves to be, but, as they insist, as innocent and eternal as the changeless truth, or we're mere walking shadows with about as much hope for immortality as a disappearing snowflake or the morning dew.

The only cost of accepting our innocence is the willingness to relinquish our demand for a specialness that, by definition, mandates it not be true for everyone else as well. Indeed, we fear losing our invented identity, although it was never there to begin with. As a result, we find ourselves lost among the lonely, conceiving of ourselves as different in truth and maintaining our convictions through consistent worship in the church of the impossible. And yet, as the faithful in the church of the impossible, we are really the innocent caught in ignorance, with no real reason for our secret shame at all.

What we must learn to accept is that if we see others as unworthy, there is no one in greater need of forgiveness than ourselves. *ACIM*, speaking again to our complete responsibility for this perception, says,

> Everything you perceive is a witness to the thought system you want to be true. Every brother has the power to release you if you choose to be free. You cannot accept false witness of him unless you have evoked false witness against him. If he speaks not of [innocence] to you, you spoke not of [innocence] to him.[227]

So how do we set out to bring back into awareness the remembrance of our eternal inclusion in the whole? Another passage in *ACIM* answers this question:

> Yes, you are blessed indeed. Yet in this world you do not know it…. If you are blessed and do not know it, you need to learn it must be so. The knowledge is not taught, but its conditions must be acquired for it is they that have been thrown away. You can learn to bless, and cannot give what you have not. If, then, you offer blessing, it must have come first to yourself. And you must … also have accepted it as yours, for how else could you give it away?[228]

This passage then follows with,

> How could you learn what has been done for you, unknown to you, unless you do what you would have to do if it *had* been done for you?

In other words, "[h]ow could you learn what had been done for you" (that your innocence and true identity have been kept completely safe), "unknown to you" (because you've fallen asleep and dreamed yourself to be a lonely self, separated from the whole), "unless you do" (right here and now, while you're still asleep and dreaming) "what you would have to do" (be kind and gentle with all) "if it had been done for you" (and everything good was all that was true)?

Since complete forgiveness is definitely possible, anyone who really cares to can learn to forgive completely. Only by forgiving completely can we come to understand that we are completely forgiven, for it is through forgiveness we find what was "unknown to us" yet already ours. Again, we must ultimately learn that true forgiveness is *of* ourselves and *for* ourselves, born in our acceptance that if the world is affecting us, *we gave it that power.* All else is mental trickery, self-deceit, and a sham.

To better understand this concept, let's revisit *can't* and *won't.* When someone is caught up in resistance to the truth and won't acknowledge the reality of something, he *can't.* And when he can't, it is impossible for him to see the problem as it is, which is that he *won't.* Even though he is choosing to be in conflict at that moment, he is quite literally blind to what he is doing. This is why there is no evil, but only bad actions based on ignorance; this is why it is fair to say that everyone is *always* doing his or her best and that, therefore, our judgments of others are nonsense. This is also why the capstone of forgiveness is realizing there is actually nothing to forgive. Can any of us really forgive the blind person who did not see? Or should we come to the realization that the person didn't see because he or she was blind? In the light of such reasoning, the reasonable, who do understand, deal calmly with others in the present of those others' *can'ts,* while the unreasonable, who don't understand, fulminate over the past of those same people's *won'ts.*

True forgiveness rests on the assumptions of personal responsibility and faith in the underlying innocence of others, and never on the speciosity of "forgiving" their guilt. The formula is simple: Anyone who is careless of the rights of others is careless of his own psychological well-being. Anyone who is careless of his own psychological well-being is truly confused. Anyone who is truly confused is, by definition, innocent. In this light, even the worst of what the guard within loves to call our sins were merely mistakes made when we did not understand what we understand now. After all, how are we going to know that the loss of our innocence is impossible if we continue to insist that others have lost theirs? Further, it is only accepting our innocence as definite that will bring us into the deeper waters of something else that needs to be undone by the redemptive power of true forgiveness: that insulting myth of an uncaring big man in the sky, who, like a Nero madly fiddling, stands idly by as the world burns with hatred and the fires of rage. There is no such thing as a faulty creator and his cracked creation, no permanence to the dream of alienation from reality, no *you* divided in interests and different from *me*, nor any real *us* being separated and apart from the trunk. This, and not the guard within's hysterical tale of punishment due for transgressions that were never actually made in truth, and, therefore, never made at all, is what speaks for the "Not Two"—and for me and for you.

"A Belief to Be Undone"

And now we near the conclusion of our journey through many grim examples of a mightily disturbed world, along with better ways to interpret all that we misunderstood before. "To awaken or not to awaken?" has become our only real question. Yet, even as we begin to inwardly stir, we continue to hear the calls to war, in the world or in the mind the same; they are still fierce, but fainter now, less compelling than before, as we accept the difficult lesson that we can't find ourselves without looking directly at the guilty guardians of sleep. And so we determine to watch them when they arise until they disappear, instead of losing ourselves in their cold, heartless labyrinth of analysis and despair.

We still need to pay careful attention to our feelings and words and tone and actions, accepting that there will continue to be times when we'll stumble and fall. But apology and forgiveness will always be there to assist us in returning to the awareness that the real conductor (reason) of our lives and our return home never changes its kindly disposition toward us, no matter how often we forget and momentarily turn away from love without interruption that has no end.

And so, in a justly renewed confidence in our inner strength, without either guilt or false modesty to impede us, we find in the simplicity of Goethe's little poem the answer we've sought since space between us appeared, and time and delay seemed to begin:

> Turn toward clarity
> Flames of love, speed!
> Those damned by deed
> Are healed by verity—
> Joyous retrieval
> From earthly evil—
> They find impunity
> In cosmic unity.[229]

As we trudge along on our journey across the cold high desert of our wavering fortitude, with flickering faith in the goodness we follow like a distant star, Goethe's gentle words enter our minds like a brotherly benediction: "Joyous retrieval (to gain back or find again) / From earthly evil— / They find impunity (exemption from punishment, harm, or loss) / In cosmic unity (a condition of accord or oneness[230])." And what is this but a reiteration of what the beneficent and the wise have been assuring us of all along: that we are integral and constituent parts of an undifferentiated whole, forever without flaw or deviation, always welcome in the home we've never left, needing only to undo our judgments of others that are the shadows of the ones we still hold against ourselves. And it is here in this unavoidable bereavement of the nature of the false self that *ACIM* offers a replacement for its loss of peace and grimness with these assuring words: "What you think you are is a belief to be undone."[231]

A *belief* to be undone. To those willing to challenge all previously acceptable, dark notions of what makes sense, this impossible place in which we act out our fantasies of searching for enemies to destroy instead of brothers to love cannot be seen to represent the truth. Therefore, to them, the images that haunt it so ingeniously cannot be seen as truthful either. Not only is this place broken, it is, to repeat what Dickens said, bedlam. And because it is bedlam, it must be unreal.

What, then, *is* real? According to the wise, the light of innocence that shines beyond all our uncertain dreams and bad memories to the contrary; *that* is what is real—because it alone is changeless and always true.

When I was a young boy, I woke up early one morning to what was, for the city, a strange absence of noise. It was light out, but very quiet, and when I looked out the window, I just whispered, "Wow!" It had snowed heavily during the night, and as far as I could see, everything—every street, every tree, every car, every lamppost—was completely covered in a pristine blanket of snow. It was so beautiful, and so fresh and clean and lovely that, in a plenitude of perfect quiet, it spoke volumes as a reminder of the landscape of our forever home. And in the outpouring of that stillness and its loving song of silence, here are the first and last words of the melody it still sings softly to everyone, including you:

> *All thoughts of the violation of*
> *your eternal purity are untrue.*

My gratitude goes first to Kathy, for her constant gentleness and love; to Ken and Gloria, for their friendship and all they have taught me; to Chris Zook, for his invaluable editorial work and insights; to Lynn Everett, for her immeasurable contributions; to my parents, my children, my sister, and my brother; to my late ex-wife; to Mike P., who, without knowing it, inspired me to write all this down; and to so many others who, over the years, have helped me in so many ways. Thank you.

Endnotes

1   Cited in Albert Camus, *The Myth of Sisyphus and Other Essays* (New York: Vintage Books, Random House, 1991), 194.

2   Cited in Gary Marcus, *Kluge: The Haphazard Evolution of the Human Mind* (New York: Houghton Mifflin Company, 2008), 1.

3   Camus, *The Myth of Sisyphus*, 20.

4   Cited in Michael Lewis, *The Big Short: Inside the Doomsday Machine* (New York: W. W. Norton & Co., 2010), epigraph.

5   Plato, *The Collected Dialogues of Plato*, ed. Edith Hamilton and Huntington Cairns, trans. Lane Cooper (Princeton, NJ: Princeton University Press, Bollingen Series, 1971), 7.

6   Arthur Schopenhauer, *Arthur Schopenhauer—Essays and Aphorisms*, trans. R. J. Hollingdale (New York: Penguin Books, 1970), 119.

7   Charles Dickens, *The Complete Works of Charles Dickens: David Copperfield, v. I* (New York: Cosimo Classics, 2009), 202.

8   William Shakespeare, *Hamlet.* (Danbury, CT: Harvard Classics, Grolier, 1980), 132.

9   Cited in Ernest Becker, *Escape from Evil* (New York: Simon & Schuster, 1975), 151.

10 Bob Woodward, *The War Within: A Secret White House History 2006–2008* (New York: Simon & Schuster, 2008), 361.

11 John Crawford, *The Last True Story I'll Ever Tell: An Accidental Soldier's Account of the War in Iraq* (New York: Penguin Group, 2005), excerpts taken from pp. xi, xiii, xiv, 23, 139–141, 204–205, 210, 212, 218–220.

12 David Bellavia with John R. Bruning, *House to House: An Epic Memoir of War* (New York: Simon & Schuster, 2007), 16–17, 19.

13 Ibid., 312–313, 316.

14 Sebastian Junger, "Return to the Valley of Death," *Vanity Fair* (October 2008).

15 Chris Kyle and Scott McEwen, *American Sniper: The Autobiography of the Most Lethal Sniper in U.S. Military History* (New York: HarperCollins, 2012), 6.

16 Karl Malantes, *What It Is Like to Go to War* (New York: Atlantic Monthly Press, 2011), 26, 30, 160.

17 Carl Hoffman, *The Lunatic Express: Discovering the World … via its Most Dangerous Buses, Boats, Trains, and Planes* (New York: Random House, 2010), 84–91, 94.

18 Cited in Kenneth Wapnick, *Parents and Children, Part II* (Temecula, CA: Foundation for *A Course in Miracles*, 2007), 71.

19 From the song "All God's Chillun Got Rhythm," written by Walter Jurmann, Gus Kahn, and Bronislaw Kaper, and first performed by Ivie Anderson in the Marx Brothers 1937 film *A Day at the Races.*

20 Kenneth Wapnick, *Form versus Content: Sex and Money* (Temecula, CA: Foundation for *A Course in Miracles*, 2005), 76.

21 J. Krishnamurti, *Letters to the Schools*, v. 2 (Ojai, CA: Krishnamurti Foundation of America, 1981), 11.

22 Bob Woodward, *State of Denial: Bush at War, Part III* (New York: Simon & Schuster, 2006), 406.

23 Ibid., 408.

24 Cited in Doris Goodwin, *Team of Rivals* (New York: Simon & Schuster, 2005), 699.

25   Corrie ten Boom, *The Hiding Place* (Uhrichsville, OH: Barbour Publishing, Inc., 1998), 204.

26   Plato, *The Collected Dialogues of Plato*, 290.

27   Ibid., 297.

28   Ibid., 576.

29   Said by Portia in William Shakespeare, *The Merchant of Venice* (Roslyn, NJ: Black's Reader Service, 1972), 243.

30   Epictetus, *The Discourses of Epictetus* (Mount Vernon, NY: Peter Pauper Press, 1948), 30.

31   Robert Burns, from the poem "Man Was Made to Mourn," in *Poems of Robert Burns* (New York: Gramercy Books, 1994), 44. The complete line reads "Man's inhumanity to man / Makes countless thousands mourn!"

32   Plato, *The Collected Dialogues of Plato*, 349.

33   Ibid., 1,247.

34   *A Course in Miracles (ACIM)*, 2nd ed. (Glen Ellen, CA: Foundation for Inner Peace, 1992), Text, 651.

35   Wapnick, *Parents and Children*, 70.

36   Leo Tolstoy, *Wise Thoughts for Every Day: On God, Love, Spirit, and Living a Good Life* (New York: Arcade Publishing, 2005), 220.

37   Claude Anshin Thomas, *At Hell's Gate: A Soldier's Journey from War to Peace* (Boston: Shambala Publications, Inc., 2006), 3.

38   Ibid., 19–20.

39   Ibid., 20.

40   Ibid., 41, 74.

41   Ibid., 102–103.

42   Ibid., 103.

43   Will Hutton and Anthony Giddens, eds., *Global Capitalism* (New York: The New Press, 2000), x.

44   Dr. Vandana Shiva in *Global Capitalism*, 112.

45   John Perkins, *Confessions of an Economic Hit Man* (New York: Plume–Penguin, 2006), ix.

46   Ibid., xxi–xxv.

47 J. Krishnamurti, *The First and Last Freedom* (San Francisco, CA: HarperCollins, 1975), 31–33.

48 Becker, *Escape from Evil*, 109.

49 Kenneth Wapnick, *Form versus Content*, 98.

50 Gregory David Roberts, *Shantaram* (New York: St. Martin's Press, 2003), 3.

51 Victor Frankl, *Man's Search for Meaning* (Boston: Beacon Press, 2006), 65.

52 Cited in Bertrand Russell, *A History of Western Philosophy* (New York: Simon & Schuster, 1972), 608–609.

53 *The New Columbia Encyclopedia* (New York: Columbus University Press, 1975), 733, 1077, 2044.

54 *ACIM*, Workbook, 237.

55 Marcus Aurelius, *Meditations* (New York: Penguin Group, 2006), 73.

56 Cited in William Strunk and E. B. White, *Elements of Style* (Needham Heights, MA: Pearson Publishing Group, 2000), 8.

57 Louis Ferrante, Unlocked: *The Life and Crimes of a Mafia Insider* (New York, NY: Harper Collins, 2008), 250–252.

58 James W. Loewen, *Lies My Teacher Told Me* (New York: Touchstone, Simon & Schuster, 2007), 116.

59 Terrence Des Pres, *The Survivor* (New York: Oxford University Press, 1976), 77, 53, 44–45.

60 Ibid., 83–84.

61 William Shakespeare, *As You Like It* (Roslyn, NY: Black's Reader Service, 1994), 257.

62 George Vaillant, MD, *Spiritual Evolution: A Scientific Defense of Faith* (New York: Broadway Books, a division of Random House, 2008), 150.

63 Cited in Hubert Dreyfus and Sean Dorrance Kelly, *All Things Shining* (New York: Simon & Schuster—Free Press, 2011), 24.

64 Russell, *A History of Western Philosophy*, 680.

65   Jon Ronson, *The Psychopath Test: A Journey through the Madness Industry* (New York: Riverhead Books—Penguin Group, 2011), 122.

66   Jeffrey Gettleman, "Albinos, Long Shunned, Face Threat in Tanzania." *New York Times,* June 8, 2008. Retrieved from http://www.nytimes.com/2008/06/08/world/africa/08albino.html?pagewanted=print

67   Quoted in Stephen T. Asma, *The Gods Drink Whiskey: Stumbling toward Enlightenment in the Land of the Tattered Buddha* (New York: HarperCollins, 2006), 196.

68   Terrence Des Pres, *The Survivor,* 96.

69   Shakespeare, *Hamlet,* 41.

70   Becker, *Escape from Evil,* 107–108, 110–111.

71   Schopenhauer, *Essays and Aphorisms,* 124.

72   Becker, *Escape from Evil,* epigraph.

73   *The Dhammapada,* trans. Gil Fronsdal (Boston: Shambala Publications, 2005), 28.

74   Shakespeare, *Hamlet,* 108.

75   Will Durant, *The Story of Philosophy* (New York: Simon & Schuster, 1961), 180.

76   Ibid., 449–450.

77   Ibid., 83–84.

78   *The Koran,* (New York: Bantam Dell, division of Random House, 2004), 56, 57, 105.

79   Kenneth Wapnick, *Journey through the Workbook of* A Course in Miracles (Temecula, CA: Foundation for *A Course in Miracles,* 2005), vol. 5, 1.

80   John Heilemann and Mark Halperin, *Game Change: Obama and the Clintons, McCain and Palin, and the Race of a Lifetime* (New York: HarperCollins, 2010), 129.

81   Mark Twain, *My Autobiography* (Mineola, NY: Dover Publications, Inc., 1999), 253–254.

82   Epictetus, *The Golden Sayings* (Whitefish, MT: Kessinger Publishing, 2001), 70.

83 Epictetus, *Discourses*, 135.

84 Ralph Waldo Emerson, from the essay "Self Reliance." Cited in *The New Dictionary of Cultural Literacy, Third Edition*, eds. E. D. Hirsch, Jr., Joseph F. Kett, and James Trefil (Boston: Houghton Mifflin Company, 2002).

85 Durant, *The Story of Philosophy*, 216.

86 Kenneth Wapnick, *Forgiveness: "A Many Splendored Thing,"* workshop given 8/20/2011 at the Foundation for *A Course in Miracles*, Temecula, California.

87 Epictetus, *Discourses*, 135–136.

88 Friedrich Nietzsche, *Why I Am So Wise* (New York: Penguin Books, 2004), 46.

89 R. J. Hollingdale, *Arthur Schopenhauer—Essays and Aphorisms*, 22–23.

90 Ibid., 65.

91 *Bhagavad Gita* (New York: Bantam Books, 1986), 36, 37, 64.

92 Cited in Durant, *The Story of Philosophy*, 246.

93 Misha Glenny, *McMafia: A Journey Through the Global Criminal Underworld* (New York: Random House, 2008), 105–10.

94 *ACIM*, Text, 445.

95 Becker, *Escape from Evil*, epigraph.

96 Sam Harris, *The End of Faith, Religion, Terror, and the Future of Reason* (New York: W. W. Norton & Co., 2005), 98.

97 Ibid., 86.

98 Tolstoy, *Wise Thoughts for Every Day*, 73.

99 Cited in Michael Korda, *Hero: The Life and Legend of Lawrence of Arabia* (New York: HarperCollins, 2010), 344–345.

100 Ibid., 420–421.

101 Robert Morgan, *Boone—A Biography* (Chapel Hill, NC: Algonquin Books, 2007), 305.

102 Ibid., 306–307.

103 Ibid.

104 Bellavia, *House to House*, 122–123.

105 Ibid., 201–207.

106   Cited in Sam Harris, *End of Faith*, 144.

107   Plato, *The Collected Dialogues of Plato*, 829.

108   Loewen, *Lies My Teacher Told Me*, 226.

109   Ibid., 54–57.

110   Epictetus, *Discourses*, 12, 28.

111   Friedrich Nietzsche, *Thus Spoke Zarathustra* (Oxford: Oxford World Classics, 2005), 160.

112   Sebastian Junger, *War* (New York: Hachette Book Group, 2010), 25, 144, 145, 146, 155, 233, 268.

113   Anthony Swofford, *Hotels, Hospitals, and Jails* (New York: Hachette Book Group, 2012), 237.

114   Jay Dobyns, *No Angel: My Harrowing Undercover Journey to the Inner Circle of the Hells Angels* (New York: Crown Publishing, 2009), 15.

115   Susan Casey, *The Wave* (New York: Doubleday, a division of Random House, 2010), 175–176.

116   David Finkel, *The Good Soldiers* (New York: Farrar, Straus and Giroux, 2009), 248, 222–223, 282.

117   Sarah Bakewell, *How to Live: Or a Life or Montaigne in One Question and Twenty Attempts at an Answer* (New York: Other Press, 2010), 207.

118   Cited in *The National Tribune*, Washington, DC, November 26, 1914.

119   *Bruce Catton's America*, ed. Oliver Jensen (New York: American Heritage Publishing Company, Inc., 1979), 128, 137, 107.

120   Sri Nisargadatta, *I Am That: Talks with Sri Nisargadatta* (Durham, NC: Acorn Press, 1973), 331.

121   *ACIM*, 523, 440.

122   William James, *Pragmatism and the Meaning of Truth* (Cambridge, MA: Harvard University Press, 1975), 118–119.

123   Quoted in William Safire, *Lend Me Your Ears: Great Speeches in History* (New York: W. W. Norton & Co., 1997),550.

124   Schiller cited and commented on in James, *Pragmatism and the Meaning of Truth*, 298.

125 Paul Austin, *Something for the Pain: One Doctor's Account of Life and Death in the ER* (New York: W. W. Norton & Co., 2008), 292–293.

126 Webster's Ninth New Collegiate Dictionary.

127 *The Koran*, 56, 57.

128 *The Holy Bible,* Deuteronomy 13:6. Verse Reference Edition (Philadelphia: A. J. Holman Co., nd).

129 Jon Krakauer, *Under the Banner of Heaven: A Story of Violent Faith* (New York: Anchor Books, Random House, 2004), ix, 69, 70, 71.

130 Sam Harris, *The End of Faith*, 84–85.

131 James Joyce, *A Portrait of the Artist as a Young Man* (New York: Penguin Books, 1992), 128–131.

132 Stephen Greenblatt, *The Swerve: How the World Became Modern* (New York: W. W. Norton & Co., 2011), 108.

133 Ibid., 108.

134 Webster's Ninth New Collegiate Dictionary.

135 Daniel Kahneman, *Thinking Fast and Slow* (New York: Farrar, Straus and Giroux, 2011), 199, 201.

136 Cited in Michael J. Clarke, *Awakening to World Disorder and Climate Realities* (Victoria, Canada: Trafford Publishing, 2008), 370.

137 Quoted in Eduardo Galeano, *Mirrors: Stories of Almost Everyone*, trans. Mark Fried (Philadelphia: Perseus Group, 2009), 56–57.

138 Kenneth Wapnick, *The Journey Home: "The Obstacles to Peace" in* A Course in Miracles (Temecula, CA: Foundation for *A Course in Miracles*, 2000), 102.

139 Ralph Waldo Emerson, *Nature and Other Writings* (Boston: Shambala Publications, Inc., 2003), 49, 50, 72.

140 Nietzsche, *Thus Spoke Zarathustra*, 67.

141 Krishnamurti, *The First and Last Freedom*, 134–135, 152–153.

142 Camus, *The Myth of Sisyphus*, 60, 94.

143 Kenneth Wapnick, *From Futility to Happiness—Sisyphus as Everyman* (Temecula, CA: Foundation for *A Course in Miracles*, 2008), 120–121, 137.

144 William Goldman, *Which Lie Did I Tell?: More Adventures in the Screen Trade* (New York: Vintage Books, Random House, 2000), 134.

145 David Carr, *Night of the Gun* (New York: Simon & Schuster, 2008), 114–115.

146 *ACIM*, Text, 499–501.

147 Rick Springfield, *Late, Late at Night* (New York: Simon & Schuster, 2010), 3.

148 Sugar Ray Leonard, *The Big Fight: My Life in and out of the Ring* (New York: Penguin Books, 2011), 294.

149 William Blake, *The Marriage of Heaven and Hell* (Toronto, Canada: Dover Publications, 1994), 33.

150 Steve Fainaru, *Big Boy Rules: America's Mercenaries Fighting in Iraq* (Philadelphia: Perseus Group, 2008), xiii, xv, 1, 2, 64, 86, 116, xv.

151 D. Keith Mano, *Horn* (Boston: Houghton Mifflin Company, 1969), 330–331, 332–338.

152 Fyodor Dostoevsky, *Notes from the Underground* (New York: Random House, Bantam Classics, 1974), 34.

153 Wapnick, *From Futility to Happiness,* 120.

154 Aldous Huxley, *Island* (New York: HarperCollins, 2002), 40–42.

155 Kenneth Wapnick, *"What It Says": From the Preface of* A Course in Miracles—*A Commentary* (Temecula, CA: Foundation for *A Course in Miracles*, 2005), 7–8, 24.

156 *ACIM*, Text, 496–498.

157 Sigmund Freud, *Introductory Lectures on Psycho-Analysis* (New York: Liveright Publishing Corp., 1977), 216–217.

158 Sigmund Freud, *The Interpretation of Dreams* (New York: Avon Books, 1965), 133.

159 Wapnick, *Journey through the Workbook of* A Course in Miracles, vol. 5, 90–91.

160   Robert M. Pirsig, *Zen and the Art of Motorcycle Maintenance* (New York: HarperCollins, 2008), 102.

161   J. Krishnamurti, *Total Freedom* (New York: HarperCollins, 1996), 177.

162   Nietzsche, *Thus Spoke Zarathustra*, 68.

163   Krishnamurti, *Total Freedom*, 224–225.

164   Thomas Cleary, ed., *The Zen Reader* (Boston: Shambala, 1999), v–vi.

165   J. Francis Stroud, ed., *The Way to Love: The Last Meditations of Anthony de Mello* (New York: Doubleday, 1995), 5–8.

166   Eileen Button, "Thou Shalt Not Turn Me into a False Idol … " *Newsweek*, December 4, 2006.

167   Will Durant, *The Greatest Minds and Ideas of all Time* (New York: Simon & Schuster, 2002), 66.

168   Wapnick, *Journey through the Workbook of* A Course in Miracles, vol. 1, 52, 55.

169   J. Krishnamurti, *Freedom from the Known* (New York: HarperCollins, 1969), 91–93, 114–116.

170   Cleary, ed., *The Zen Reader,* 102, 133, 139.

171   *The Holy Bible*, Ecclesiastes 8:15.

172   Freud, *Introductory Lectures on Psycho-Analysis,* ix.

173   Plato, *Socrates' Defense* in *The Collected Dialogues of Plato*, 16, 17, 21, 23.

174   Ibid., *Phaedrus,* 520.

175   Michael Kodas, *High Crimes: The Fate of Everest in an Age of Greed* (New York: Hyperion HarperCollins, 2008), 152–153, 172–173, 240–241.

176   Kenneth Wapnick, *A Tale Told by an Idiot: Macbeth, Guilt, and A Course in Miracles* (Temecula, CA: Foundation for *A Course in Miracles*, 2004), 21–22, 72–74.

177   Plato, *The Collected Dialogues of Plato*, 499, 501–502.

178   Kenneth Wapnick, *A Tale Told by an Idiot*, 72–74.

179   Walt Whitman, *Leaves of Grass* (New York: Crown Publishers, 1961), 106.

180   Ibid., 72.

181   Epictetus, *The Handbook* (Indianapolis: Hackett Publishing Company, 1983), 14.

182   Wapnick, *The Journey Home*, 292, 295–296.

183   Krishnamurti, "A Wholly Different Way of Living, Ninth Dialogue with Dr. Allan W. Anderson," February 1974. Retrieved from http://www.jkrishnamurti.com/krishnamurti-teachings/view-text.php?tid=1109&chid=813

184   Michael Grant, *History of Rome* (New York: Charles Scribner's Sons, 1978), 205.

185   *ACIM*, Text, 116–117.

186   Nietzsche, *Why I Am So Wise*, 6.

187   *ACIM*, Text, 95.

188   Ibid., 99.

189   Nietzsche, *Thus Spoke Zarathustra*, 59.

190   Cited in James Miller, *Examined Lives: From Socrates to Nietzsche* (New York: Farrar, Straus and Giroux, 2011), 305.

191   Ibid., 328.

192   John Burdett, *Bangkok Tattoo* (New York: Vintage Books, Random House, 2006), 211.

193   Plato from *Phaedo* in *The Collected Dialogues of Plato*, 40.

194   Yogananda, *Autobiography of a Yogi* (Los Angeles, CA: The Self-Realization Fellowship, 2000), 42.

195   *ACIM*, Workbook, 161.

196   Asma, *The Gods Drink Whiskey*, 197.

197   Plato, from *The Republic*, 812–813; and *Timaes*, in *The Collected Dialogues of Plato*, 1,152.

198   Sri Nisargadatta, *I Am That*, 220.

199   Krishnamurti, *The First and Last Freedom*, 56; and *The Awakening of Intelligence* (New York: HarperCollins, 1975), 141.

200   *ACIM*, Text, 166–167.

201   Whitman, *Leaves of Grass*, 106.

202   Mathew Arnold, "Dover Beach" in *Selected Poems* (New York: Penguin Books, 1994), 103.

203 Shakespeare, *Hamlet*, 120.

204 Michael Talbot, *The Holographic Universe* (New York: Harper-Collins, 1992), 153.

205 From *Discourse on Method* (1637). Cited in *Bartlett's Familiar Quotations*, 523.

206 Goethe, *The Goethe Treasury*, (Mineola, NY: Dover Publications, 2006), 42.

207 Ramana Maharishi, *The Spiritual Teachings of Ramana Maharishi* (Boston: Shambala Publications, 1972), 10.

208 Kenneth Wapnick, *The Message of* A Course in Miracles (Temecula, CA: Foundation for *A Course in Miracles*, 1997), 152–153.

209 William Shakespeare, *Macbeth* (Danbury, CT: The Harvard Classics, Grolier Enterprises Corp., 1980), 388.

210 Jalal al-Din Rumi, "The Dream That Must Be Interpreted" in *The Essential Rumi*, trans. Coleman Barks (New York: HarperOne, 2004), 112.

211 Robert Powell, *The Real Is Unknowable, The Knowable Is Unreal* (Berkeley, CA: North Atlantic Books, 2005), 7.

212 Cited in Laura Huxley, *This Timeless Moment: A Personal View of Aldous Huxley* (Berkley, CA: Celestial Arts, 1968), 289.

213 Sri Nisargadatta, *I Am That*, 258.

214 J. Krishnamurti, *Krishnamurti's Journal* (New York: Harper Row, 1982), 28, 74.

215 Whitman, *Leaves of Grass*, 63.

216 Kary Mullis, *Dancing Naked in the Mind Field* (New York: Pantheon Books, Random House, 1998), 69–70.

217 Talbot, *The Holographic Universe*, 2, 158–159.

218 Quoted in Durant, *The Greatest Minds and Ideas of all Time*, 56.

219 *ACIM*, Text, 594.

220 Shankara, *Shankara's Crest-Jewel of Discrimination: Timeless Teachings on Nonduality*, trans. Swami Prabhavanada and

Christopher Isherwood (Hollywood, CA: Vedanta Press, 1970), 127, 131.

221 Cleary, ed., *The Zen Reader*, 99–100.

222 Stephen Mitchell, *The Second Book of the Tao* (New York: Penguin Books, 2009), 148.

223 Edgar Allan Poe, *The Works of Edgar Allan Poe* (New York: W. J. Widdleton, 1871), II, 40.

224 Michel de Montaigne, *Essays*, Book I, cited in *Bartlett's Familiar Quotations*, 165.

224 Becker, *Escape from Evil*, 1–2.

226 Ibid.

227 *ACIM*, Text, 207.

228 *ACIM*, Text, 270.

229 Johann Wolfgang Goethe, *Faust*, trans. Walter Kaufmann (New York: Random House, 1990), 485.

230 Webster's Ninth New Collegiate Dictionary.

231 *ACIM*, Workbook, 157.

Bibliography

A Course in Miracles. 2nd ed. Glen Ellen, CA: Foundation for Inner Peace, 1992.

Arnold, Mathew. *Selected Poems*. New York: Penguin Books, 1994.

Asma, Stephen T. *The Gods Drink Whiskey: Stumbling toward Enlightenment in the Land of the Tattered Buddha*. New York: HarvperCollins, 2006.

Aurelius, Marcus. *Meditations*. New York: Penguin Group, 2006.

Austin, Paul. *Something for the Pain: One Doctor's Account of Life and Death in the ER*. New York: W. W. Norton & Co., 2008.

Becker, Ernest. *Escape from Evil*. New York: Simon & Schuster, 1975.

Bellavia, David, and John R. Bruning. *House to House: An Epic Memoir of War*. New York: Simon & Schuster, 2007.

Bhagavad Gita. New York: Bantam Books, 1986.

Blake, William. *The Marriage of Heaven and Hell*. Toronto, Canada: Dover Publications, 1994.

Burdett, John. *Bangkok Tattoo*. New York: Vintage Books, 2006.

Burns, Robert. *Poems of Robert Burns*. New York: Gramercy Books, 1994.

Button, Eileen. "Thou Shalt Not Turn Me into a False Idol.… " *Newsweek*, December 4, 2006.

Camus, Albert. *The Myth of Sisyphus and Other Essays*. New York: Vintage Books, Random House, 1991.

Carr, David. *Night of the Gun*. New York: Simon & Schuster, 2008.

Casey, Susan. *The Wave: In Pursuit of the Rogues, Freaks and Giants of the Ocean*. New York: Doubleday, 2010.

Clarke, Michael J. *Awakening to World Disorder and Climate Realities*. Victoria, Canada: Trafford Publishing, 2008.

Cleary, Thomas, ed. *The Zen Reader*. Boston: Shambala Publications, 1999.

Crawford, John. *The Last True Story I'll Ever Tell: An Accidental Soldier's Account of the War in Iraq*. New York: Penguin Group, 2005.

Des Pres, Terrence. *The Survivor*. New York: Oxford University Press, 1976.

The Dhammapada. Translated by Gil Fronsdal. Boston: Shambala Publications, 2005.

Dickens, Charles. *The Complete Works of Charles Dickens: David Copperfield, v. I*. New York: Cosimo Classics, 2009.

Dobyns, Jay. *No Angel: My Harrowing Undercover Journey to the Inner Circle of the Hells Angels*. New York: Crown Publishing, 2009.

Dostoevsky, Fyodor. *Notes from the Underground*. New York: Random House, Bantam Classics, 1974.

Dreyfus, Hubert, and Sean Dorrance Kelly. *All Things Shining*. New York: Simon & Schuster—Free Press, 2011.

Durant, Will. *The Greatest Minds and Ideas of All Time*. New York: Simon & Schuster, 2002.

———. *The Story of Philosophy*. New York: Simon & Schuster, 1961.

Emerson, Ralph Waldo. *Nature and Other Writings*. Boston: Shambala Publications, 2003.

Epictetus. *The Discourses of Epictetus*. Mount Vernon, NY: Peter Pauper Press, 1948.

———. *The Golden Sayings*. Whitefish, MT: Kessinger Publishing, 2001.

———. *The Handbook.* Indianapolis: Hackett Publishing Company, 1983.

Fainaru, Steve. *Big Boy Rules: America's Mercenaries Fighting in Iraq.* Philadelphia: Perseus Group, 2008.

Ferrante, Louis. *Unlocked: The Life and Crimes of a Mafia Insider.* New York: HarperCollins, 2008.

Frankl, Victor. *Man's Search for Meaning.* Boston: Beacon Press, 2006.

Freud, Sigmund. *The Interpretation of Dreams.* New York: Avon Books, 1965.

———. *Introductory Lectures on Psycho-Analysis.* New York: Liveright Publishing Corp., 1977.

Galeano, Eduardo. *Mirrors: Stories of Almost Everyone.* Translated by Mark Fried. Philadelphia: Perseus Group, 2009.

Gettleman, Jeffrey. "Albinos, Long Shunned, Face Threat in Tanzania." *New York Times,* June 8, 2008.

Glenny, Misha. *McMafia: A Journey through the Global Criminal Underworld.* New York: Random House, 2008.

Goethe, Johann Wolfgang von. *Faust.* Translated by Walter Kaufmann. New York: Random House, 1990.

———. *The Goethe Treasury.* Mineola, NY: Dover Publications, 2006.

Goldman, William. *Which Lie Did I Tell?: More Adventures in the Screen Trade.* New York: Vintage Books, Random House, 2000.

Goodwin, Doris. *Team of Rivals.* New York: Simon & Schuster, 2005.

Grant, Michael. *History of Rome.* New York: Charles Scribner's Sons, 1978.

Harris, Sam. *The End of Faith: Religion, Terror, and the Future of Reason.* New York: W. W. Norton & Co., 2005.

Heilemann, John, and Mark Halperin. *Game Change: Obama and the Clintons, McCain and Palin, and the Race of a Lifetime.* New York: HarperCollins, 2010.

Hirsch, Jr., E. D., Joseph F. Kett, and James Trefil, eds. *The New Dictionary of Cultural Literacy.* 3rd edition. Boston: Houghton Mifflin Company, 2002.

Hoffman, Carl. *The Lunatic Express: Discovering the World … via its Most Dangerous Buses, Boats, Trains, and Planes.* New York: Random House, 2010.

The Holy Bible, Verse Reference Edition. Philadelphia: A. J. Holman Co., n.d.

Hutton, Will, and Anthony Giddens, eds. *Global Capitalism.* New York: The New Press, 2000.

Huxley, Aldous. *Island.* New York: HarperCollins, 2002.

Huxley, Laura. *This Timeless Moment: A Personal View of Aldous Huxley.* Berkley, CA: Celestial Arts, 1968.

James, William. *Pragmatism and the Meaning of Truth.* Cambridge, MA: Harvard University Press, 1975.

Jensen, Oliver, ed. *Bruce Catton's America.* New York: American Heritage Publishing Company, Inc., 1979.

Joyce, James. *A Portrait of the Artist as a Young Man.* New York: Penguin Books, 1992.

Junger, Sebastian. "Return to the Valley of Death." *Vanity Fair,* October 2008.

———. *War.* New York: Hachette Book Group, 2010.

Kahneman, Daniel. *Thinking Fast and Slow.* New York: Farrar, Straus and Giroux, 2011.

Kodas, Michael. *High Crimes: The Fate of Everest in an Age of Greed.* New York: Hyperion HarperCollins, 2008.

The Koran. New York: Bantam Dell, 2004.

Korda, Michael. *Hero: The Life and Legend of Lawrence of Arabia.* New York: HarperCollins, 2010.

Krakauer, Jon. *Under the Banner of Heaven: A Story of Violent Faith.* New York: Anchor Books, Random House, 2004.

Krishnamurti, J. *The First and Last Freedom.* San Francisco: HarperCollins, 1975.

———. *Freedom from the Known.* New York: HarperCollins, 1969.

———. *Krishnamurti's Journal.* New York: Harper Row, 1982.

———. *Letters to the Schools,* v. 2. Ojai, CA: Krishnamurti Foundation of America, 1981.

———. *Total Freedom.* New York: HarperCollins, 1996.

Kyle, Chris, and Scott McEwen. *American Sniper: The Autobiography of the Most Lethal Sniper in U.S. Military History.* New York: HarperCollins, 2012.

Leonard, Sugar Ray. *The Big Fight: My Life in and out of the Ring.* New York: Penguin Books, 2011.

Lewis, Michael. *The Big Short: Inside the Doomsday Machine.* New York: W. W. Norton & Co., 2010.

Loewen, James W. *Lies My Teacher Told Me.* New York: Touchstone, Simon & Schuster, 2007.

Maharaj, Nisargadatta. *I Am That: Talks with Sri Nisargadatta Maharaj.* Edited by Sudhaker S. Dikshit. Translated by Maurice Frydman. Durham, NC: Acorn Press, 1973.

Maharishi, Ramana. *The Spiritual Teachings of Ramana Maharishi.* Boston: Shambala Publications, 1972.

Malantes, Karl. *What It Is Like to Go to War.* New York: Atlantic Monthly Press, 2011.

Mano, Keith D. *Horn.* Boston: Houghton Mifflin Company, 1969.

Marcus, Gary. *Kluge: The Haphazard Evolution of the Human Mind.* New York: Houghton Mifflin Company, 2008.

Miller, James. *Examined Lives: From Socrates to Nietzsche.* New York: Farrar, Straus and Giroux, 2011.

Mitchell, Stephen. *The Second Book of the Tao.* New York: Penguin Books, 2009.

Morgan, Robert. *Boone—A Biography.* Chapel Hill, NC: Algonquin Books, 2007.

Mullis, Kary. *Dancing Naked in the Mind Field.* New York: Pantheon Books, 1998.

Nietzsche, Friedrich. *Thus Spoke Zarathustra.* Oxford: Oxford World Classics, 2005.

———. *Why I Am So Wise.* New York: Penguin Books, 2004.

Perkins, John. *Confessions of an Economic Hit Man.* New York: Plume-Penguin, 2006.

Plato. *The Collected Dialogues of Plato.* Edited by Edith Hamilton and Huntington Cairns. Translated by Lane Cooper. Princeton: Princeton University Press, Bollingen Series, 1971.

Poe, Edgar Allan. *The Works of Edgar Allan Poe.* New York: W. J. Widdleton, 1871.

Powell, Robert. *The Real Is Unknowable, The Knowable Is Unreal.* Berkeley, CA: North Atlantic Books, 2005.

Roberts, Gregory David. *Shantaram.* New York: St. Martin's Press, 2003.

Ronson, Jon. *The Psychopath Test: A Journey through the Madness Industry.* New York: Riverhead Books—Penguin Group, 2011.

Rumi, Jalal al-Din. *The Essential Rumi.* Translated by Coleman Barks. New York: HarperOne, 2004.

Russell, Bertrand. *A History of Western Philosophy.* New York: Simon & Schuster, 1972.

Safire, William. *Lend Me Your Ears: Great Speeches in History.* New York: W. W. Norton & Co., 1997.

Schopenhauer, Arthur. *Arthur Schopenhauer—Essays and Aphorisms.* Translated by R. J. Hollingdale. New York: Penguin Books, 1970.

Shakespeare, William. *As You Like It.* Roslyn, NY: Black's Reader Service, 1994.

———. *Hamlet.* Danbury, CT: The Harvard Classics, 1980.

———. *Macbeth.* Danbury, CT: The Harvard Classics, 1980.

———. *The Merchant of Venice.* Roslyn, NY: Black's Reader Service, 1972.

Shankara. *Shankara's Crest-Jewel of Discrimination: Timeless Teachings on Nonduality.* Translated by Swami Prabhavananda and Christopher Isherwood. Hollywood, CA: Vedanta Press, 1970.

Springfield, Rick. *Late, Late at Night.* New York: Simon & Schuster, 2010.

Stroud, J. Francis, ed. *The Way to Love: The Last Meditations of Anthony de Mello.* New York: Doubleday, 1995.

Strunk, William, and E. B. White. *Elements of Style.* 4th ed. Needham Heights, MA: Pearson Publishing Group, 2000.

Talbot, Michael. *The Holographic Universe: The Revolutionary Theory of Reality*. New York: HarperCollins, 1992.

Ten Boom, Corrie. *The Hiding Place*. Uhrichsville, OH: Barbour Publishing, Inc., 1998.

Tenney, Lester L. *My Hitch in Hell—The Bataan Death March*. Washington, DC: Brassey's Inc., 1995.

Thomas, Claude Anshin. *At Hell's Gate: A Soldier's Journey from War to Peace*. Boston: Shambala Publications, 2006.

Tolstoy, Leo. *Wise Thoughts for Every Day: On God, Love, Spirit, and Living a Good Life*. New York: Arcade Publishing, 2005.

Townsend, Dabney. *Hume's Aesthetic Theory: Taste and Sentiment*. New York: Routledge, 2001.

Twain, Mark. *My Autobiography*. Mineola, NY: Dover Publications, Inc., 1999.

Vaillant, MD, George. *Spiritual Evolution: A Scientific Defense of Faith*. New York: Broadway Books, 2008.

Wapnick, Kenneth. *Form versus Content: Sex and Money*. Temecula, CA: Foundation for *A Course in Miracles*, 2005.

———. *From Futility to Happiness—Sisyphus as Everyman*. Temecula, CA: Foundation for *A Course in Miracles*, 2008.

———. *Glossary Index*. Temecula, CA: Foundation for *A Course in Miracles*, 1982.

———. *The Journey Home: "The Obstacles to Peace" in* A Course in Miracles. Temecula, CA: Foundation for *A Course in Miracles*, 2000.

———. *Journey through the Workbook of* A Course in Miracles. Temecula, CA: Foundation for *A Course in Miracles*, 2005.

———. *Parents and Children, Part II*. Temecula, California: Foundation for *A Course in Miracles*, 2007.

———. *A Tale Told by an Idiot: Macbeth, Guilt, and* A Course in Miracles. Temecula, CA: Foundation for *A Course in Miracles*, 2004.

———. *"What It Says": From the Preface of* A Course in Miracles—*A Commentary*. Temecula, CA: Foundation for *A Course in Miracles*, 2005.

Whitman, Walt. *Leaves of Grass*. New York: Crown Publishers, 1961.

Woodward, Bob. *State of Denial: Bush at War, Part III*. New York: Simon & Schuster, 2006.

———. *The War Within: A Secret White House History 2006–2008*. New York: Simon & Schuster, 2008.

Yogananda. *Autobiography of a Yogi*. Los Angeles, CA: The Self-Realization Fellowship, 2000.